Pedagogical Tact

Phenomenology of Practice

The series *Phenomenology of Practice* sponsors books that are steeped in phenomenological scholarship and relevant to professional practitioners in fields such as education, nursing, medicine, pedagogy, clinical and counseling psychology. Texts in this series distinguish themselves for offering inceptual and meaningful insights into lived experiences of professional practices, or into the quotidian concerns of everyday living. And texts may reflectively focus on methodological issues and dimensions of the philosophic and human science underpinnings of phenomenological research. Proposals for the series are welcome. For details, please contact Series Editor Max van Manen at vanmanen@ualberta.ca.

Series Titles

Vol. 1: *Pedagogical Tact: Knowing What to Do When You Don't Know What to Do*, Max van Manen

Pedagogical Tact
Knowing What to Do When You Don't Know What to Do

Max van Manen

LONDON AND NEW YORK

First published 2015 by Left Coast Press, Inc.

Published 2016 by Routledge
2 Park Square, Milton Park, Abingdon, Oxon OX14 4RN
711 Third Avenue, New York, NY 10017, USA

Routledge is an imprint of the Taylor & Francis Group, an informa business

Copyright © 2015 Taylor & Francis

All rights reserved. No part of this book may be reprinted or reproduced or utilised in any form or by any electronic, mechanical, or other means, now known or hereafter invented, including photocopying and recording, or in any information storage or retrieval system, without permission in writing from the publishers.

Notice:
Product or corporate names may be trademarks or registered trademarks, and are used only for identification and explanation without intent to infringe.

Library of Congress Cataloging-in-Publication Data is on file.

ISBN 978-1-62958-274-0 hardback
ISBN 978-1-62958-275-7 paperback

Contents

Preface   11

1. The Primacy of Pedagogy   15
   Missed Moments of Pedagogical Tact?   15
   A Pedagogical Moment   17
   What Is Pedagogy?   18
2. Experiencing Pedagogy Vicariously   21
   Virtual Pedagogy in Cinema   22
   Virtual Pedagogy in Fictional Literature   26
3. The Nature of Pedagogy   33
   The Pedagogical Moment   34
   Entering the Child's World of Possibility   35
   The Practical Moment of Acting Pedagogically   37
   Phenomenological Pedagogy   39
   How Do We Know What Is Best?   41
   The Goal of Pedagogy   42
   Ontotheology and the Pedagogy of Character   45
   The Irreducibility of Pedagogy   47
4. The Pedagogy of Reflective Practice   49
   The Relation Between Reflection and Action   49
   Kairos Time: The Perfect Moment: The NOW   51
   The Novice Teacher   53
   The Experienced Teacher   55
5. Observing with Pedagogical Eyes and Ears   61
   Seeing Children Pedagogically   62
   Pedagogical Care Experienced as Devotion and Worry   64
   Experiencing Responsibility in the Face of the Unique   68
   Caring for the Faces of Those Who Are Faceless   73
6. Pedagogical Tact   77
   People-Sense and Child-Sense   77
   The Nature of Pedagogical Tact   78
   Personal Pedagogies   80
   The Immediacy of the Moment   81
   The Pedagogical Meaning of Discipline   84
   Confusing the Possible with the Desirable   86
   Tact Is Not Ruled by Rules—Yet Tact Is Not "Unruly"   89
   Pedagogical Understanding   92
   The Pedagogy of Teaching   97
   To Live Is to Touch and to Be Touched   103

7. Pedagogical Con-tact   107
   Modes of Contact   111
   Meaningful Learning   117
   Pedagogical Relation   119
   The Reflexive Nature of Pedagogy   122
   The Paradoxical Nature of Pedagogy   123
   Pedagogical Atmosphere   126
   Presentative and Representative Contact   129
   How Do Children Experience Our Presence?   131
   The Pedagogy of Being (What We Teach)   133
   Virtual Contact   136
8. Pedagogical Regard and Recognition   139
   Pedagogical Aspects of Being Seen and Being Known   142
   Regions of Regard and Relations to the Self   144
   Who Am I?   147
   The Secret Self   150
   Phenomenological Pedagogy   152
9. The Phenomenology of Student Experience   157
   Orienting to Student Experience   159
   Naming the Experience of Naming   160
   How to Gain Access to Student Experience   165
   What Is Named When We Speak of "Experience"?   167
   The Pedagogical Significance of Orienting to Student Experience   169
10. Cyber-Pedagogy   171
    The Inner Self   171
    Cyber-Pedagogy and the Search for Self-Identity   172
    Constant Contact and Digital Intimacy   175
11. Pedagogical Knowing and Acting   179
    The Ethics of Responsibility   181
    The Embodied and Temporal Nature of Practical Knowledge   182
    Knowing What to Do When You Don't Know What to Do   184
    Presence and Hope in an Uncertain World   190
    Damages   194
Appendix A: Ethical-Pedagogical Perspectives   195
    Deontological Pedagogy   196
    Utilitarian Pedagogy   197
    Consequentialist Pedagogy   198
    Contractualist Pedagogy   198
    Virtue Pedagogy   199
    Situational Pedagogy   200
    Relational Pedagogy   201

Appendix B: Historical Notes   203
    Human Science Pedagogy   204
    Wolfgang Klafki   206
    John Dewey   207
    Johann Friedrich Herbart on Pedagogical Tact   208
    Languages of Pedagogy   213
    Pedagogy Without *Paides*   215
    A Continually Unfolding of a Language and Practice of Pedagogy   218
    Pedagogy and the Philosophy of Caring   219
    Thematic Elements of Pedagogical Thoughtfulness and Tact   225

References   227

Index   233

About the Author   239

For Luka and Jude

It works!
(the child has stopped crying)
... but did I do right?

I know it sounds absurd
but please tell me who I am
("The Logical Song," Supertramp)

The pedagogical question:
How are we to act and live
with others, young and old,
in times of uncertainty and contingency,
realizing that we are apt to do damage?

More Praise for *Pedagogical Tact*

Van Manen's latest book Pedagogical Tact is a true work of art, elevating classroom pedagogy to an unheralded level of fascination, and revealing the committed teacher as a truly gifted and unique professional.
 —Frank Crowther, University of Southern Queensland

Having experienced a journey of insights and understandings from Max van Manen's writings on phenomenology and pedagogy since the mid-1970s, I see Pedagogical Tact as an elegant culmination that weaves together five central themes of his work, beautifully illustrated, and highly accessible for educators, childcare workers, and others who are interested in improving education at any level: the meaning and being of child sense, personal pedagogy, interpretive reflectivity, onto-theology, and pedagogical ethics are desperately needed as a necessary antidote to the autocratic, mechanistic, surveillance-oriented policies and practices that dominate schooling today.
 —William H. Schubert, University of Chicago

While The Tact of Teaching provided the initial inspiration for our popular Dutch program "Pedagogical Tact for Teachers," Max van Manen's new book deepens the phenomenon of (con)tact even further—doing so at a pleasant pace and with profound thought, and thus instilling and strengthening the swift in-the-moment-tact that a teacher, parent or school leader needs in everyday situations, and sensitizing our awareness of the truly human, truly vulnerable beauty of the teaching vocation.
 —Luc Stevens and Geert Bors, NIVOZ (Netherlands Institute for Educational Matters)

Pedagogical Tact is a masterful synthesis of Max van Manen's explorations of the relational qualities of work with children, the relational work that carries educational experience. It is a critique of much contemporary thinking about schools and an introduction to thinking in ways that go beyond critique. It is a must-read.
 —Ian Westbury, University of Illinois at Urbana-Champaign

This book demonstrates that pedagogy is a powerful practice in the caring contact of the adult-child relations. Children's lives are not fully visible to us, and yet we live in the same world. Through vocative examples and sensitive experiential reflections Max van Manen shows how pedagogical thoughtfulness and tact are urgently required of all adults who carry caring and formative responsibilities for children and youths.
 —Tone Saevi, NLA Høgskolen, Bergen, Norway

Preface

Dear Reader, this book does not need to be read in a sequential order. I have aimed to develop thematic chapters on pedagogical thoughtfulness and tact that can be read independently and in any order, though the opening chapters do begin with some introductory topics. There are five main pedagogical elements woven throughout the various chapters that explore how pedagogical thoughtfulness and tact may become conditioned in our personal lives (as teachers, parents, childcare professionals, and others) who carry pedagogical responsibilities for the young.

These thematic pedagogical elements are (1) *Child-sense*: possessing the active and reflective sensitivity to sense what goes on in the life of a child or young people in a particular and concrete situation, (2) *Personal pedagogy*: developing the self-reflexive awareness of one's own personal background and emotional make-up that contributes to a sensitive personal pedagogy, (3) *Interpretive reflectivity*: the intuitive or phenomenological reflectivity that helps to understand the lived meanings of certain phenomena or experiences in a child's or young person's life, (4) *Ontotheology*: the ontotheological awareness of what are the contemporary cultural forces that seem to shape not only the character of young people but also the pedagogical character of the adult in positive and negative modalities and directions, and (5) the personal and professional ethic that distinguishes "good" from "bad" ways of supporting and dealing with children and youths in particular situations and predicaments.

I will show that the notion of pedagogy, in the contemporary sense of this book, enjoys little currency in the present educational English language community. But the advantage of the dearth of a language of pedagogy is that it allows for a reinterpretative use of the terms "pedagogy" and "pedagogical tact," and a more sensitive attuning to the reality of adult–child relations. In this book the specification of meaning of the concept of pedagogy is not inconsistent with aspects of the long historical tradition of pedagogy in continental educational thought. But, the new language of pedagogy does not refer narrowly to a science or techniques of teaching, the production of learning outcomes, or curricular programs and competencies. Rather, pedagogy in the contemporary sense has to do with the personal relational and ethical aspects of teaching and bringing up children and youths: the pedagogy of teaching, parenting, grandparenting, etc.

The new pedagogy is that more elusive notion that lies at the heart of teaching and all other childcare practices. But even though pedagogy is a somewhat difficult subject to study and practice, a professional pedagogical perspective on teaching should be mandatory for all education. It forces us to try to see and understand the complexity of classroom and school experiences as a formative reality for children's and young people's growth, learning, and transformative becoming.

We need to restore to education its proper pedagogical impulse and meaningfulness. The notions of pedagogical thoughtfulness, reflection, and tact have preoccupied me for many years. Pedagogy lies at the heart of the formative process of growing up and the educational development of human potential as well as the unique character of each person. We must aim for depth and richness. But as parents, teachers, policy makers, and educational leaders, we neither serve our children nor their classroom teachers and school administrators well when we only focus narrowly on "learning outcomes" and "testable results" that fail to acknowledge that deep and rich educational experiences cannot properly and adequately be described in terms of programs of learning and school productivities. In our increasingly technologically mediated worlds, the personal and relational dimensions of teaching-learning and interacting are at risk.

I was "blessed" to receive my own early schooling in an inner-city school. None of us came from middle-class homes with hope of further education. I was very lucky to encounter some teachers who gave me a chance at further education that my other school friends unfortunately did not receive. These early life experiences prompted my fascination with a novel such as *Ciske the Rat* (see Chapter 2) that I read several times as a young adolescent. My heart hurts for the hundreds and thousands of children who are orphaned by wars, who suffer from abuse, disease, or starvation, or who are recruited as child soldiers in distant lands. Their miseries press on our collective conscience for a guilt we cannot wash off. Yet it is not my intent to infuse a particular social cause into this pedagogical text. Stories from and about children were gathered from a variety of schools and from a variety of backgrounds and social contexts. In putting their experiences into words young people come to know their experiences and in reflecting on their experiences young people come to know what they mean to them.

I hope readers of this text will personally recognize an impulse that has motivated me over many years to remain focused on and guided by the philosophical perspective of life meaning, the methodology of existential reflection on lived experience, and the inspirational motivation that bring us to the study of pedagogy in the first place. I think this is the same impulse that brings young people to opt for a pedagogically charged career: teaching, education, counseling, social work, psychology, health science, and so forth. I genuinely feel that pedagogy is the vocational calling that lies at the origin of humanity and at the heart of our humanness and our purpose for being human in a fragile but fascinating world.

PREFACE

About the Cover Image

Into the Water! (1898), by Virginie Demont-Breton, The Royal Museum of Fine Arts, Antwerp, Belgium.

The cover painting *Into the Water!* by Virginie Demont-Breton, portrays a mother and her two children at an ocean beach. For many children, playing on the sandy beach and splashing in the shallow water is an adventurous and pleasurable activity. But this mother has difficulty with her toddler, who resists being taken into the water. The mother pulls the child's arm with a strong stride to force him to walk on his own feet. But we see from his whole physically tensed body that he is tenaciously struggling to stop her. Simultaneously he is clutching her skirt as if to seek security in holding onto her. He is burying his head in his mother's clothing. But the mother's demeanor seems firm and not at all playful. Is the little boy simply being recalcitrant? It would not be very helpful to call it a battle of wills.

This painting may be seen as an apt metaphor for pedagogical tact (or the lack of it) in situations in which an adult has to know what to do when not really knowing what to do. Although the image here is of a small infant, the metaphoric quality of the image applies to all ages and pedagogical situations and relations.

We need to try to understand what this moment may be like for the mother as well as for the child. Perhaps the mother wants to introduce the child to the pleasures of the beach? Perhaps she aims to simply let him experience the water on his feet? We do not see the face of the toddler. Is he crying? Is he scared looking at the wide ocean stretching out in front of them? Is he afraid of the water? Is the water too cold? Does he not like to get his feet wet? Or does he just want to go home? The small infant on the mother's shoulder looks unstirred by all the turmoil. It is a classic painting of a recognizable pedagogical moment of a caring parent who attempts to draw her child into the world.

The mother seems determined and may feel that she is doing what is best for her child. What emotions motivate her? And what is her child experiencing right there? Does the mother understand and recognize the meaning and significance of her child's distress? Her hand holds her child's hand in a firm, full-fisted grasp. She appears intent to have him experience this wondrous water world. But the child does not appreciate her intent. Should the mother stop and reflect on her attempt to take an unwilling child into the water? Or does she feel at the end of her rope? If her gestures do not seem tactful, they sure raise questions of pedagogical tact. Should she try to be a bit gentler and more patient in persuading him to venture a few steps into the water?

How many of us have not experienced times when we were coerced or influenced by an adult (a parent, teacher, or other caring adult) to be or do something we did not want to be or do? Or we experienced times when we were prevented to do something we wanted to do? Perhaps it was for the best? Or perhaps not? The latency of some tactless pedagogical actions of a parent or teacher may still haunt us for the rest of our lives. At the hand of many evocative experiential practical examples, this phenomenological text asks: What role does or should pedagogy play in schools, families, communities, and in our media-mediated worlds that are increasingly being rationalized and ruled by instrumentalist managerial, technocratic, and economistic policies, forces, and values? This book on pedagogical thoughtfulness and tact aims to complement and reflectively enrich teaching- and learning-oriented texts and childcare literature in educational, psychological, health science, and childcare-oriented programs.

Acknowledgments[1]

I thank the numerous school students and their teachers who have shared their experiences with me in writing and research projects that were generously funded by the Social Sciences Research Council of Canada. I also thank my graduate students, who have shared their personal experiences and their phenomenological reflections on pedagogy and pedagogical stories with me.

Over the years I have benefitted from ongoing discussions with many friends and colleagues about pedagogical issues and the fragilities of the future for our own children. Unlike other academic or political involvements, pedagogy is always a very personal concern. In a sense teachers do not care for abstract children; they care for the actual children with whom they live and for whom they personally hold educational and pedagogical responsibilities, here and now.

I sincerely thank my friends and colleagues Catherine Adams, Geert Bors, Frank Crowther, Teresa Dobson, Bas Levering, Wilfried Lippitz, Tone Saevi, and others who have contributed to or commented on aspects or topics of this text. And I thank my publisher, Mitch Allen, for believing in the importance of pedagogy in our personal and professional lives.

I thank my wife, Judith van Manen, a gifted teacher, for her pedagogical insights and sensitivities. And I am grateful to my son Mark, who thoughtfully recalls childhood stories (some of which I might rather forget), and to my son Michael and daughter-in-law Miep, who exemplify how to be thoughtful parents to our grandchildren, Luka and Jude. I thank them all for their love and incredible accomplishments and for showing me tactfully the need to remain humble for often not knowing what to do when I had to know what to do as a parent or grandparent in life's predicaments.

---

[1] I thank the Hal Leonard Corporation for permission to use lyrics from *The Logical Song*, words and music by Rick Davies and Roger Hodgson, copyright © 1979 ALMO MUSIC CORP. and DELICATE MUSIC. All Rights Controlled and Administered by ALMO MUSIC CORP. All Rights Reserved Used by Permission. *Reprinted by Permission of Hal Leonard Corporation.*

Chapter One

The Primacy of Pedagogy

Missed Moments of Pedagogical Tact?

At a pleasant social evening some friends are sitting around talking about a symphony orchestra that is playing in town. Edward, a retired businessman, expresses his admiration for the concertmaster. Some other people join in talking about the challenges of being a successful musician. Then Edward takes the floor again:

> You know, this is a memory that has obsessed me my entire life. Until recently I have not been able to talk about it with anyone because it is so hurtful. Even as an adult, sharing it would have brought me to tears. When I was sixteen years old, after studying violin for a number of years, I realized that I could never really be good enough. I just lacked something. I could not really excel. So I decided to give it up. My father was very unhappy about my decision. He tried to change my mind. But I refused. I told him that I knew that I would never be able to play the instrument properly. Angrily, my father took the violin from my hands. He hung it on the wall of the living room and said, "From now on, whenever you look at this violin, you will know what a failure you are in my eyes." I felt horrible. After several weeks my mother took the violin down from the wall. She felt sorry for me. But the empty spot could not be taken down. It haunted me: I was a failure in my father's eyes. The memory of that moment has troubled me all my life. Therefore, I have always told my own kids that they should do whatever they feel is right for them and not what they may feel I expect from them. My father never took his words back about me being a failure, even though eventually I became the successful head of a large company. But now, at the age of eighty-two, I finally feel that I have dealt with my secret pain or, at least, that I can share it here with you.

Edward's story shows how the latency of pedagogical moments can affect us for the rest of our lives, whether we are consciously aware of it or not. We can easily recognize the significance of the occurrence of *negative* pedagogical moments. At times we may still blame certain adults from our childhood

---

Pedagogical Tact: Knowing What to Do When You Don't Know What to Do, by Max van Manen, 15–20. © 2015 Taylor & Francis. All rights reserved.

for their neglect, their negative influences, or past harmful actions that still haunt us. These blames and accusations also constitute the pedagogical narratives of our lives. And they may determine our own pedagogies.

But hopefully each of us can also recognize what good pedagogy can do when we gratefully acknowledge the love and care we received from a mother, father, teacher, or some other significant adult who worried about us and was there for us when needed. This is especially clear when we reflect on the happiness, successes, and blessings we experienced in our families as children and in classrooms as students. We may recognize the consequences of pedagogy when we become aware of the latent, lasting, and lingering effects of the events that make up the innumerable often-forgotten experiences, foggily fragmented and half-remembered pedagogical happenings in our childhoods. The latent values of these events mean that they have formative—and yet often untraceable—consequences for our unfolding sense of self, personal identity, secret interiorities, and for who and what we (have) become.

How many of us are still longing for the father's recognition or the mother's appreciation that still somehow drives what we do and what we hope to make of ourselves? This powerful pedagogical theme of the latent significance of an adult's approval in our lives is a poorly recognized and a little understood pedagogical phenomenon. Even those who have developed conflicts or messed up relationships with their parents may at times realize to their surprise (or even chagrin) how this father's regard or this mother's love is still a deep-seated object of desire that makes us do or achieve things that give positive meaning to our lives. We recognize these pedagogical latencies in the lives of famous authors such as Franz Kafka or Marcel Proust who suffered from dysfunctional relations with their fathers. But no doubt we can recognize the entanglements of recognition and (dis) approval in our own lives or in the lives of others close to us.

Theories of extrinsic and intrinsic motivation and reward are existentially simplistic mechanisms that fail to realize that the long-term latency of pedagogical events belongs to the silent secrets of the narrative themes of our lives. Some parents place high expectations on their child, expectations that the child may or may not be able to live up to. Other parents claim not to pose expectations, but the children experience them nevertheless and perhaps even more compellingly. Again, other parents may truly not entertain any expectations, or so it seems. But how do their children experience the lack of expectations? Only pedagogically-sensitive teachers may surmise the consequences of such potential entanglements of expectations when during a parent-teacher conference they encounter the parent in the child and the child in the parent.

We simply cannot predict in childhood how the latency of pedagogical influence is felt and realized throughout life, even when this particular child has meanwhile become an adult. Of course, the child also influences the adult. The pedagogical relation is complex, and in part it signifies also a process of self-development and self-understanding for the adult. The mother, father, grandparent, teacher, psychologist, nurse, counselor, pediatrician, and those others who care for children learn to understand themselves in new ways as they are prompted to reflect on themselves and their interactions with the children for whom they care.

A Pedagogical Moment

In a poem entitled the "Bearhug," Michael Ondaatje (1979, p. 104) describes how his son had been calling him from the bedroom for a goodnight hug and kiss. Ondaatje is a loving father but he is busy with something and so he yells "okay" to his son—that he will be there in just a moment. Then, after finishing, he finally and absentmindedly walks into his son's bedroom, and what does he see? His son is standing there, expectantly, with his arms outstretched and a huge smile on his face. He is ready for the ritualistic good-night bearhug. In the next stanza, Ondaatje gives a sensitive poetic description of the way a parent hugs a child. But then, almost as an afterthought, two short lines trail the end of his poem:

> How long was he standing there
> like that, before I came?

Between the calling of his young son and this lingering moment of reflecting, Michael Ondaatje experiences a pedagogical moment. A pedagogical moment that takes the form of personal responsiveness: the father acts (says "goodnight" to his son, though after letting him wait rather long), and he reflects (asks himself, "What was it like for my son to have to wait like that?" And by implication, perhaps, "Should I have been a bit more attentive?"). The goodnight kiss may seem a simple ritual, but in actually it can be filled with psychological and pedagogical significance, as, for example, the many references and studies about the goodnight kiss in Marcel Proust's writings attest (1981)—in his staying awake while waiting for his mother to come and whose kiss would finally be able to put Marcel to sleep, his father's disapproval of him, and the psychoanalytic entanglements.

Unlike Proust's interpreters, Ondaatje does not seem to want to make a psychoanalytic issue out of this childhood incident. And yet Ondaatje alludes to the implied meanings of this common, significant childhood moment (the child cannot sleep and calls to the parent for a goodnight hug; Ondaatje dawdles, and dawdles some more, and then, finally, comes to the child's bed). Ondaatje makes this moment into a pedagogical incident by wondering how long his son had been waiting for him. And he prompts us to reminisce what this moment may be like for the child. How many of us did not have childhood experiences like this—as parent or as child: waiting for the goodnight hug or kiss? Of course, one might hear the irritated adult refrain that parents should not always have to be at the beck-and-call of their children, that children should not be spoiled, that overprotectiveness may unwittingly create children who remain emotionally too dependent on their parents, and, of course, that children should learn that they sometimes have to wait for their parent to be available.

But it is quite clear from the poem that Ondaatje did not deliberately let his son wait for the goodnight hug (e.g., this kid is just too demanding—I don't want to be too overprotective). But these considerations show the thoroughly ethical nature of pedagogy. Ondaatje's poem has such a pointed pedagogical significance in that it shows how the reflexive turn of his afterthought is a pedagogical wondering: What was his child's experience of waiting like? What calls in the calling of the child for his father? What kind of waiting was this? How does this waiting condition the child's experience of the pleasure of the anticipated hug and kiss? How good is such goodnight bear hug? How is this waiting and the goodnight kiss experienced as a portal for sleep?

Pedagogical experiences occur in situations when and where adults stand in pedagogical relations with children or young people. These situations do not need to be uncommon. Usually pedagogical moments happen in ordinary situations when an adult is required to act pedagogically. It is a matter of acting pedagogically responsibly and appropriately in everyday situations. Sometimes, if not commonly, in our daily living with children we are required to act instantly, in the spur of the moment. As a rule, we do not have time to lean back in our chair and deliberatively decide what to do in the situation. And even when there is time to reflect on what alternative actions are available and what best approach one should take, in the pedagogical moment one must act immediately, even if that action may consist of holding back.

What Is Pedagogy?

So what, then, is pedagogy? Well, this is a question that does not really seem to need an academic answer. Anyone knows what pedagogy is who has received the attentive care and worries of a mother, a father, a teacher, a grandparent, or some other adult who, at various times, played a supportive and formative part in our young lives. Without the pedagogical support from these adults, we simply could not and would not be who we are, or, worse, we would not even be alive today.

So don't we already know what pedagogy is? The answer is paradoxical: we do and we don't. We do because parenting (and teaching) is the oldest profession in the world. Child rearing is as intrinsic to human life as is feeding, clothing, caring, sex, and sheltering. Pedagogy inheres and is rooted in our phenomenological response to the child's natural vulnerability. In spite of the historical atrocities human beings have inflicted on their offspring, we recognize that there is a need to do right with the young child. (Call it instinct, sentimentality, culture, motherhood, or paternity—call it whatever you wish.) It is the poverty of social science that it fails to see an obvious given: the young child, by virtue of his or her very vulnerability, tends to bring out the best in grown-ups.

Yet, in a sense we don't know what pedagogy is because the phenomenon of pedagogy is ultimately a mystery when we push for a more originary understanding of pedagogy. The primal meaning of pedagogy is beyond rational understanding. The child is born crying, and the parent experiences the cry as an appeal, as a transforming experience to *do* something: to hold the child, protect her, smile, and perhaps worry whether everything is all right. This first overwhelming sensual and sensitive sensibility that a new parent experiences is often this ability of a seemingly natural responsiveness: response-ability, the unfolding of our pedagogic nature. As new parents, before we have a chance to sit back and reflect on whether we can accept this child, the child has already made us act. And luckily for humankind, this spontaneous needfulness to do the right thing usually *is* the right thing. As we reach to hold the child (rather than turn away and let it perish), we have already acted pedagogically.

When living side by side with adults, children soon prompt increasingly reflective questions. In other words, as soon as we gain a lived sense of the pedagogic quality of parenting and teaching, we start to question and doubt ourselves. Pedagogy *is* this questioning, this doubting. We wonder: Did I do the right thing? Why do some people teach or bring their children up in such a different manner? We are shocked when we see or hear how children are physically or psychologically abused. We also may notice with distress how many children are more subtly ill treated or abused. We see this all around us in shopping places, in public transportation locations, in the neighborhood, in newspapers, and on the street.

From the history of child psychology and child studies we know that young children, who do not experience a minimum of proper care, tend to do poorly in life. Abandoned babies in crowded orphanages that lacked adequate nursing care have died from the simple deficiency of loving touch and affection—they perished from lack of contact. Children who must somehow grow up while surrounded by neglect or, worse, by suffering abuse and maltreatment may be doomed to be damaged for the remainder of their adult lives.

The simple point is this: it is pedagogy that makes the crucial difference in a child's life. Pedagogy involves us in distinguishing actively and/

or reflectively what is good or right and what is life enhancing, just, and supportive from what is not good, wrong, unjust, or damaging in the ways we act, live, and deal with children. In this sense pedagogy is the experience of the good, the meaning of the good, of goodness. A positive pedagogy of parenting and teaching may promise a life with adequate doses of meaningfulness, happiness, and healthy and responsible relations with others. The good of pedagogy is not some social product or educational outcome but rather goodness itself: goodness *of* and *for* this or that child or these young people. This goodness must constantly be recognized, realized, and retrieved in particular actions in concrete and contingent situations and relations. In the words of Levinas: "Only goodness is good" (1995, p. 61).

Upon reflection the meaning of pedagogy in the adult-child relation is profoundly enigmatic. The inceptual phenomenon of the pedagogical relation is probably the most elemental dimension of human existence. So, in this book I use the term "pedagogy" to refer to this primordial adult-child relation that is biological and cultural, ancient and present, mundane and mysterious, sensuous and sensitive to the ethical demand as it is experienced in pedagogical relations, situations, and actions. As well, the relational affect for the child or young person is constitutive of the relational ethics between the adults who are caring for the child. This relational ethic intends fidelity, love, trust, mutual dependency, and the acceptance of caring responsibility of the adults for their child and for each other.

CHAPTER TWO

Experiencing Pedagogy Vicariously

Such diverse authors as Martin Langeveld, Klaus Mollenhauer, Otto Bollnow, Hannah Arendt, and Bernard Stiegler see pedagogy rooted in the ethical sphere of the adult-child relation and the cultural contexts that shape the pedagogical relation. Pedagogy derives its impetus in the responsibility that adults carry for children or young people who cannot yet be charged with certain responsibilities themselves.

Pedagogical theorizing and practice differ from other social disciplines and practices in that they always orient to the child's or young person's lifeworld and growing up toward maturity. But the ethics of professional pedagogical theorizing and practice is not really possible without the support of empirical and theoretical insights from other disciplines: psychology, sociology, childhood studies, anthropological studies of children's cultures, jurisprudential knowledge of children's rights, the humanities, and other human and social science that are relevant to our understanding of children.

Pedagogy, as theoretical social science, studies the ethically sensitive realities and formative experiences of children: How are children to live and grow up at home, at school, and in other childrearing settings? How are personal and societal realities of children and childhood pedagogically perceived in everyday life, social theory, and media and technologies of communication? How do adults interact with children in pedagogically positive or negative ways? How are pedagogical responsibilities interpreted in parental, educational, legal, and medical environments? For example, we may ask: How are children regarded in newspapers, novels, or movies? How are children depicted in movies differently in culturally different cinema? What are the ethical implications and consequences of these perceptions?

Pedagogical seeing of children in movies differs from ordinary cinematographic watching in that "seeing movies pedagogically" is always an ethically engaged watching and watchfulness. Pedagogical seeing is sensitive to the

---

Pedagogical Tact: Knowing What to Do When You Don't Know What to Do, by Max van Manen, 21–31.
© 2015 Taylor & Francis. All rights reserved.

ways that adults are involved in children's lives (van Manen, 1979, 1982, 1984, 1990). As we observe the lives that adults live with children, we may study family, community, neighborhood, and school or classroom life from these various pedagogical perspectives. We may reflect on the nature of the *pedagogical relation* that exists between the adult(s) and the children. We may observe how the pedagogical relation becomes actualized in *pedagogical situations*. We may notice how the relation and the situation contribute to a *pedagogical atmosphere*. We may study the *pedagogical actions* for their ethical significance. And we may try to trace how events carry latent *pedagogical significance* that may manifest itself later in life.

Virtual Pedagogy in Cinema

Cinema, poetry, novels, and other arts offer us opportunities to experience pedagogical moments prereflectively and thus make them available for our reflective attention. Just as with the Ondaatje poem in the opening chapter, we may vicariously gain pedagogical understandings through the virtually mediated immediacy of cinematic experiences.

In the classic movie *The Browning Version* (Gitlin and Scott, 1994), Albert Finney in the teacher role of Mr. Andrew Crocker-Harris gives a painful farewell speech to the students and staff of a British boys' school at which he had been teaching for eighteen years. The viewer of the movie is quickly impressed that Crocker-Harris is an expert in the classic languages he teaches and is exacting and demanding of the learning he expects of his pupils. So why apologize? He apologizes because he realizes he failed not in his curriculum expertise or instructional standards but for the fact that his teaching lacked pedagogical attentiveness:

> I am sorry.... I am sorry because I have failed to give you what it is your right to demand of me as your teacher, sympathy, encouragement, humanity. I have degraded the noblest calling a man can follow—the care and molding of the young. When I came to this school I still believed that I had a vocation for teaching. I knew what I wanted to do, and yet I ... I did not do it. I can offer no excuses; I have failed, and miserably failed. And I can only hope that you can find it in your hearts—you and the countless others who've gone before you—to forgive me for having let you down. I shan't find it easy to forgive myself. (Excerpt from the movie *The Browning Version*)

No matter how old fashioned the apology of Crocker-Harris may sound and how antiquated his expression of "molding of the young," there is something in his speech that should give us pause: that teaching and caring for children—whether as professional educator or as parent—is indeed the noblest calling that any human being can follow in his or her life. And yet there is something even more stirring in this apology. We should also give pause to the realization that undoubtedly, in our pedagogical lives with children, we commit to failings about which we may not find it easy to forgive ourselves. A profound failing of Mr. Andrew Crocker-Harris is a problem that is common in many schools: the teacher teaches to the heads of the students but fails to be sensitive to their hearts. He fails to see that they are not just "learners" but also full human beings in the process of personal becoming: becoming worthwhile persons for whom classic languages may have special significance in their present and later personal and social lives.

Pedagogical failings do not refer here to poorly applied techniques of teaching and curricular competencies; rather, these failings have to do with the personal relational and ethical aspects of teaching: the pedagogy of teaching. Pedagogy is that more elusive and invisible dimension that lies at the heart of teaching and all other childcare practices. But even though pedagogy is a difficult subject to study and practice, gaining a pedagogical perspective on teaching should be mandatory for all teachers. It forces us to try to see and understand the complexity of classroom and school experiences and events as a formative reality that encompasses the many influences and factors that play a role in the students' transformative becoming of educated grown-ups.

Watching movies in which the pedagogical relation between children and adults is at the center is a revealing activity. It permits us to take a reflective glance at situations, relations, and events that tend to elude us in everyday living. Especially when we watch scenes that mirror and uncannily exemplify our own lives, sometimes so recognizably, we cannot help but admit our own failings. Film critics rarely if ever view the movies they discuss from a pedagogically sensitive perspective. They rarely have an eye for the ways that childhood and children are portrayed in the cinema of yesterday and today. If they did, they would notice the sense of hope, tragedy, and humor that hangs over all of our lives. There is not a single honest film about children that does not show, directly or indirectly, the good as well as the damage we do as adults to children. Even though we may generally approach our vocation with loving pedagogical intentions and sentiments, we cannot help but do wrong at times—and oddly we often fail at those moments when we assume that we act out of caring responsibility.

The movie *The Class* (Arnal, Benjo, Letellier, and Scotta, 2008) shows the disillusionments and occasional triumphs of a pedagogically well-intentioned teacher. In contrast with the British upper-social-class setting of *The Browning Version*, *The Class* portrays a multi-ethnic French school in a low-income neighborhood. François Begaudeau, who plays himself as the teacher François Marin, wants to deal with his students in an open and respectful manner. He engages them in his lessons through dialogue and conversation, but things continually go wrong. This movie clearly shows how the ongoing interactions, the constantly changing relations, and the shifting situations in the classroom constitute the experiential reality and sphere within which all instruction and curriculum-mandated teaching takes place. The pedagogical atmosphere of the classroom seems composed of modulating waves of attention and distraction, washing over the complex life and dynamics of interiorities and exteriorities within which teaching and learning occur.

The individual events of teaching and learning cannot really be culled from the total sphere within which it all takes place. As we observe the goings on and as we focus here and there on the students and teacher, we should wonder: How are these students really experiencing the situations? What if anything is this student "learning" in this moment? What about that student? What events may have lasting consequences for the student? What is the teacher's awareness of what is taking place while involved in a routine exposition or a challenging exchange? How does the "personality" of the class as a social entity moderate the experiences of the various individual children and the teacher?

Sometimes teachers say one thing but do another. It is one thing to know that every student needs to feel respected, but what if the body language, the tone of voice, or the eyes of the teacher do not express such willingness to respect? So how is it that this teacher, François Marin, can feel so dedicated, can so eloquently express insights into students' lives and share with his colleagues how children should be positively regarded and understood while also, in his interactions with the students, he often seems to be saying and doing something entirely the opposite. He frequently does not seem able to evoke the right tone for teaching what he is trying to teach. He seems to be caught between his desire for maintaining a reciprocal relation with his students and the authoritative social structure of the institution in which they find themselves.

The teacher attempts to motivate the students to show interest in his lessons on grammar and composition, but the students seem more motivated to question his knowledge, sincerity, authority, and true intentions with a boring subject that seems irrelevant to their lives. The school is intent on producing productive citizens, but the students do not accept that motivational agenda. We quickly get to know some of the individual student characters: an umbrageous Arab girl who constantly seems to feel slighted, an intelligent and energetic African boy who seems to have his own agenda, a smart but cautious Asian boy, and many other vivacious students whose motivations seems to fluctuate in many directions except that of the goal of the lesson. This entire tumultuous scene makes evident how problematic it is to speak of "motivating" students for learning certain subjects. Can we ever really ascribe causal significance, inner life, and sustained meaning to the phenomenology of motivation? Or is "motivation" just a term of a discourse that pretends to make sense of how and why people act the way they act?

In one of the last scenes of *The Class*, at the end of the last day of school, the teacher asks students to tell what they feel they had learned during the school year. Some students joke, and others share some of their interests. When the buzzer goes, they all file out of the classroom. But one student lingers and stays behind. She approaches the teacher at his desk. She is obviously distressed. She confesses to the teacher that she is worried because "I did not learn anything." The teacher Marin doesn't seem to understand: "What? That doesn't mean anything." He explains that it may be difficult to think and remember what she has learned.

—But I don't understand.
—What do you mean?
—I don't understand what we do.
—In French?
—In everything.
—You can't say you don't understand anything in any subject. That is not true.
—I don't want to go to vocational school.
—There's no question of that yet. You are moving on to next year. You'll have plenty of time to think about your future. Vocational school isn't an absolute certainty. It all depends on how you do next year.
—But I don't want to. (Excerpt from the movie *The Class*)

This is such a wrenching and critical scene because, again, the teacher Marin fails to fully recognize the pedagogical significance of the moment. Some students suffer through our schools, day after day, week after week, month after month, while none of their teachers has an inkling of the daily drowning desperation that is the consequence of having lost touch with the lessons, not being noticed, not being understood, and not being worried about. In this instant the teacher fails to say or do whatever it is that the girl needs to hear. It is a failure to make contact and to reach out when it is so desperately needed and wanted.

Movies like *The Browning Version* and *The Class* are so pedagogically powerful because they make "indirectly" visible what seems to be largely invisible in the educational literature. First, they make visible the invisibility of pedagogy itself. Pedagogy can only be seen and felt indirectly and often only interpretively from life's happenings. They make visible the slight gestures, the significant glances, the atmospheric qualities, the conspicuous hints, and the numerous other physiognomic and relational subtleties that betray or intimate emotions and intentions that often contradict what we are actually saying or claiming to do. Such movies may show viscerally that the dynamics of interacting with children depends on pedagogy: the ability to distinguish actively and reflectively what is good from what is not so good in our interactions with the children for whom we carry responsibility.

Virtual Pedagogy in Fictional Literature

During my visit to the Netherlands I have managed to locate an old, yellowed copy of the trilogy by the Dutch author Piet Bakker. The books are out of print now. And this copy, which I recovered from an antique bookstore, upon opening, pours out the same papery scent that my parents' books possessed. When I was a young adolescent, these books were already secondhand. The aging pages show brown spots like the skin of my mother's hands. I recall how turning the dry and fragile pages would release this not unpleasant musty odor. This slight smell of stale paper dust and dried glue somehow belong to the story of the life of Ciske and his teacher. The story belongs to my childhood. But it also confronts me with my own aging, my mortality in the light of the youth of my own children and grandchildren. And as I now skim the pages of this book, I virtually skim through the memories of my early school years.

How do children enter our adult lives? How do they acquire significance, concreteness, reality? As I reread the opening lines from the novel *Ciske the Rat*, the story and atmosphere revisit me with a vague vividness that characterizes childhood memory. I am rereading a childhood reading. I am reading my childhood.

And that is how *Ciske the Rat* came to our school:

> "Today we are going to receive something that will give us much joy," mocked Maatsuyker, the school principal, as we were just finishing our morning cup of coffee before the start of school. "A transfer. Boy, oh boy, he has quite a reputation for criminal behavior already. In and out of juvenile court. Fighting with a knife.... And he will be in your class, Bruis!"
>
> The latter was meant for me. I regarded him somewhat coolly because Maatsuyker was in the habit of acting rather pompously and overbearingly. Especially toward me, because I had only been teaching for a fortnight. He knew that he could not impress the other teachers, but with me he was still playing up his authority.
>
> Maatsuyker looked at me with a certain glee, which annoyed me. He immediately passed me some pedagogical advice:
>
> "If I may counsel you, then let him know immediately who is boss. Put him up against the wall and use your hands if you have to. That kind of kid only has respect for physical authority, if you know what I mean. Give him a licking so he will think twice trying anything with you."
>
> "No way," I replied curtly. "Then the kid knows instantly that in truth you are afraid of him."
>
> "A nice challenge for Bruis!" said Ms. Tedeman. "Bruis still has ideals. Well, you can practice your pedagogic skills, young man."
>
> Ms. Tedeman is a likable spinster teacher in her fifties. She has lost some of her enthusiasm for teaching, but she still has her heart in the right place for the fifty-plus children in her class. [my translation] (Bakker, 1944, p. 7)

From my present point of view, the author, Piet Bakker, was led more by a sense of realism and humanity than by a motivated understanding of pedagogy. And yet what was so appealing in these stories was the difficult but growing caring relation between a less-than-perfect teacher and a troubled child. Did I, as a child, identify with Ciske? Or did I identify with his teacher?

> Jorisse nodded to Ms. Tedema's words. He had a story. "When, last year, we went on a field trip, a police van stopped at the station just about six yards from our group. And out of the car emerged a heavily shackled fellow. Of course the children were all eyes. And the chap scarcely saw me and he shouts, "Hi teacher!" Indeed, it was a former student of mine! And what does the schlemiel do? He starts singing: Row, row, row your boat. . . . ! And suddenly I see him in front of me! The third desk near the window. A nice boy with brown eyes and a gray sweater. A pleasant open face. So then it really bothered me when I saw him being led away by two cops. I mean I did not get upset by my former student but by those cops. No, don't laugh so stupidly! I felt that those men should keep their hands off one of my kids. Crazy, of course. And then I looked at the children around me. They stood there so charmingly with their backpacks and their cheery clothes, and I thought, God knows who of you will end up in one of those police vans. Yes, that was a lousy start of a day's outing with my class." [my translation] (Bakker, 1944, p. 8)

The Ciske trilogy awakened my desire to become a teacher, to want to make a difference in the lives of children. But I was perhaps twelve years old then, still a child myself. Can a child have a pedagogic interest in the welfare of another child? I believe that as a child, I developed a caring relation to Ciske. But the relation was a reader's experience. I understood something I could not yet explain. The story of Ciske spoke to me, but I could not tell why it had such appealing power. It simply "spoke" to me. Do I have words for the experience now? How can a teacher communicate what it means to develop a caring relation to children?

What I realize now is that this book is structured like a composite of stories, anecdotes. Bruis is the authorial voice, and he tells anecdotes about Ciske—about his own life as a teacher with the child Ciske, as if he were entering in a diary everything that seemed worthwhile recounting as it happened during the day. What makes the stories so effective is that they each seem to tell something important about teaching, about the failures, promises, disappointments, and possibilities of our pedagogic living with children. Yes, fictional stories are so powerful, so effective, so consequential in that they can explain things that resist straightforward explanation or conceptualization. They explain indirectly by evoking images of understanding of the significance of an experience.

> "There he is," Maatsuyker suddenly announced. At the end of the hallway stood the Rat. Leaning against the wall. His head hardly reaching the coat pegs.

> A smallish boy. Maatsuyker right away walked up to him, like a man who had an important mission to fulfill. There he stood: big, enormous, and assuming in front of that little Rat. A blush of anger crept to my face when I saw how, without any ado, he dealt the boy a slap in the face. And I heard him shout in a high-pitched voice, "Can't you properly take your hat off your head?! That is what we are used to here. Remember that! Hat off, stinker!"
>
> The jerk! All children walk in the hallway with their hats on. The kid was utterly surprised by the unexpected attack. Maatsuyker wanted to reach out again, but slyly and smoothly, the Rat ducked away from his flailing arm, and before Maatsuyker knew, the Rat skittishly ran away. And then I saw how he had obtained his nickname. That sly shifty escape had something animalistic, really like a rat that is hunted by a yelping dog.
>
> But just as he wanted to run onto the street, Vermeer walked through the door. He always arrives a bit later at school because he has to take his daughter to kindergarten. Vermeer caught the Rat in his arms and carried the struggling and kicking boy to Maatsuyker.
>
> "Come on, little deserter!" he smiled. At that point I quickly walked up in order to prevent any more incidents. I was furious! That stupid and awkward Maatsuyker had ruined my intention to greet the Rat normally, like I would have greeted any other newly transferred student to my class. [my translation] (Bakker, 1944, pp. 8–9)

The Ciske triology is hardly an example of high literature. In Holland this genre is called "folk novels." And the three volumes were among the dozen or so books that my parental home possessed during my elementary school years. How these books entered our house I do not know. By the time I developed a hunger for words they were simply there on a small shelf next to an ornamental ironwork statue that my father had welded for a hobby. My parents never seemed to pay much attention to the books (my father only read newspapers), and so I moved several of them to a corner under the eaves of my tiny bedroom. Consequently, I had finished reading the Ciske novels (as well as an adult text on human sexuality and other less memorable works) before I had completed grade five. For several years the Ciske novels were among the most frequently reread texts in my modest but steadily growing library.

> "I'll take him to my class right now," I said resolutely. And without waiting for a response from the dumbfounded Maatsuyker, I turned to the Rat: "Let's go, mate!" For a moment he looked at me. He had large gray eyes. Eyes with a wild glance. And yet incredibly beautiful. Those eyes in that pale face with lank, colorless hair and thin lips. Those eyes were the only thing really striking in that shabby child's body.
>
> In that glance there was something like, "What do you big guys all want from me?!" and I could not help but wink at him, in which he probably read, "Just let them drop dead, Rat! Come on along!" Because he walked very tamely beside me through the corridor. [my translation] (Bakker, 1944, p. 9)

The Ciske novels were well suited to my circumstances. I attended an inner-city Dutch school where a street-kid like Ciske would not have felt out of place. There were several Ciskes in my class. Often these kids evoked in me a mixed sense of pity and fear. Pity because I sensed that they were not loved by anyone, at home or at school. Fear because I sensed their growing hardness and immunity to the damaging effects of the poverty, abuse, and neglect around them. Ironically, as a child I did not fully realize that my elementary school had been an inner-city school of questionable quality until I became a teacher many years later. Then I received my first teaching appointment at the same school, but not after I was warned about the rough-trade nature of this lower working-class school whose students simply were not destined for higher goals such as grammar school or academic high school, preparing for university or professional career. Few finished high school at all. Most students were children without a "future."

> To be honest, my meaningful wink was meant more as a protest against the meddlesome interference of Maatsuyker than as a sign of sympathy for the kid. Maybe also because I felt ashamed for the school. The school is, for the children, a piece of civilization. Our modes of conduct need to be decent. Even the littlest beggar has a right that his teacher is a considerate, gentle person. I am not at all opposed—and neither are the children—to the occasional rap. But Maatsuyker does it in such a brutish, vulgar manner.
>
> So when we entered the classroom, Johnny Verkerk screamed, "Sir, that's the Rat!" And then I did really the same as Maatsuyker, because promptly Johnny received a rap on his knuckle-hard skull. "Finish your math," I growled. "I did not ask you for any advice, did I?"
>
> There shone a certain contentment in those big, gray eyes of the Rat. [my translation] (Bakker, 1944, p. 9)

I am an older adult now, and as I continue to reread pages from the Ciske novels, I gain some insight into the charm of this text. This child, Ciske, is an enigma. He is the original stranger, the child who brings the adult to puzzlement because the adult does not understand the child and does not know what to do with the child. The child is as unfathomable, as bewildering as a wild animal. And yet in so many ways this child is the product of an adult world. The adult does not realize that he is already deeply involved in the child's problems.

> I harbor genuine envy to those real and experienced teachers such as Vermeer and Jorisse. They seem to know almost immediately and naturally what tone to use with any particular student. I don't in the least. I still have to learn that from a few hundred children. And they unfortunately are my guinea pigs—that is their bad luck.
>
> When the Rat stood at my desk, the class was quietly working on the math problems that I always put on the board before school starts to please the eager kids. But I could not help noticing how continuously some eyes wandered

toward the Rat. The latter was standing there, as an accused who is determined to keep his mouth shut in front of the Bench's Magistrate.

"Well, tell me, what is your name, comrade?" I said as naturally as possible. But the Rat must have detected something unnatural, something artificial or phony in my voice, because he looked at me with those strange eyes and remained silent. "You won't suck me in that easily!" that face said. [my translation] (Bakker, 1944, p. 11)

How does one find the right tone, the right words for each child? That is surely the question at the heart of our pedagogic lives. The teacher's task is not merely to find an opening, a way of reaching the child. As if it is not difficult enough to detect what language, what words, what gestures, what kind of tone can breach the barriers that separate any particular child's world from an adult's understanding and good intentions. The teacher must also do something with the language. The teacher's aim is not to battle, to penetrate, to violate the child's inner nature; rather, the teacher's intent is pedagogic—to establish a pedagogical relation wherein it is possible to distinguish what is good and what is not good for the child.

Damn, what incredible eyes that boy has in his head! Pearl gray with dark, scintillating pupils. An ill-omened glow smoldering in those eyes. The eyes of a wild creature!

"Well, that is babyish," I responded with an air of indifference. "You don't even dare to say who you are?"

Again he looked at me with a stony stare, and then I did something stupid. "Perhaps you would rather tell your name to the man from the hallway?" I said mockingly. What an ass I was to resort to Maatsuyker as some kind of bogeyman! I became annoyed when the Rat haughtily shrugged his shoulders. His face did not betray the least amount of fear. I said curtly, "Go and sit in that front desk, boy-with-no-name!"

Henry Berg moved over as if someone with the plague was coming to sit next to him. I knew for sure that he would come to school tomorrow with a note from his mother "that she does not appreciate her son to have to associate with such riff-raff." The Rat walked to his desk. Impassively. I had suffered my first defeat. "Take out your reading books," I instructed the class. [my translation] (Bakker, 1944, p. 11)

That is how the novel *Ciske the Rat* begins. A journey into the lifeworld of "a child without a future." Or at least without any prospect that I, even as a child myself, understood as "no future"—delinquency and crime. And so the rest of the book reads like a pedagogical thriller. How can a teacher make a difference in the life of a child-without-a-life? Here is a child who seems to desire no future because he lacks already a life worth living. There are no rules, no principles of knowledge that can tell the teacher what to say or how to say or do the right thing when the child is there. What is the difference that makes a difference between a life and no-life? Does this sound sentimental? Does this appear naive to my present adult reading? I take the Ciske novels back to my new "home," Canada.

As I talk with teachers, I hear many anecdotes about teaching, school, and the children or adolescents they teach. Sometimes the stories are inspiring, reflecting the joys of teaching and living with children. Sometimes the stories are disturbing; they may resemble the life of Ciske. Except that there is now a heightened reality to the stories I hear because most often I already know these children—not fictionally, but concretely, in flesh and blood. Many present-day stories we hear about through the media and people in our lives are stories that are more desperate even than the story of Ciske.

CHAPTER THREE

The Nature of Pedagogy

Although we should be able to recognize the meaning and significance of pedagogy from our childhood experiences, it should also be pointed out that we may be not fully able to grasp what pedagogy means as an active and reflective ethic until we have ourselves lived with children or young people for whom we hold responsibilities. For example, just because we have been students and have spent many years in schools and other educational institutions, this does not mean we really know what it is like to be a teacher. The same is true, of course, for families. We may not fully understand what it is to be a mother or a father until we have lived the caring life of a mother or father ourselves. And yet there are many teachers, social workers, nurses, pediatricians, and other childcare professionals who have developed a wonderful sense of pedagogy without having had children of their own.

To reiterate, pedagogy can be generally described as distinguishing what is good or right from what is bad or wrong (not good or inappropriate) in our ways of acting and interacting with children. Of course, in our everyday living with children we do not always know how to distinguish actively and reflectively what is good from what is not good (or less good) for children. In certain situations and predicaments we may question and doubt ourselves or admit that we may not know what is best for this child or these children.

But the point is that this doubt and uncertainty belongs to pedagogy and shows us the profoundly ethical nature of pedagogical thinking and acting. Without this ethical uncertainty pedagogy would be reduced to a set of techniques, recipes, or rules. Teaching, parenting, and caring for children are never simple affairs that can be handled by means of rules and recipes. Situational predicaments that can be "solved" by techniques and procedures are not ethical predicaments. And so pedagogy is both the tactful ethical practice of our actions as well as the doubting, questioning, and reflecting on our actions and practices.

We also know what pedagogy is in the daily care and worry we feel for the children in our care: a never-ending caring worry that flares up especially in times of difficulty, misfortune, adversity, or hardship. Pedagogical worry

---

Pedagogical Tact: Knowing What to Do When You Don't Know What to Do, by Max van Manen, 33–48.
© 2015 Taylor & Francis. All rights reserved.

seems to belong to being a mother or a father, and to the responsibility we feel for children with whom we stand in relations of *in loco parentis*.

The Pedagogical Moment

"I really would like to hear you practice the violin," says mother. A sour situation. What is supposed to be a satisfying experience—fun even—for both the parent and the child becomes pure obligation. Already mother's voice bears a tone of anticipated disappointment. Each day is another battle. And one can hear the parent think, "Why can this child not show some enthusiasm, some gratitude for all my sacrifice?"

But the child hears something quite different. Mother wishes he would play the violin with enthusiasm. But also, quite clearly, Mother does not really enjoy the violin practice. It is a chore for her too. This is evident from the businesslike manner in which the daily practice is set in time and space. Violin practice is a contractual encounter between this mother and this child, and both wish it were over before it even starts. Both approach the practice with apprehensive tenseness. Soon the child says, "I'm tired, Mom. Can I do it later?" The violin is held with resignation, and nothing is more unbecoming than an unwilling body holding an awkward musical instrument.

Children are sensitive to subtle signs of mood and atmosphere. Undeniably, making music together is not really being enjoyed in this family. Mother says angrily, "All right, that's it. I'm sick and tired of your attitude. Maybe we should sell your violin or give it to some child who knows how to appreciate music."

Elsewhere in the same neighborhood a father lifts a cello out of its case. He lovingly tunes it. There is a certain patience and discipline in his gestures. No rushing. This is a special moment, a kind of interlude, a time to be enjoyed for its own sake. The cello sings a languid song. This is not a call to duty but an enticing invitation. There is something compelling in the way the house fills up with melody. The body is responsive, follows the music. Laura walks into the room and looks, listens, smiles. Then, as surely as the cello sings, she opens her violin case and sets the instrument to her chin and shoulder. The tones harmonize. Instantly the ten-year-old finds the right entrance to her father's melody. The father looks surprised. Remarkable! Well done! But he actually had expected this: he had carefully selected the right chords. Soon certain tonal phrases are exchanged, picked up, repeated. The ear tastes them for their roundness, fullness, and blend: "Now try it like this. Yes, on the E-string."

In this situation making music together is hard to distinguish from practice and exercise. In this home too, practice is a daily ritual. But with this father and daughter, practice time is experienced as a healthy workout that elevates the spirit. In this case routine is not only the following of a voluntary and familiar path but also brings something precious: harmony, rhythm, and melody feed both body and mind. This is not to suggest, however, that we should not have sympathy for the mother. For both the mother and the father there will be times when practice resembles drudgery.

What do these examples show about the pedagogy of bringing up children? Simply this: pedagogy is both a complex and a subtle affair. Pedagogy is the ability to actively distinguish what is good or appropriate from what is less suited or inappropriate for children or young people in a particular moment: a pedagogical moment. The pedagogical moment is that exact instant of a pedagogical situation or relation when a pedagogical action is required. Specific rules or even general principles for acting are difficult to formulate. Some adults seem to strike just the right tone with children. Others constantly flounder in their dealings with them. The difference is not necessarily that some adults have read more about parenting or teaching than others. Reading educational literature can provide important knowledge, but that knowledge tends to be external. It does not necessarily make us more thoughtful or more tactful in our day-to-day relations with young people. The practice of cultivating one's pedagogical thoughtfulness and tact is the response to the challenge of approaching each situation with respect and attentiveness. Tactful educators have developed a caring attentiveness to the unique: the uniqueness of each child, the uniqueness of each situation, and the uniqueness of each individual life.

When thoughtfulness and tactfulness coincide, a peculiar quality emerges that has as much to do with who we are as with what we do in a pedagogical moment. It is a knowledge that issues from the heart as well as from the head. We can imagine the mother from the above example complaining to the father who plays the cello. The father says to her, "Why don't you sing along or play along?" Now imagine that the mother takes this advice to heart. Will it work? Perhaps. We can never predict the success of an action. No two children are alike or experience a situation in exactly the same manner. What is even more important: Would the mother be able to generate the same invitational atmosphere as the father? The difference may lie in the most fragile and subtle details.

And unfortunately (or, perhaps, fortunately) there are no specific rules that will ensure the right kind of thoughtfulness, sensitivity, and tact. Pedagogical sensitivity is sustained by a certain kind of seeing, listening, and responding to a particular child or group of children in ever-changing situations. Tact in our relationships with children may grow from this basis of thoughtfulness and sensitivity.

Entering the Child's World of Possibility

Children are not there for us—we are there for them. Yet they come to us bearing a gift: the gift of experiencing *the possible*. Children are children because they are in the midst of the primal process of becoming. They tend to experience life as possibility: anything can happen. Parents and teachers act pedagogically when they consciously show the child possible ways of being. They can do this if they realize that adulthood itself is never a finished project. Life forever queries us about the way it is to be lived: "Is this what I should be doing with my life? Is this how I should spend my time?" No one can reawaken these questions in us more powerfully and more disturbingly than a child. All one has to do is watch and listen to children and learn from them. In this children are our teachers. As teachers and parents, we willingly open ourselves to children. This means that we do our utmost to understand what it is like to be in the world as a child. More concretely, I do my very best to understand the situation of this child. How does this child experience life in its multifaceted dimensions?

Placing oneself beside one's student or child is something very personal, and it can be a fragile act. Take the case of Joey and his grandparents. Joey is four, and his grandparents live a long way away. Naturally they want to make the most of any visit. So when they go for an errand, they take Joey along in their big shiny car. Joey is excited. There are many buttons on the dashboard. There are many new places to see and questions to ask: "What is that building, Grandma? Look at that dog! What's this button for, Grandpa?"

But his questions fall mostly on deaf ears. The grandparents are having their own conversation, and they only occasionally throw a comment or question in Joey's direction, like candies to keep him occupied and pacified. Joey's words are not really attentively heard. They like to have him along, but they do not invite him to be present in a personal sense. When Joey comes home, he is unusually quiet, and only after some prodding does he remark, "I had nobody to play with."

In sharing my life with this child I cannot avoid becoming an example. As an adult, I embody possible ways of being for the child. I see the child trying on my gestures, my ways of seeing and doing things, my ways of reacting, my ways of spending time. And as I see that happening, I am confronted with my own doubts. Is this the way I want my child to act and be? And if not, is it the way I want myself to act and be?

This is how the child becomes my teacher. As he or she tries out possibilities, I am reminded of the possibilities still open to myself. In this experience of pedagogical possibility lies the truth of the cliché that children make us feel young again. Children, in their trying out, express that there is hope, that there is possibility of living life differently—and better. And once again I am stimulated to grasp that hope for my own life.

There is a paradox here: I experience this child's life as more important than my own, and the result is that I must now take a closer look at my own. I must question and reshape it. Before I had this child, I could abuse myself with bad habits if I wished. I could live life quite unaware of the deep needs of others. But because I live with and love this child, I can no longer live comfortably with my old self. The education of the child turns into self-education.

Some educators believe that their own education is complete. They will probably try to impose a taken-for-granted set of beliefs and values. Inevitably such "education" turns into a pedagogy of oppression and manipulation—an authoritarian form of domination of adults over children. The "completed" educator tends to see children as incomplete. No need, then, to listen to children. Impossible to learn from them.

The Practical Moment of Acting Pedagogically

In a lecture about pedagogical acting, Langeveld (1975) tells how an accident happened right in front of him when a twelve-year-old girl calls her father, whom she sees on the other side of the street.

> "Hello Daddy!" she calls out, waving to a man on the opposite side of the road, who waves back to her. He then steps from the pavement to meet his daughter and, before her very eyes, he is run over by a car. He is killed, but she does not yet know. Soon she will: already she screams loudly. Later she'll go on crying and seeing the image of her father's death happening in front of her. She has an irrational feeling of guilt: she *knows* she is not guilty, but she called his name, she waved to him and then he stepped off the pavement and it happened. (1975, p. 9)

Langeveld asks his audience: What does one do in a situation like this? Of course, some people may hurry by and not get involved. But Langeveld shows that we likely cannot help but react. The situation asks for a personal response: to be available to the girl who is in need of help. Langeveld defines a pedagogical situation as the complexity of givens in terms of which we must act. He does not use the term "pedagogical moment" in his work, but what he describes is a pedagogical moment. Confronted with such situation, one has to act in the moment. The philosopher Levinas calls the ethical experience wherein you cannot help but respond *responsibility for the other* (Levinas, 1969). And indeed, Langeveld describes how a "personal response" becomes a "pedagogical response of response-ability":

> What, now, did you do walking behind the girl whose father was run over by a car? People hurried to the place of the accident. Should this girl see her father crushed and bleeding? *Before you* knew *what you were doing, you had already decided,* and you had taken the girl's hand in order to prevent her from approaching that horrible sight. "Let us go quickly to find your mother. . . . Where do you live? Where is she?" [emphasis added] (1975, p. 9)

Of course, we can argue about the reasonableness of Langeveld's actions. But judging his response is less important here than noticing that he inadvertently shows us what the structure of a pedagogical moment looks like.

First, we can learn from this anecdote that the pedagogical moment is embedded in a situation in which something pedagogical is expected of us and we subsequently are oriented to that which is in the best interest or "good" of this child. We must do something. Second, Langeveld's story shows that, commonly, the pedagogical moment does not permit us to step back from the situation. In the interactive moment of teaching or parenting or dealing with children in one way or another, there is no time to deliberate rationally and morally, considering one point of view and another, weighing what are the various possibilities and consequences of action that this situation offers us. Reflective deliberation assumes the use of some form of practical reasoning to thus arrive at a morally and relationally responsible decision about how best to approach a situation and then to act on this decision.

But this kind of deliberative reflection in action—critically comparing, sorting of alternative means and ends, weighing the consequences, deciding what one should do, and then acting on it—rarely can be employed in pedagogically interactive and relational situations. When we are teaching (discussing, listening, showing, interacting with) a group of children or dealing with a single child, we tend to be relationally "captive." Quite literally our mind is not our own. And thus we have the saying, "We give the other a piece of our mind." Pedagogical moments commonly consist of immediate actions, and thus it is not surprising that Langeveld (1975) says,

> *Immediately* you brought the child into a different life situation: a mother, a house. *Immediately* you assured her that people were looking after her father: "Shall I go and have a look"? "No," you added *immediately*, "no, let us first find your mother, as you live just around the corner." [emphasis added] (p. 9)

Langeveld himself does not comment on the curious "immediacy" of the nature of pedagogical acting; rather, he uses the anecdote to reflect on the practical ethics of pedagogy. He shows how pedagogy asks, demands something of adults. He goes on to suggest that it demands reflection on the meaning and significance of pedagogical notions such as the child's experience of risk and safety, and the child's need for security, reliability, and continuity. These values, he suggests, are basic to being pedagogically responsive and responsible acting in our everyday relations and situations with children. To a certain extent, in an increasingly complex and risky environment, children need to be able to experience the world as *secure*, to depend on certain adults as being *reliable*, and to experience a sense of *continuity* in their social relations with those who care for them.

But Langeveld (1975) also warns that there exists no closed or universally acceptable rational system that would tell us how we should behave with children in our everyday actions and how we should rationally justify our pedagogical approaches and methods. What is reasonable to one person may appear unreasonable to another person, says Langeveld. Instead, he attempts to locate the norms of pedagogical acting in the concrete and contingent experiences of everyday living with children. We further need to realize that these norms may differ from place to place, from time to time, from situation to situation, and from culture to culture.

The street accident story is an event that might happen to any of us. And Langeveld *shows* us more than he actually *tells* us. He shows that, although we say, "Before you knew what you were doing, you had already decided," this is actually not a process of reflective decision making in terms of which reflection in action is usually portrayed. And in this feature our living with children at home or in the community does not differ fundamentally from life in classrooms. As professional pedagogues, teachers, just like parents, are expected to act immediately, though thoughtfully, and in a pedagogically appropriate manner with children.

Thus, pedagogy first of all refers to our active everyday living with children as parents, teachers, school principals, childcare workers, and so on. In everyday life we practice a certain pedagogy, and of course, the pedagogy of the home is different from the pedagogy of the classroom, or the pedagogy of the office of the psychologist, the pediatrician, the nurse, or the social worker.

In his primer, *Concise Theoretical Pedagogy* (1943/1979), Langeveld defines pedagogy in ethical terms that places as central its lived meaning and experiential meaningfulness:

> Pedagogy is a science of experience; it is a human science, indeed it is an ethical human science that is conducted or studied with practical intent.... [It] is a science of experience because it finds its object (the pedagogical situation) in the world of lived experience. It is a human science because the pedagogical situation rests on human intent.... It is ethical because it distinguishes between what is good and what is not good for a child.... It is practical because all this is brought to bear in the practical process of [*opvoeding*] bringing up and educating children. (p. 178)

In essence a pedagogue could be considered an ethicist—an ethicist who specializes in questions and concerns that may emerge in pedagogical situations, relations, and actions. Langeveld (1943/1979) describes pedagogy as a human science. But his special approach to this human science became known as phenomenological pedagogy (for a brief entry, see van Manen and Adams, 2014).

Phenomenological Pedagogy

Langeveld systematically explores the main themes and terms of pedagogy. For him theorizing is not some kind of abstract, disembodied, intellectual activity; rather, it is a reflective clarifying of the experiential elements of pedagogical reality as it is lived at home, at school, and in the community. Some of the main themes are carried by questions such as: What does it mean to help children grow up? What is the nature of the pedagogical encounter? What is involved in pedagogical authority, responsibility, and trust? Why is pedagogy something we cannot avoid in life? What are the limits of pedagogy? How can substitutive responsibility (by the adult for the child or youth) be justified, and what does it mean? What are the means and ends of pedagogy? Langeveld explores this project in great depth and nuanced detail:

> It is concerned with gaining phenomenological insights into the structural dimensions of pedagogy and concurrently with determining the essential meanings of the most fundamental phenomena in the totality of this field of study (i.e., pedagogy as bringing up children and young people). (1943/1979, p. 182)

Phenomenology is not just a method that one can employ like a set of procedures; rather, it is an attitude that relies on the attentive perceptiveness, creative insight, and interpretive sensitivity of the person. The phenomenological attitude comprises a fascination with the uniqueness, the particularity of an experience or phenomenon.

A new parent is not moved to love for his or her child by abstractions but by the concreteness of his or her experiences: experiencing the vulnerability of the newly born in holding the infant, the first smile of the child, the tenderness one feels when looking in the child's face, the worry when the child falls ill. Thus, a phenomenology of pedagogical parental love is not primarily pursued through a theoretical discourse or a conceptual analysis of the notion of motherly or fatherly care; rather, it is pursued through attempts to awaken the experience as we live it and make contact—through concrete examples and reflection—with the living sensibility of its uniqueness.

Phenomenology is oriented to the lifeworld as we immediately experience it—prereflectively rather than as we conceptualize, theorize, categorize, or reflect on it. It is the study of lived or experiential meaning and attempts to describe and interpret these meanings in the ways that they emerge and are shaped by consciousness, language, our cognitive and noncognitive sensibilities, the ontics of meaning, and our personal, social, and cultural pre-understandings (for methodological explications see Vagle, 2014; van Manen, 1997, 2014). Phenomenology can be adopted to explore the unique meanings of any pedagogical experience or phenomenon, such as the experience of care, recognition, patience, encouragement, hope, respect, humbleness, and so forth. The practical significance of phenomenological pedagogy is the thoughtfulness and tact it affords in pedagogical situations and relations.

How Do We Know What Is Best?

It is a sobering realization that although we may strive to do what is best for our children, often we do not know what is best. Hopefully many adults can say that they have encountered some inspiring teachers in their lives and that they have been blessed with loving parents who did "good" by them. And yet some of us would also admit that we have been damaged by those same caring people. Perhaps they were too demanding. Or they did not ask enough of us. Perhaps they were too protective. Or they gave us too much slack. Perhaps they did not want to make the same mistakes as their own parents did and therefore are now making other mistakes.

It is obvious that every newborn needs to be cared for simply to stay alive and grow. Langeveld points out somewhat provocatively but in all seriousness that we are not born human but that all newly born babies must be brought into humanness by those who care for them. Without such primal pedagogical care, children will perish or suffer from irreparable damage for the rest of their lives. In other words, pedagogy is not just some skill, such as skills of teaching; rather, it is a human necessity that cannot be avoided.

"*Agogic, -agogue, agogy,*" are rare Greek root words that mean or connote "guiding, eliciting, drawing forth, accompanying, helping, assisting, leading." *Agogy*, as a social science, studies how people change; *agogical* practices provide directions for interventions in helping people transform themselves and develop self-responsibility and mature independence. Pedagogy is the *agogy* of children (*paides* means child); ortho-pedagogy is caring for children who have special problems or handicaps (such as in the context of special education). Andragogy is the *agogy* of adults (*andra* means older). For example, university or other adult-oriented educational programs have an *andragogical* focus. We can also speak of *agogical* care when concerned with caring for the elderly, such as in nursing homes. An interesting question is, of course: what forms of knowledge, qualities, and ethical values are required for someone involved in *agogical* practice?

We may read in newspapers a story about workers in nursing homes who have abused or neglected elderly people in their care. A judge has ordered the healthcare workers to take "sensitivity training." The judgment is certainly well meaning and seems to understand that an agogical intervention is needed. But technoscientific concepts such as "sensitivity training" pretends that "sensitivity" is something that can be imparted through "training" sessions. This is a problematic proposition: Can sensitivity be taught or trained? We may have to admit that agogical development is not served well by "skill" or "competency" training. Agogical sensitivities such as affects, feelings, ethical values, and tactfulness cannot be trained in an instrumental manner, but, if approached with openness, willingness, and commitment, they can be developed through phenomenological reflections and evocations, but only in those who are receptive to it.

Just as science cannot "understand" phenomena of love and friendship, it also cannot use scientific concepts and procedures to explain and understand the phenomenon of pedagogy. Why? Because pedagogy is a field of study that is driven by pathic sensibilities. Pathic aspects of pedagogical practice concern "affects"—affects of thoughtfulness, tact, sensitivity, and the ability to grasp what goes on in the inner life of the other. Today many young people endure childhoods of abuse, neglect, abandonment, and poverty—without love, respect, or sensitivity. They are likely to grow up as damaged goods. Similarly, young people who are brought up without having been sensitized toward the fears, pains, and suffering of others around them may fail to grow up into compassionate and empathic persons.

Some adults are so afraid of being and setting a bad example for children that they refuse to be an example at all. And yet it is quite impossible not to be an example, whether positive or negative. We cannot help but be examples in the very way that we are present and interact with children. In our own living with young people we cannot help but "show" how a life is to be lived. So we cannot NOT be examples. We are always ethically involved with young people. But we must choose whether and how our involvement is pedagogically sensitive and reflective.

How should we understand and deal with the influence that virtual milieus exert on the development, cognitive, emotional, and moral growth of young people? What is the significance of online social relations and intimacies between adolescents and pre-adolescents? What are positive and possibly problematic issues of social networking technologies in young people's lives, and how should parents and other educators interpret and deal with such issues? How much responsibility should young people carry in making important decisions about their own futures? How much stress and imposition are adults justified in exerting on young people in the development of supposed talents, such as learning to play a musical instrument? To what extent is a teacher justified in probing the inner lives and private thoughts of his or her students? How should governments and childcare institutions deal with youth criminality? All these types of questions, and numerous others like them, fall within the domain of pedagogy. Such general issues tend to express themselves in particularized, immediate, and concrete issues in everyday life.

The Goal of Pedagogy

Pedagogy is the caring task of raising and educating children. Practices of educating children cannot really be separated from raising children. Even teachers who see it mostly as their task to "deliver" the government-mandated curriculum are inevitably relationally involved with their students. Most of us do not remember a favorite teacher for the math, English, or science lessons they taught but for their pedagogical qualities and actions in teaching their subjects. This depiction sounds perhaps embarrassingly sentimental and even antiquated—but so be it! Pedagogy should not be timid for declaring itself the core component of teaching as education.

The difference between pedagogy and "instruction" or "curriculum" is that pedagogy has no external goal outside of itself which would serve certain societal interests such as the educational institution, political agendas, the economy, the corporate sector, or other interest groups. In a sense, the goal of pedagogical action is not a predetermined outcome but the caring action itself—and this action is in service of the best interest of this child or these children. Pedagogical action that is motivated by the external setting of learning outcomes and achievement goals inevitably turns into instrumental action—action in the service of calculative ends. It may seem provocative to say this, but pedagogy does not need externally-motivated goals and objectives.

However, pedagogy does have internal goals that determine the appropriateness of how to act with children and young people. The internal goals depend on how pedagogy is understood in its originating significance. For example, if pedagogy is understood as "leading" children into the world of their community and culture, then the question becomes: Who will lead them where and why? If pedagogy is understood as "preparing" children for tomorrow, then the question becomes: What does it mean to prepare for and deal with tomorrow, which tomorrow? If pedagogy is understood as assisting children to face and interpret the meaning of experiences and events that they will encounter in their lives, then the question becomes: How do we accompany children in situations in which they encounter the forces and phenomena of living?

Especially in our complex contemporary world it is clear that not all knowledge inherent in the various cultures can be passed on to young people without selecting, shaping, organizing, and structuring that knowledge for teaching and learning. And at the base of these selecting, shaping, organizing, and structuring criteria are situated powerful philosophical assumptions about the relation between knowledge and reality.

John Amos Comenius's famous *Orbis Sensualium Pictus* (*The World of Things Obvious to the Senses, Drawn in Pictures*, 1611/2011) was the first school textbook presenting knowledge especially selected and designed to represent the real world. Ever since Comenius, educationalists and curriculum scholars have argued about what knowledge and skills are most worthy to include in the curriculum and how this knowledge should be selected, captured, structured, and organized in policy statements and bodies of knowledge to be presented through various media, technologies, teacher activities, learning experiences, and educational environments.

Pedagogical action is always a matter of dealing with ethically charged situations that are contingent in the here and now. Therefore, pedagogy should not be confused with didactics, instruction, or curriculum activities, which must, at times, indeed be rightfully preoccupied with determinate goals and outcomes. And yet pedagogy should play a role in curriculum development, in the planning of teaching and learning programs, and in lesson planning. The didactic selection, organizing, and structuring criteria of curriculum as well as teaching and learning programs should find their inception in the concern of what is best for this child or these children. In addition to pedagogical concerns there will also be considerations at play that have to do with the nature of society, knowledge, politics, tradition, the economy, the job market, and so on.

Traditionally pedagogy draws a distinction between being a child and being an adult. Being a child means that one still has unknown and unfulfilled potentials that will be realized, whereas the adult already has made many choices. And, of course, the developing and growing child will increasingly make certain qualities and characteristics one's own. For example, we do not yet know whether this child or young person will become a true reader and perhaps even an author, but the adult will already have determined or realized such properties, though it is always possible that a person who was never interested in reading or rarely would read a novel or other literary material suddenly develops a passion for words or a talent for literature. It is also the case that an adult who decides to go back to school for further study at a later age may first have to "unlearn" knowledge by opening him or herself to new forms of knowledge and the critical or philosophical attitudes that are associated with this knowledge. The adult who opens up to new views and vistas must let go of old, established views before he or she can truly dedicate him or herself to new intellectual and ethical challenges.

Within this broader existential sense of learning, pedagogy does have goals. We want our children to grow toward a life of meaningfulness, personal and social responsibility, and happiness. The internal goals of pedagogy have to do with the questions of what it means to be human and what it means to grow up toward adulthood. Langeveld (1943/1979) described this pedagogical goal as "self-responsible self-determination," in which, as Levering (2014) points out, the emphasis is placed on an acceptable determination of a meaningful form of adulthood. But the present-day view of the pedagogical goal of self-responsible self-determination is that adulthood is not determined by a determinate set of norms that one has acquired or taken upon oneself but that adulthood means that one is now being held accountable for what one has made of oneself. Thus, a pedagogical goal is not oriented toward a defined determination or state of adulthood but rather toward tasks of responsibility that one cannot yet demand of a child or a young person who has not yet reached the juridical, ethical, cognitive, and thoughtful emotional maturity.

To reiterate, the goal of pedagogical action is not a goal in the sense of an external outcome, such as the results on a test. That is why, for example, praise should be practiced with an eye of what is good or appropriate in this moment. Blind praise or praise that is given because we believe in a certain principle (praise is good for the child's self-esteem, praise makes the child achieve at higher levels, praise always feels good, praise increases the child's learning outcomes, etc.) is problematic because the principle or goal may not be appropriate in the contingent moment in which we find ourselves. Pedagogy requires that we are constantly thoughtful about the way we recognize or "see" the child who is with us at this moment and in this situation or circumstance against the broader goal of human becoming.

As a child-sensitive ethics, pedagogy is concerned with what is "good" or "best" for children and young people, even if this means at times to declare that we are at our wits' end with some such questions. Pedagogy asks of us what roles different adults and young people themselves should play in young people's lives. It would be wrong to argue that children's future is none of our business because young people should determine for themselves what world they want to build. As Hannah Arendt (2006) pointed out, such an argument underestimates the degree to which young people are already trapped in a world that is much older than they are and older even than their parents and forbearers.

Ontotheology and the Pedagogy of Character

Finally, at a more fundamental level, the goal of pedagogy is determined by the ethics and values of the (implicit or explicit) philosophy of life of the parent, teacher, or childcare person. And yet we may not always be very aware of our own perspective thoroughly saturated with technocratic, calculative, and materialistic values that have the power and effect of a dominant and pervasive theology on our being. This ontotheology is what we need to be aware of since it shapes the way we organize our lives and our schools.

Most parents would want their children to be and become happy and successful in life. But does that mean we want to help them become competitive, striving for personal advantages and economic success for themselves? Social commentators have pointed out that our Western culture is driven by an ontotheology of self-centered values that easily lead to selfishness, greed, a striving for personal wealth, a lack of empathy for the suffering of others, and so forth. David Brooks (2015) observes that we live in a time and society that encourages us to think about how to have a great career but leaves many of us inarticulate about how to cultivate the inner life, the character of the person. Perhaps happiness is not the central value of the goal of pedagogy; perhaps we should tactfully aim to move the young person into a form of life that provides the satisfaction of community, sharing, and even self-sacrifice for the ones we love and for those who depend on us. In his *Empathic Civilization*, Jeremy Rifkin (2009) suggests that we need to reorient the ontotheological view of life and nature that is embedded in our educational systems, business practices, capitalist economies, and political culture.

The consumer marketplace encourages us to live by a utilitarian calculus that is insensitive to the social and economic harm that it does to others (Brooks, 2015). Social commentators have pointed out that ironically it is the sociopaths and psychopaths acting as CEOs, financial speculators, Wall Street–type brokers, and leaders of money companies who enjoy dismantling and fusing companies while, in the process, wrecking the pension plans of the people working for these companies. The phenomenon of pathological ruthlessness is especially disconcerting when we realize that sociopaths comprise 4 percent of the general population (Stout, 2006). In other words, 4 percent of ordinary people have an often undetected mental state that lacks a capacity for empathy, altruism, and emotional sensitivity to human suffering. Of course, it does not mean that psychopaths and sociopaths must be dangerous criminals. No doubt we all have people in our community of friends and circle of co-workers that function normally though lacking in pro-social values and emotional sensibility. And yet, assigning people with diagnostic labels is no doubt hazardous.

M. E. Thomas, in her book *Confessions of a Sociopath* (2013), describes how she knew that her own experiences while growing up were different from those of others. Her childhood was positive and caring. She was never abused or neglected. But she did not get why people around her would be emotionally moved by certain events while she felt indifferent herself. She describes how she was intrigued by people's vulnerabilities and how she enjoyed playing games, manipulating people, and engaging in risky behaviors. In spite of these secret realizations, she presents as a rational and highly intelligent woman, and she has become a very successful attorney and law professor. She regularly publishes in law journals. But, because she knows she is different in her relations with friends and lovers, she sought medical opinions. She has been diagnosed as "highly psychopathic".

If it is appropriate to typify people as psychopathic or sociopathic, then this raises the question of whether individuals who seem to lack empathy and emotional sensitivity are fit to be with children. It raises also the question of what pedagogical tact should do when confronted with young people who seem overly egocentric, who display excessive self-esteem, and who lack empathy and emotional responsiveness.

The reference to psychopaths and sociopaths is only used here as an example of the different forms character can take. Some aspects of character may be hard to influence, and therefore it is compelling to see how Thomas provides a rich account of her experiences that may yield phenomenological insights into phenomena of ego-centrism, sensation seeking, interpersonal dominance, and so forth. Yet it seems that she has positively adapted to her "disorder."

In some sense almost all people, young and old, have character issues. Perhaps, sometimes or many times, one tends to be too selfish, too greedy, inconsiderate of the welfare of others, uncooperative, aggressive, untrustworthy, and so forth. In fact, in a Western culture that encourages competition and personal greed, the pedagogical challenge may be to move young people in directions that are more pro-social and supportive of others at the cost of self-interest.

The Irreducibility of Pedagogy

The proper pedagogical approach is to ask ourselves as adults: How, then, do we help nudge the world (politically, ecologically, and ethically) in directions that young people can indeed exert their influence and realize their ideals? But this pedagogical influence is not meant to sacrifice this moment for some future goal; it means that the value of our action lies already in this moment. It means that we may increasingly nudge young people toward social ethics, mutual dependence with others, self-critical responsibility, and knowing their place in communities of responsibility—but we must realize our pedagogical intent in the now. The question is: What forms of ethics and politics are helpful in thinking and acting pedagogically?

Pedagogy is not just a juvenile-oriented sort of ethics. Pedagogical studies, opinions, and judgments are almost always supported by insights and knowledge from other fields: child studies, psychology, law, sociology, anthropology, history, and so forth. Because in essence pedagogy is always already an ethics, pedagogical action and reflection must be willing to be doubly ethically accountable: it must ethically reflect on itself as a child-sensitive ethics. In other words, pedagogy must be able to ask the question of what kind of ethics is the appropriate source for thinking and acting in pedagogically (ethically) sensitive situations.

Understanding basic principles of child development is helpful. For example, it would obviously be inappropriate to accuse and punish small children for lying when they are not yet ready to understand the difference between truth telling and lying. Although pedagogy cannot do without knowledge of other social sciences, it cannot be reduced to any one of these sciences. And pedagogy differs from other professional practices such as clinical psychology, medicine, social work, jurisprudence, child psychology, anthropology, and political science in that it is ultimately concerned with the ethical and moral problems of how we should inquire into how to live responsibly and caringly with children.

Yet pedagogy is often confused with psychology. But just because developmental psychology shows, for example, that children are able to read at a very early age does not mean that children should learn to read at a very early age, especially if the time spent in early reading is at the cost of oral dialogic interaction with others. In verbal interactions with others, children learn all kinds of logics (turn taking, argument, conversational relations, expressivity, etc.) that are not afforded by solitary reading experiences and that may be considered pedagogically important. Similarly, studies may show us cognitive and emotional consequences of meeting others primarily through social networks mediated by screens. But they cannot tell us what is best for children and what we should do with particular children. Only pedagogical reflection can do so.

In this sense pedagogy is an independent discipline. Other social and human sciences may give us insights into empirical, scientific, political, and ethical questions of, for example, child development, children's illness and health, jurisprudence of youth criminality—political, social, historical, or cultural practices and issues related to dealing with and caring for children. But ultimately none of these human and social sciences can tell us what to say or do or how to act with a child in a particular circumstance. Pedagogy is autonomous as a professional practice and a theoretical discipline of child ethics in the sense that it cannot be reduced to any of those other social sciences or disciplines.

Yet it is clear that the domain of pedagogy intersects with other fields. For example, pediatrics and clinical child psychology are also involved in reflections and actions that fall within the ethical sphere of pedagogy. The Canadian "Encyclopedia on Early Childhood Development" gives advice to parents about how to deal with newborn babies and toddlers. Such sources may provide helpful insights into growth and development patterns of young children. For example, parents can read about the importance of mother-child attachment and how to gauge whether a child is feeling secure and protected.

Chapter Four

The Pedagogy of Reflective Practice

The Relation Between Reflection and Action

The term "pedagogy" carries the connotative meaning of discretion, prudence, judgment, caution, and forethought. So at first glance there is nothing provocative to the idea that reflection is central to the pedagogy of teaching. It is in the very nature of the pedagogical relation that the teacher reflectively deals with students rather than doing so unthinkingly, dogmatically, or prejudicially. Reflective thinking is important not only as a tool for teaching but also as an aim of education, said John Dewey, as "it enables us to know what we are about when we act. It converts action that is merely appetitive, blind, and impulsive into intelligent action" (1964, p. 211). However, to suggest that teachers need to be reflective practitioners begs the question that we know what the process of reflection consists of.

The concept of reflection is challenging and may refer to a complex array of cognitively and philosophically distinct methods and attitudes. Dewey's ideas about the nature of reflection alone give us ample opportunity to feel provoked (1933). He argued that reflection consists of several steps, including (1) "perplexity, confusion, doubt" due to the nature of the situation in which one finds oneself; (2) "conjectural anticipation and tentative interpretation" of given elements or meanings of the situation and their possible consequences; (3) "examination, inspection, exploration, analysis of all attainable considerations" that may define and clarify a problem with which one is confronted; (4) "elaboration of the tentative hypothesis suggestions"; and (5) deciding on "a plan of action" or "doing something" about a desired result (1973, pp. 494–506). A proper sequencing of such reflective steps makes up reflective experience, which in turn can lead to analysis and evaluation and then to further reflective action. For Dewey,

---

Pedagogical Tact: Knowing What to Do When You Don't Know What to Do, by Max van Manen, 49–60.
© 2015 Taylor & Francis. All rights reserved.

"thinking is the accurate and deliberate institution of connections between what is done and its consequences" (p. 505).

But knowledge of reflective methods alone is not sufficient; there must be a union of skilled method with attitudes. Dewey spoke of the need for developing certain qualities or traits of character such as open-mindedness or sincerity, wholehearted or absorbed interests, and responsibility as well as the need for a habit of thinking in a reflective manner (1964, pp. 224-228). He further made distinctions between theoretical judgments and judgments of practice, though he hastened to point out that practical judgments too are by their very nature intellectual and theoretical. The form of reflection involved in practical situations only differs in that it has a specific kind of subject matter—it is concerned with "things to do or be done, judgments of a situation demanding action" (1916, p. 335). But in making this distinction Dewey passed over the more recent observation that reflection in action may have a logic of its own. Donald Schön has suggested that phrases such as "thinking on your feet" and "keeping your wits about you" suggests not only that "we can think about doing something but that we can think about something while doing it" (1983, p. 54).

The notion of reflection is further complicated by the temporal dimensions of the practical contexts in which the reflection occurs. The thinking on or about the experience of teaching and the thinking within the experience of teaching seem to be differently structured. Retrospective reflection on (past) experiences differs importantly from anticipatory reflection on (future) experiences (van Manen, 1991). In contrast, contemporaneous reflection in situations allows for a "stop and think" kind of action that may differ markedly from the more immediate "reflective" awareness that characterizes, for example, the active and dynamic process of a class discussion, a lecture, a conflict situation, a monitoring activity, a one-on-one, a routine lesson, and so forth.

It is especially this active contemporaneous type of reflection that is probably the most challenging dimension of teaching, as it is "reflection" in the very moment of acting that seems to be a puzzling phenomenon (van Manen, 1991, 1992). By focusing on this dimension of the task of teaching, I do not want to undervalue in the slightest degree the formative relevance and practical significance of reflection on the experiences that educators share with children. The notion of reflection is implied in the very meaning of pedagogy that, by definition, signifies that teaching is done in an intentional manner that constantly distinguishes what is good or most appropriate from what is bad or inappropriate for this child or those children in particular circumstances. Specifically, it is highly worthwhile to explore the methodology and practical applicability of phenomenological reflection in the pedagogical lifeworld (van Manen, 1997, 2014).

The question is: How reflective is the active moment when the teacher is engaged with the children in his or her charge? Or how reflective can it be?

And how appropriate is the image of reflection in action (thinking about doing something while doing it) as evoked by Schön and others? It is true that at times, when there is a lull in the activity of teaching and the teacher can momentarily stop from participating, hang back, or step away from the classroom situation in order to reflect on what needs to be done next, one can speak of reflection in a fuller sense of the term. But even in such situations it would appear that reflection is only limited and restricted to the task at hand rather than take into consideration the full range of possibilities of interpreting what is going on, understanding the many possibilities of action, considering alternative courses of action, weighing their various consequences, deciding on what must be done, and then actually doing it, as suggested by Dewey.

In the daily life of teaching children teachers often feel they are constantly on the spot. And in the spur of the moment only limited true reflection seems possible. When the teacher is "live," then thirty-some pairs of eyes may be registering his or her every move and mood. This quality of engaged immediacy certainly seems to be a main factor that contributes to the common phenomenon of teacher fatigue and enervation. We should not underestimate the complexity of this immediate situatedness of teaching as practical action. This also means that we cannot take for granted that teacher thinking or critical reflection is a unidimensional or simple concept. It appears, then, that in everyday life the practice of pedagogy can only be reflective in a qualified and circumscribed sense.

One could even say that, ironically, in the active or dynamic situation of teaching we cannot help but be "unreflective" in the curious sense that the classroom teacher must constantly act on the spot and cannot step back and postpone acting in order to first reflect on the various alternatives to this action and consequences of the various alternatives. And even the teacher who has carefully reflected about what to do or not to do in each and every case must in the end commit him or herself to some action or non-action. Thus, a teacher who acts is always a dogmatist: while acting, one can only do one thing at a time.

Kairos Time: The Perfect Moment: The NOW

Nevertheless, the acknowledgment that the active practice of teaching is too busy to be truly reflective does not mean that teaching is condemned to Dewey's warning of blind impulsivity or routine habit. Teachers feel they can act with students in the classroom with more or with less thoughtfulness. While they are involved in teaching, good teachers "thinkingly act" and often do things with immediate insight. As teachers, we sometimes catch ourselves about to say something but then hold back before we have completely committed ourselves to what was already "on our lips." Other times the situation we are in seems to "tell" us, as it were, how we should act. Having to act in the immediacy of the moment may be referred to as Kairos time. Kairos is the mythological Greek god of the instant of the moment or timeless time (Hermsen, 2014).

We all know Chronos, the father of Zeus, but the strange thing is that Kairos is little known. Since ancient times a Kairos moment has been described as a transformative moment of chance depending on our ability and willingness to seize the opportunity that is offered within it (Murchadha, 2013). Kairos moments are pure, perfect, unpredictable, and uncontrollable moments that possess possibility. Kairos moments may yield insights and clarity but are often brought on by pain, agony, and feelings of frustration and desperation. Kairos moments force us to be absolutely present to ourselves and to the meaning and significance of what we are facing. So the Greek term *Kairos* refers to the timely time (Marramao, 2007). It cannot be measured. It is the perfect time, the qualitative time, the supreme moment, the NOW. If Kairos comes in your direction, he will race by on his wild wings. At that "eyewink" moment you have the chance to grab him by the hair as he flies by, but the moment he has passed you, you are too late. You may reach out for his hair, but your hands will slip off his bald skull.

Francesco Salviati—Time as Occasion (Kairos) (1543—1545), Palazzo Vecchio Museum

This is a provocative image but one that is striking and clarifies the human predicament when something hangs in the balance: of needing to deal with a crisis that confronts us in the now but that will be too late to face when the now has passed. Kairos may spontaneously jolt us into a moment of wonder and awe at something we thought we knew. But Kairos also demands of us the right thing at the right time—only the right action at the right time will do. If you hesitate, then the Kairic moment has passed, and all you will be left with is regret.

The upshot of all this is that pedagogical reality is often beset with Kairos moments. We have to act even if we do not know how to act. Thus, teacher thinking and teacher reflection are challenging notions that need phenomenological, philosophical, conceptual, and empirical exploration. The phenomenological question is: Where and how does the experience of reflection enter the reality of the pedagogical lifeworld? How is reflection in action experienced? And how may this be different from the conceptualizations of reflection in action as found in the literature? What kind of reflection or thinking, if any, is possible in practice? And what are the forms of knowledge or skills that inform or constitute Kairos moments and Kairos time?

The Novice Teacher

It is long known that beginning teachers typically encounter problems in the interactive reality of teaching. Let me first paint an ideal condition: a well-prepared student-teacher has acquired excellent subject-matter expertise, successfully studied theories of child development, and has become thoroughly knowledgeable about sound models of teaching and classroom management. The new teacher has honed his or her practical and reflective skills with successful peer-teaching exercises and classroom observations and has developed a critical understanding of philosophical, political, and professional educational issues. Finally, upon entering the classroom in earnest, the novice teacher has conscientiously prepared to meet the students with innovative, well-structured, finely tuned, and smoothly paced lessons and units.

But it is not uncommon that, in spite of this excellent preparation, great frustration is encountered: now, facing the students, the new teacher finds, to his or her disillusionment, that all this planning still falls short of what is required by the classroom reality. And somehow the hard-won knowledge base of subject matter, teaching skills, educational theories, and curriculum programs still does not live up to the Kairotic demands of the pedagogical life in the classroom.

What the teacher discovers is not that his or her knowledge base is false or useless; in fact, the new teacher may even have felt a smug sense of superiority over some of the "old-fashioned" senior teachers. Yet something seems wrong. The acquired knowledge base somehow does not fit. How else can one explain the awkwardness one feels when the great lesson plan fizzles? When the class seems unresponsive? When you feel that the kids do not seem to like or respect you? When, instead, one feels like a stranger, a fake, an outsider? When one simply does not know how to deal with situations that change before you had a chance to actually realize what was going on?

And so the novice teacher wonders, "Why is it that I have learned all this math, that I know all this methodology, but when Liz insisted that the stuff was too difficult, that she and other kids just did not get it, I simply was not able to really help them? Why is it that I received top marks in my courses on educational psychology, but when Jane broke down and told me to 'get lost' when I tried to help her, I did not know what to say? How is it that the teacher next door can command the students' attention just by looking at them, but with all my knowledge of classroom management and discipline, I do not know how to hide my feelings of uncertainty when Sean smirks at me or when Mona utters derogatory remarks or when some kids seem to invent a thousand tricks of stalling, disrupting, and not participating in the lessons? Why do I feel exhausted from constant preparation, time spent on marking, but, in comparison with all my hard work, many kids seem unwilling to complete their homework and unprepared to work even half as hard as I do? How can it be that I try so hard to put into practice what I learned about motivation and enrichment, but I felt totally deflated when a parent today told me that her son feels bored in my class? How strange that I had to learn so much about teaching and learning, but much that goes on in school has so little, if anything, to do with teaching?"

> As I made my way reluctantly toward the door I fought to suppress a rising feeling of panic. Why was I always anxious before class? It wasn't that I was unprepared; on the contrary, I had the good fortune to be teaching *Macbeth*, a text with which I felt completely familiar and comfortable. I knew my material and my method implicitly. I also knew that the class would be receptive—they always were. What was it then? Why this incessant feeling of pre-class panic? Perhaps it was my acute self-consciousness, my feeling that the students would view my every move with critical eyes, my sense that upon leaving the staffroom I would enter their world, their domain, and that I would be judged according to their criteria. I felt vulnerable. Perhaps that was it: vulnerability. But, then, teaching demands vulnerability—I would have to become accustomed to it.
>
> With new resolve I calmed my rising panic and stepped boldly into the hallway. Taking the first step is always the worst, I told myself, striding with firm steps toward my class. I smiled benevolently to a group of students at their lockers, nodded at a staff member, retrieved a crumpled piece of paper and deposited it in the garbage, all was done smoothly, I was in control. I smiled to myself, nobody could see through this composed exterior. I would be fine.

Just then a familiar, vulgar whistle reached my ears, suggestively drawn out and accompanied by a scurrying of feet. I froze momentarily, my confidence had evaporated. The surrounding students had turned expectantly toward me, grinning, waiting for my reaction. In an instant I decided on my course of action. I ignored the whistle and proceeded down the hallway, blind to my surroundings, poker-faced—but was my face flushing red?

The students arrived, slid into their seats and turned toward me in anticipation. Many of them had been in the hall. I wondered what they were thinking. As if in answer to my thought a hand went up at the right of the class. I nodded absentmindedly to elicit Heather's question.

"Ms. Overton?" She addressed me in a mocking, wheedling voice that carried with it an implicit warning that her comment would not be of a friendly nature. I braced myself. She timed her remark impeccably, waiting for every ear to be attuned to her voice before proceeding with exaggerated innocence.

"Simon really loves it when you wear that outfit!" With a subtle movement of her head she indicated Simon, slouched in his chair and grinning smugly. Again I felt my face flush.

Somehow I glossed over the situation and managed to get through the next hour, although I scarcely know how. Ever since then I have never again worn a dress while teaching.

Beginning teachers often seem to feel the tension or the "poor fit" between what they learned about teaching and what they discover is required in the practice of teaching. How to deal with potentially embarrassing situations? One does not want to overreact. But glossing over the incident may not be the best response either. Would a light joking response have been effective? Of course, it all depends on the emotional make-up, the self-confidence, and the personal pedagogy of the teacher.

Teacher educators have generally become quite aware that the tried "knowledge into practice" model of teacher training falls short of effective professional preparation. The concept of the teacher as a reflective practitioner is, in part, a response to the sense that an epistemology of turning technical theory into useful practice does not seem sensitive to the realization that the readiness to take advantage of Kairos moments must play an active and dynamic role in the ever-changing challenges of the school and classroom. Yet much of teacher preparation remains stuck in the traditional epistemology of practice and suffers from practical flaws as far as the interactive reality of the classroom is concerned.

The Experienced Teacher

The recurring theme in teacher testimonials is that the life of teaching is hectic. Yes, indeed, it is hard to pace oneself. Yes, it is unpleasant to eat your lunch while supervising the computer room and library and hallways at noon, and it is especially unpleasant not to have enough time to make it to the bathroom before the bell goes again. Yes, it requires inventiveness to somehow respond to or push off the many pressures and demands made on you by administration, parents, students, colleagues, and yes, it is difficult to give teaching all that it takes and still have enough time and energy left to attend to your own loved ones at home.

Moreover, cutbacks and underfunding of education in many districts are causing all kinds of pressures among teachers:

> My preparation time has been cut back to the contractual minimum. I have been assigned to teach additional high school courses, for which I have neither expertise nor interest. The enrollment in all my classes is at maximum. And it seems that every day we have so many problems in our schools that we are required to attend lengthy staff meetings several times a week. I rarely get home in time to make supper.
>
> Then there are the daily morning "student needs" conferences, lunch-hour supervisions, phone calls to and from parents, and all kinds of other ad hoc meetings.
>
> Many days I cannot even get to the bathroom before the afternoon school buzzer because three out of five days I have lunch-hour supervision, which leaves me exactly ten minutes for dealing with contingencies, getting coffee, and eating my own lunch in the staffroom.
>
> Moreover, my husband and kids at home complain because I spend many of my evening hours dealing with more than 150 weekly student writings, assignments, and projects.
>
> I have been feeling so down and besieged that I simply can no longer see how I can do my job with any degree of adequacy. So when individual students at school come to me for extra help or to discuss their problems, I now tend to react in ways that sometimes surprise me when I reflect on it afterward.
>
> On more than a few occasions I have told students to back off, take charge of their own affairs, and expect no special treatment from me.
>
> What disturbs me most is that my relationship with my students seems to become less personal. Things are just not as they should be.
>
> Yet as I tell these things, I feel guilty and quite mixed up about it all.

I am not just interested in portraying the generally frenzied nature of the life of classrooms; rather, I like to focus on the peculiar phenomenological structure of practice and the immediacy that characterizes almost every minute of the ongoing activity of teaching.

We could walk into any classroom at almost any time and notice the involved nature of the practice of teaching. Whether the teacher is explaining something to the whole class, initiating an activity, monitoring group work, holding a class discussion, responding to a student's work, or trying to deal with some enthusiastic, restless, or "disruptive students," what may strike us is the lack of space and time for the teacher to take required distance from any of these situations in order, in the Deweyan sense, to reflect, decide, and act on why and what it is that he or she should really do or not do in any of these circumstances.

When one asks teachers how they do this, how they handle things from moment to moment, they tend to answer in generalities. This is indeed difficult to describe. And if one insists with the question, then teachers may respond with a story, a complaint, a self-deprecating joke, an anecdote, or an observation. Let me offer one of these anecdotes. It is quite an ordinary story, reflecting a situation that is only memorable because it seems to show that often success in teaching is measured in little victories. But the brief account also contains a Kairotic element that speaks to the immediacy of practical acting. The teacher preambles the story with a few contextual comments about the student in order to make her anecdote intelligible.

> There is this student, Tony, in one of my grade nine classes, and he is constantly trying to mobilize other students around him to disturb or boycott the class. Tony will make silly comments. He tries to avoid having to do assignments. He will ask questions that do not appear to make sense. He will act as if he does not understand what is going on. He rarely concentrates.
>
> We were having a class discussion and brainstorming ideas for a solution to a problem. Students were invited to make suggestions. A brief discussion would follow, and then I listed each useful idea on the board. When it was Tony's turn, he made a suggestion that obviously was meant to poke fun. However, in a flash, I said, "Yes, that is very good Tony . . ." I treated and discussed his comment seriously and added it on the board to our list. Tony was obviously surprised and thrown off guard. But I could see in his face that he did not seem displeased that he had contributed positively. He became more focused, participated in the discussion, and lasted for the rest of the lesson.

Teachers will tell many such stories. The accounts often seem to portray the reality of teaching as a mundane and unglamorous process. But what is most interesting is that these stories are at odds with the methodological, philosophical, and theoretical accounts of "teacher reflection in action" and "teacher decision making" as we find them in the professional literature and research reports.

Does the concept of teaching as reflective decision making aim at a plausible and attainable reality? Many teachers have given me testimonials that are at odds with the concept of teaching as deliberative reflection in action. It is true, of course, that when you ask a teacher, "What made you decide to act in this way?" the teacher will readily give reasons. Teachers admit that they must be making countless decisions throughout the day. But when you ask the same teacher how much reflective thinking really went into each of these many "decisions," the teacher will equally readily admit that in actual fact you do not really make decisions in that sense;

rather, you say and do what is appropriate in a thoughtful kind of way in the instant of the moment. One university teacher confided that, at times, he quite purposefully tries to reflect on what he should say or do while saying and doing it. "But," he said, "doing this quickly became highly frustrating."

> I felt that I become artificial and, in fact, the reflectiveness with which I approach the students, the class discussion, the presentation, or the classwork that I do becomes an obstacle for a smooth lesson. So instead of improving my teaching, it worsens.... Sometimes the result is that I grow more self-conscious, and I become aware of the students looking at me and judging me. Then I experience a kind of split sense of self—a self as observed and objectified by others and a self trying to deal with this situation.

As a result of the emphasis on reflective practice in teacher-education programs, student teachers have been pressed to live up to the expectation that good teachers are reflective teachers. But they have not always learned where and how the reflective process should enter the life of teaching. Some beginning teachers receive the strong message that they should not only be reflective in the pre-active and the post-active phases of teaching but that, in the thick of classroom action, teachers should be constantly thinking about why and what they are doing while they are doing it, constantly considering alternatives to their aims and methods, constantly being prepared to alter their course midstream, constantly reflecting on the significance of student behavior, and constantly taking into consideration alternative interpretations of what is going on with students, socially and psychologically, in their learning of subject matter.

Even with the best of intentions, things do not happen that way. What makes true reflection in action difficult is that life in classrooms is contingent, dynamic, and ever-changing: every moment, every second is situation specific. Moments of teaching are ongoing incidents that require instant actions. As Tony's teacher suggested, one must quite literally act "in a flash." In some languages the term "moment" (*Augenblick* in German, *ogenblik* in Dutch) literally translates as "in the twinkling of an eye." Indeed, the reality of pedagogical acting takes place at this Kairotic level of temporal immediacy that does not permit a reflective stepping back from or out of the situation in order to consider the various alternatives and consequences of those possible alternatives in concrete, ever-changing situations.

Again, I am not suggesting that good teachers act without thought. But we have not really examined the nature of this "thought." Although immediate acting does not consist of distancing oneself from a situation as one would do in post hoc reflection on experience, to a certain degree we can maintain a reflexive dialogue between the I and the self. The I monitors, as it were, what the self does while doing it. One teacher described how her thoughtfulness is something more like a mood, an attitudinal state of mind in relating to students:

When I walk into my classroom, I am aware that I adopt quite purposefully an attitude of tolerant forbearance toward my students and my class. In that sense I am quite different in class from how I am with my kids at home. And yet I am not just acting or playing a role all day long. That would be too tiring and too exacting of my energies and resourcefulness. In school I employ another side of myself from what I show at home.

With my own family I am quite aware that in certain situations with my kids I should not act impulsively, and therefore, I quite literally may "count to ten" sometimes, or take "time out" before I say or do something that I might later regret. But in the classroom it is usually impossible to take time out. Although there are moments when I take a breath and almost force myself to count to ten. Of course, I rarely make it to ten. There are thirty students in this class, and you can't walk away from it or turn your back and take a break. You must get on with what you are doing. And so my attitude of forbearance provides me with a patient alertness and tolerance so as not to act and interact with my students in a manner that is impulsive, careless, or unthinking.

A phenomenology of tactful action may reveal several styles of intuitive practice: from acting in a largely self-forgetful manner to a kind of running inner speech that the interior eye of the ego maintains with the self. This split awareness of self manifests itself as a kind of natural schizophrenia whereby one part of the self somehow dialogues with the other part. Teachers often say things such as "part of me wanted to complete the lesson and another part of me knew that I should stop and deal with the concern that had arisen."

In everyday life in classrooms the thousand and one things that teachers say, do, say, or not do all have normative pedagogical significance. Not only the ends or goals of education but also the means and methods used all have pedagogical value and consequences for learning. Any teaching situation could pose innumerable questions of how to act: What is appropriate, and what is less appropriate with these children? What should one say in this or that situation? How does one enter a classroom? How does one close the door? How and what atmosphere is created by the many seemingly innocuous things that teachers and students do? How does this work differently with different kids and different cases? How does the teacher address the class? Where does he or she stand, sit, or move around? What speech climate is created? What tone of voice? When should a teacher be silent? What glance? What gesture? Which teaching techniques and what evaluation approaches are pedagogically more appropriate in particular circumstances? What type of experience is good for children here? And what material is less good for them? Should this difficult subject matter be taught? Should it be made easier? How easy? What kind of difficulty is good for this student? And what about that student? How much pressure is too much? What kind of discipline is right in this situation? And what expectations may be inappropriate? What should one do now? Any of these questions may be posed or occur to teachers, but if they do present themselves, then they usually occur upon reflection on the situation in which one found oneself. In real situations the teachers must constantly and instantly act in a manner that hopefully demonstrates a thoughtful considerateness.

CHAPTER FIVE

Thoughtful Observing with Pedagogical Eyes and Ears

As I walk past a school playground, I see a child skipping rope. I pause and smile. I see a youthful bounce, the commanding rhythm of a rope—and perhaps a memory. I recognize this rhyme. Times do not change. When the child stops, I still feel the snap against my feet. Regret fills me. I wish I could revisit my old school playground. But then I come to myself. My childhood place is thousands of miles away. It is not likely I will see it again as I knew it. I turn away from that child and resume my walk. I saw a child, a rope, a game. Sight and sound collaborated to make me feel the rope against my feet. Then I saw regret, nostalgia. Then I went on my way.

The teacher sees Diane skipping rope. He sees much more than a passerby can see, for he has known her for more than a year. She skips away from the other children, and he wonders what it will take for Diane to become one of them. She is academically the highest achiever of her class, but her achievements are not the product of some irrepressible raw intelligence; Diane earns her accomplishments with a grim fervor that saddens the teacher. She has an overachieving mother who fosters ambitious goals. Diane's mother intends to have herself a gifted daughter. Diane complies. She earns her mother's favor, but at the price of childhood happiness, her teacher thinks. As the teacher sees her skipping, he observes her tenseness and contrasts it with the relaxed skipping of the others. It is the same tenseness that betrays her anxiety with every assignment, every test. Diane marches rather than skips through the hoops of life.

The teacher also sees how Diane's eyes are turned to a half dozen girls who skip together with a big skipping rope. One of the girls returns her glance and gestures for Diane to come. Diane abruptly stops. The rope hits her feet and she turns away, toward the school door.

What does the teacher see? A lonely girl who can relate to classmates only by constantly measuring herself by competitive standards. If only she

---

Pedagogical Tact: Knowing What to Do When You Don't Know What to Do, by Max van Manen, 61–75.
© 2015 Taylor & Francis. All rights reserved.

could develop some personal space, some room to grow and develop social interests just for herself, away from her mother. The teacher is hopeful, for in Diane's eyes he has spotted desire—a desire to be accepted by her classmates. Who knows, some "thoughtfulness," some pedagogical tact may just nudge Diane closer to the shared social space of her possible friends.

We are contrasting the way a passerby sees a skipping girl with the way a teacher sees Diane. The teacher has a pedagogical interest in the life of this child. He stands in pedagogical relationship to her, and he cannot help but see the child as a unique and whole human being involved in self-formative growth.

Seeing Children Pedagogically

So how does a teacher see children? Is there a unique pedagogical way of seeing children, different from the way other people would see them? A strange question, perhaps. Given that seeing is a sensory act, don't we all see children the same way? For example, we see the same figure, the same movement, the same child skipping rope or painting a picture. But we never see anything purely. How and what we see depends on who and how we are in the world. How and what we see in a child is dependent on our relationship with that child.

There is an acute danger in thinking professionally about children. Child psychologists, instructional consultants, curriculum developers, resource personnel, principals, school counselors, evaluation specialists, and learned professors are all in danger of thinking and talking about children in abstract ways, in categories. The theoretical language of child "science" so easily makes us look past each child's uniqueness toward common characteristics that allow us to group, sort, sift, measure, manage, and respond to children in preconceived ways.

For instance, once I call a child "attention deficit disorder," once I see a child as a "behavior problem" or a "low achiever," or once I refer to him or her as someone who has a specific "learning style," a particular mode of "cognitive functioning," then I am inclined immediately to reach into my portfolio of professional tricks for a specific instructional intervention, a behavioral therapy, or a medical solution. What happens, then, is that I forego the possibility of truly listening to and seeing the specific child. Instead, I put the child away in categorical language. This language is as constraining as a real prison. Putting children away by means of technical, diagnostic, or instrumental language is really a kind of pedagogical abandonment.

Of course, no teacher can be truly attentive to each and every child in his or her classroom. An elementary school class may have 30 students; a high school teacher may see 150 students a week. And when teachers amongst themselves discuss certain students, then they may use stories and descriptors that reflect their particular experiences, interests, and views of these students, depending also on the subject the teacher teaches. Some teachers will be more perceptive than others, but in reality a teacher may only be able to be attentive to a couple of students who may need this attention at this particular time. The point is, however, that by really being attentive to this or that particular student, a teacher may be able to pedagogically see any student when the moment demands it.

A teacher is a child watcher. This does not mean a teacher can see a child "purely," without being influenced by the philosophic view this teacher holds of what it means to be human. One cannot adequately observe children without reflecting on the way one looks at them. All I am saying here is that a teacher must observe a child not as a passerby, a policeman, or a friend might; a teacher must observe a child pedagogically. This means being a child watcher who guards and keeps in view the total existence of the developing child.

Diane conducts herself in a certain way on the playground, and the teacher watches quietly and wishes he could bring her academic effort and her personal life into better harmony. The teacher thinks of specific ways that that influence might be brought to bear on Diane.

The teacher has an understanding of the child's development that is simultaneously engaged and reserved, close and distant. On the one hand, he or she must watch and watch over the child with care and concern, and herein lies both engagement and maximum subjectivity. And on the other hand, the teacher must watch the child's total field of limits and possibilities, and herein lies the need for reserve and distancing.

Teachers are oriented to children in a special way. In some ways not unlike parents, but still not quite like parents. Like a parent, the teacher is concerned with the child's maturation, growth, and learning. But the teacher has a special interest in certain aspects of a child's growth while realizing that the total development must be kept in view. By exemplifying a certain standard or norm, educators mobilize their influence to help children gain insight into their own interests.

In some sense the most personal relationship between adult and child is the parenting relationship. A woman who becomes a mother learns to observe her children with motherly eyes, with a motherly body. Can anyone observe a child quite in the same ways a mother does? And what is the nature of fatherly eyes? Can anyone else see the way a father sees his child? Only a father and mother can watch a child and watch over a child with truly fatherly and motherly eyes. But a teacher also enters a very personal relationship with a child. At the same time, there is a distancing that makes the teacher a special pedagogical observer. By knowing this child, a teacher can hold back superficial judgment about this child. The word "observing" has etymological connections to "preserving, saving, regarding, protecting."

The teacher serves the child by observing from very close proximity while still maintaining distance.

Pedagogical Care Experienced as Devotion and Worry

Every adult who works with children—every mother, father, grandparent, psychologist, teacher, nurse, pediatrician, social worker, minister—should be open to the need to experience love and worry about and for the children in their care. Common examples of pedagogical care and worry are easily found in the ordinary lifeworlds of parents and children. A mother poses a question online:

> My problem is that I find it very difficult to pass the care for my family to someone else. I don't mean just for an evening but for several days. Are they enjoying good company? Are they feeling okay? Are small conflicts properly resolved? Are they eating regularly and enough? Are they getting clean towels?
> I know this is a problem of being a worrywart, but do others recognize it, and what can I do about it? My husband is a dear father, but he is often away and is not as close to the home front as I am; he simply does not experience this "problem" the way I do.

A second mother responds to the online question:

> I do not know if there is a real solution to your query. But you can probably make it somewhat easier for yourself... by beginning to look for situations that are not problematic. You seem to be struggling with the process of letting go that begins in part already right at the birth of your first child.

The second mother seems to recognize the worrying experienced by the first. It is not just that the mother finds it difficult "to pass the care"; she really has a problem with "letting go." Next, the second mother gives suggestions for dealing with the problem in some appropriate manner. Indeed, this is often how it goes in life. Language is the way of accessing and understanding human experience. By naming and renaming experience, we bring it to awareness, (re)interpret it, and come to particular understandings or misunderstandings. The example simply illustrates that finding a language to describe our experience is a critical requisite for addressing and understanding our pedagogical predicaments.

When I ask people for concrete examples to illustrate the caring of their parents, I receive a variety of stories. A thirty-year-old woman tells how her mother had come to stay with her for a few days in the big city. When, in the evening, she returns home from late-night shift work, she finds her mother still up. Surprised, the daughter says, "Why didn't you go to bed? You knew I would be late." "Yes," her mother answers, "but I wanted to make sure you got home all right." "But, Mom, this is my life. What do you think I have been doing for the last ten years?!" "Yes, yes," the mother answers, "I can't help it. I just like to know that you are okay."

For many parents, care seems to consist of fretting and fussing and worrying and generally making a nuisance of oneself for the sake of one's children. Of course, kids at times hate this in their parents, but in the back of their minds, they also know that it would be much more terrible if there were no one to worry about them. On CBC radio we hear a broadcast interview with street children in Vancouver. One street child says, "What is most terrible being on the street is that there is nobody who has dreams about you. Ordinary kids have parents who worry about them. Nobody, neither my father nor my mother, ever worried about me, ever had a dream for me." And a fourteen-year-old foster girl says, "You know what I am afraid of? I am afraid that if I were to die, no one would really care." Of course, we should not think that caring is something that comes naturally with being a mother or a father. Children may have caring parents but still end up in government care.

It seems that when we try to recall particular moments of caring, it is often the intense experiences that stand out. But the qualities of these experiences seem characteristic also of the more mundane and common moments of caring. The following is an excerpt from the diary of Judith Minty. It could have been told by many parents. It is an example of pedagogical listening by a mother:

> My son, my middle child, the handsome one, the worst student, the one most admired by his peers, came home from football practice tonight sick, with a bellyache, half crying.
>
> Thirteen years old, short for his age, he pedals off on his bike at 5 p.m. and drags back into the house around eight every night.. . .
>
> A half-cold dinner waits for him in the kitchen. I rush him out there so that he can eat, shower, and riffle through the pages of his homework before he groans into bed. . . . And I don't forget to remind myself that if most of his friends are playing football and he isn't, then there is no one to occupy his time, nothing to do between school and bedtime.
>
> But tonight is different. He eats little, says he is sick. I tell him it was the peanut butter sandwich he ate before practice. I tell him that big Scott M across the street throws up after every practice if he eats less than two hours before. My son trudges upstairs to suffer alone.
>
> After his shower he goes to his room, where he thinks no one can hear him. But I hear him crying. I don't worry too much. He is the one who moans when he has a minor cold. Briefly, I think of appendicitis, but brush the thought away. I also think about those other times he has cried because something he couldn't cope with what was gnawing at him. I will wait awhile, see what develops. (1982, pp. 215–216)

In this recognizable family situation, we hear a mother worrying. But this is not the kind of worrying that we commonly regard as self-indulgent and useless. The kinds of things the mother does is the ordinary stuff of parenting: the things parents do and think. This worrying is not a side effect of parenting; it is the very life of it. A mother is involved in taking care of her son. In everyday life situations, caring is lived as a worrying attentiveness.

And Judith Minty knows this. She says, "I don't worry too much," but of course the point is that she does worry. Saying this to herself is as much a manner of keeping herself in check as it is a way of assuring that she should not let her own feelings and needs overshadow those of her son. She seems to know that worry can be both a way of staying in touch with her child and a way of dwelling too much on her own anxieties. She chooses the former. She worries and waits.

> When he comes downstairs, I ask him if the practice went badly today, was the coach after him? No, he just feels sick. I tell him no television—he needs to lie down in his room. The others come [his sisters] . . . [We talk but I] hear my son in the distance, still crying behind closed doors.
>
> I am reading in my bed. He appears. I put my book down. He sits at the foot of my bed, still young enough to weep in public, and tries to start. The others hover, then vanish. They know this is his crisis.
>
> "Lorie [his sister] is going to leave soon," he finally manages to blubber out. I tell him no, that she won't be going to college for years yet. [He says] "I don't want anything to change." (1982, p. 216)

Parental care is rarely an explicit fretting and more often a lingering awareness, a heedful attunement. While talking to her daughters or reading, the mother at the same time remains aware of her son's presence in the background. Did she do the right thing?

Worry, it seems, is the active ingredient of parental attentiveness. Worry—rather than duty or obligation—keeps us in touch with the one for whom we care. Worry is the spiritual glue that keeps the mother or father affixed to the life of their child. So when Judith Minty's son finally comes to talk to his mother, she expects that he will open up to her:

> The crack begins to open. "Do you want to stay just the way you are?" [I ask.] Of course he does, and nods, and then it all comes spilling, tumbling out, a waterfall full of worry and sadness and tears. As he tells it, I remember how, when he was ten, he worried about what would become of us when the sun burned itself out; how, when he was nine, he worried about having to fight in Vietnam. This tough boy-child, whom we worry about with his D+'s and C-'s has a different depth to him than our others.
>
> What will happen to him if his father dies, if I die? What will he do if he lives to be 103 and there is no family left?. . .
>
> We laugh that when he is 103, [his younger sister] Annie may be 101 and Lorie 105. I tell him that when he goes away to college, I expect him to come back

now and then. We talk about change, how people make plans to do things when they grow up, how I will miss him, but won't be lonely. And we talk about the new family that he will have when he leaves his old family. (1982, pp. 216, 217)

Notice how nicely the worrying mother takes away the worries of her child, how she indicates her worry as a mother—that she will miss him—but that he need not worry about that either. Finally she reflects to herself:

> Have I done a good job? I don't know. He is not crying any more. He tells me he has been thinking about this for a week and hasn't been able to eat much. We both laugh and agree that the not eating part was probably good for him. [He had put on too much weight.]
> It is much later now. He is sleeping. Everyone is sleeping. I hope his spirit sleeps well. (1982, p. 217)

When everyone is sleeping, the mother is still awake, thinking about her child. In some sense this wakefulness to one's child is characteristic of the life of parenting. To have children means that one will never be able to just sleep. Caring for one's children is a kind of worrying mindfulness. In some languages this worrying dimension is much more pronouncedly felt by the speakers of those languages. For example, in the Dutch language the equivalent word for "care" is "*zorgen*" which means caring as well as worrying. Similarly, "*sich sorgen um*" in German, "*omsorg*" in Norwegian, "omtänksam" in Swedish all have the connotation of a worrisome or concerned caring that cannot be adequately expressed by a single English word in everyday English language. These subtle but highly significant experiential distinctions of caring are missed by philosophical language analysis (compare Noddings 1984; 2013). Conceptual analysis fails to see that concepts are abstractions from experiences and therefore tend to lack the experiential resonance of the lived meanings of more experience-sensitive texts (see appendix 2).

The strange thing is that the more I care for this other, the more I worry and the stronger my desire to care. Desire does not mean a personal want or need; wants and needs differ from desire. I may always have wanted to buy an expensive bike, and now that I finally am able to afford my dream, I feel satisfied, or I may find that I am disappointed and that my want was not as worthwhile as I thought. At any rate, my want has been stilled. But desire that lives in my relation of care reaches beyond anything that might bring satisfaction and, thus, acquiesce the desire. For example, love is desire in this sense. Think of the lover who asks his loved one, "Do you love me?" And his love says, "Yes, you are my love and only love." The question is: What happens to desire? Chances are that a week later, a day later, or maybe even five minutes later the lover may again feel the desire to ask and say, "Yes, but do you really love me?" And again his love responds, "Yes, I really do love you." This example illustrates that true desire cannot be stilled. No answer can forever satisfy. In fact, desire feeds on itself and fans itself—think of the great love tragedies. Similarly, caring responsibility increases in proportion to the measure that it is assumed. The more I care for this person, the more I worry, and the more I worry, the stronger my desire to care.

What is also peculiar about this ethical experience of caring responsibility is that it singles me out. It addresses each person uniquely. When the voice of caring calls, then it is no use to look around to see whether it was meant for someone else. No, here is this child in front of me, and I look this child in the face. Before I can even think about it, I already have experienced my responsiveness: my respons-ability. I "know" this child calls upon me. It is undeniable: I have experienced the appeal. And this experience is a form of knowing. I am called. I am being addressed—or to use a phrase from the philosopher Emmanuel Levinas (1985): I am the one who is charged with responsibility. What makes Levinas' insights so unique is that he is the only philosopher who offers us an experiential ethics of caring responsibility that is not founded in a theory of ethics. That is why he calls it pure ethics. He shows us that in the encounter with the other, in this greeting, in this face, we experience the purely ethical before we have involved ourselves in general ethics as a form of thinking, reflecting, and moral reasoning.

Experiencing Responsibility in the Face of the Unique

What is the distinction between caring as general ethics and caring as pure ethics? An example may be found in the biblical parable of Abraham and Isaac in Genesis 22. For example, Søren Kierkegaard (1983, pp. 82–120) portrays Abraham as the great God-fearing man who was commanded by God to sacrifice his only son.

> The time came when God put Abraham to the test. "Abraham," he called, and Abraham replied, "Here I am." God said, "Take your son Isaac, your only son, whom you love, and go to the land of Moriah. There you shall offer him as a sacrifice on one of the hills which I will show you." (Holy Bible, King James version, Genesis 22)

Abraham is biblically thought of and lionized in terms of his unshakable faith. But Kierkegaard is possessed by the "shudder of thought" that accompanies trying to understand Abraham's predicament. What did Abraham think when he set out on the journey to sacrifice his son? What would it have been like to be there with Abraham on the three-day journey? How would we see Abraham raise his eyes to the hill in Moriah where the burnt sacrifice of his son was to take place? What did Abraham go through when he gathered the firewood and sharpened the knife? What possible horror did he experience when he bound his son, when he raised the knife?

The horror is that Abraham was indeed prepared to sacrifice his beloved Isaac in the face of and in defiance of any ethical standard. This horror is difficult to alleviate. Yet in Abraham's predicament we may sense the tension between two demands of caring responsibility. First, there is the demand experienced in the call that has singled me out as uniquely responsible. And second, there is the demand of the community that we must always be able to justify and account for our responsibilities, duties, and tasks in some kind of ethical manner.

Would it not have been easier for Abraham if he had at least tried to explain God's strange command to his wife and son at the outset of the journey? Kierkegaard shows that this would have been impossible. The absolute responsibility that Abraham felt toward God could not and cannot be justified in any system of ethics or by any moral principle. If anything, child sacrifice is a mad, murderous, and scandalous act, and Abraham would only have met total scorn and disbelief. So it was Abraham's fate that he had to carry this unbearable burden, this terrible secret, all by himself. Abraham had heard God's call, and it was his responsibility to heed this call.

In rereading Genesis 22, one may wonder: What would have been the significance of the fact that it was a second voice, the voice of an other, who called Abraham and who commanded him to stop and not raise his hand against his son, the son he loved so deeply?

> Then he stretched out his hand and took the knife to kill his son; but the angel of the Lord called to him from heaven, "Abraham, Abraham." He answered, "Here I am." The angel of the Lord said, "Do not raise your hand against the boy; do not touch him." (Holy Bible, King James version, Genesis 22)

Without intending to be sacrilegious, we could imagine that this is how it went: Abraham tied his son to the sacrificial stake as the biblical story said he did (see also Caputo, 1988; Derrida, 1995a; Levinas, 1969). He sharpened his knife as he must have done. Then he raised the knife and looked Isaac in the face. And at that very same moment he heard the voice and the voice forbade him to kill.

Both Caravaggio and Rembrandt have depicted the sacrificial biblical scene in their paintings. The treatment of Isaac's face is especially striking. In Caravaggio, Isaac's face is contorted with dread and fright, and the angel's face is expressive with appeal. But in spite of these very different expressions, what is most remarkable is the uncanny likeness of the two faces. Art critics have suggested that Caravaggio used the same model, Cecco Boneri, to paint both the angel and Isaac, but it has also been suggested that Caravaggio painted his own face for both the angel and Isaac. Whatever the case, Abraham is held from killing his son by staring into the face of the angel, which is identical to the face of his son.

Sacrifice of Isaac, Caravaggio (1603), Uffizi, Florence

Not only is Abraham confronted with the Levinassian face of the other; the pure ethical experience of this happening is also the pedagogical moment in which Abraham experiences the impossibility of harming his own vulnerable child. It was Isaac's face that issued the appeal to the father, just as every child's face does to his or her father or mother. Formulated differently: Abraham heard the call of pedagogy when looking into his son's face.

Strangely, in Rembrandt's painting Isaac's face is completely covered over by the clutching grip of Abraham holding him down. It is as if Rembrandt, the famous master of portraiture, did not know what to do with the face of Isaac. And so he covered up the face completely. But both Caravaggio and Rembrandt anticipate Levinas in their understanding of the significance of the face as the ethical experience of responsibility for the other and, in particular, the pedagogical sensitivity to one's child.

The reason Caravaggio and Rembrandt could show us the ambiguous role of the face is that Abraham's situation is not at all exceptional. In fact, it powerfully portrays our everyday predicament: our ambiguous relation to our own children. The French philosopher Jacques Derrida has put it very well: in a real sense we can kill our children (i.e., their singularity) in many different ways, and all of us, men and women, are like Abraham holding the knife over those who are dear to us. That is why Levinas says that "Care

The Sacrifice of Isaac, Rembrandt, 1635, State Hermitage Museum

for the death of the other is the beginning of the acknowledgement of the other" (Levinas in Rötzer, 1995, p. 65).

We need to be sensitive to the singularity of the other. And the singularity of each person comes into sharp relief against the fact of his or her individual mortality. Ironically, we are given this mortality right at birth. Therefore, Derrida (1995a) calls this "the gift of death," as it is our own mortality that belongs to each of us more uniquely than anything else imaginable. Whatever else can be taken away from us, there is one thing that belongs to us so essentially that nobody can take it away—our own death. I may give my death in sacrifice to someone else, and yet even that supreme gift cannot be substituted for their own death. Thus, it is the nonsubstitutional uniqueness of the other that I must preserve and not kill by betraying it to the general. And yet, Derrida claims, this is precisely what we do every day:

> By preferring my work, simply by giving it my time and attention, by preferring my activity as a citizen or as a professorial and professional philosopher, writing and speaking here in a public language ... I am perhaps fulfilling my duty. But I am sacrificing and betraying at every moment all my other obligations: my obligations to the other others whom I know or don't know ... also those I love in private, my own, my family, my son, each of whom is the only son I sacrifice to the other, every one being sacrificed to every one else in this land of Moriah that is our habitat every second of every day. (Derrida, 1995a, p. 69)

It seems that we constantly betray the call of caring responsibility in our efforts to be caring in the general sense of duty, as in our professional practice of teaching, psychology, social work, nursing, or medical care. Derrida articulates the dilemma in such a way that his confession of failing to be responsive to the call of his own son becomes an unsolvable predicament:

> What can be said about Abraham's relation to God can be said about my relation without relation to *every other (one) as every (bit) other [tout autre comme tout autre]*, in particular my relation to my neighbor or my loved ones who are inaccessible to me, as secret and transcendent as Jahweh.... Translated into this extraordinary story, the truth is shown to possess the very structure of what occurs every day. Through its paradox it speaks of the responsibility required at every moment for every man and woman. (Derrida, 1995a, p. 78; emphasis in the original)

In a way Derrida seems to let himself—and us—off the hook in our unique responsibility to care for the other as other. On the one hand, he suggests that we need to heed this call, and yet, on the other hand, his questioning strategy aims to show that we must constantly fail, as we cannot possibly be responsive to every other who is out there and who also makes an appeal to our caring responsibility. Because we can only worry about one thing at a time, we cannot worry about everyone and everything. So why worry? Why care in this deepened sense? Indeed, even as a teacher or as childcare professional, one would have to agree with Derrida—we cannot really see how we could worry for each child in our charge.

Does that mean we must flee into the ethical domain of a professional responsibility that says that we must subsume our caring behaviors under some general moral code? The problem with Derrida's approach is that he has already fled into language and ethics when he deconstructs the prereflective occurrence of the caring encounter. The point is that in everyday life the experience of the call of the other, of care-as-worry, is always contingent and particular. It can happen to any one of us anywhere, anytime.

Every situation like that is always contingent. I can only be here and now. In this home. In this classroom. In this street. Thus, it is the singularity of this person, this child who addresses me in my singularity.

Caring for the Faces of Those Who Are Faceless

I would like to suggest, somewhat tongue-in-cheek, that care-as-worry can be likened to an illness, a chronic condition of worrying for this other person who is dear to me, whom I love, or for whom I care and happen to feel responsible. And indeed, this condition of care-as-worry is truly somewhat like an affliction. Existentially the vulnerability of the other may be experienced as ethical pain—a pain that is symptomatic of the worrying condition engendered in the encounter with this other person who has made a claim on me. Many parents, many teachers, many nurses, many physicians, and many other helping professionals would readily agree that this worrying can be painful and troubling. But it is a form of worry that is also necessary. Why? Because worrying keeps me in touch with the presence of this other. Or, as Levinas says, "The presence of the other touches me" (1995, p. 62). And now that the ethical has entered my life, I feel I should do something, that something is demanded of me.

As a father or mother, you may recognize this care-as-worry from personal experience: from those numerous moments when you suffered almost more from the stomachache, the illness, the fear, or the anxiety experienced by your child than the child did him or herself. A teacher may feel a special responsibility for this or that student. And this care-as-worry is often expressed as, "I have to let her know that she is doing okay," or "I need to keep a special eye on him." But, of course, caring in a deeper sense can only happen where contexts, structures, teacher-student or patient-staff ratios, and schedules provide opportunities for the occurrence of genuine caring relations, even though we know that these relations cannot be planned or predicted.

Effective practice is not the primary reason to remain open to the ethical demand; also important is that caring in this deeper sense remains the source for understanding every other kind of caring. It is true that care-as-worry cannot be legislated or prescribed through protocols, and it is impossible to care deeply for every person (child, student, patient) for whom we are responsible as professionals. But the sporadic and spontaneous occurrence of this originary kind of care in singular instances provides the basis for understanding the more practical pedagogical responsibilities that we do expect from professional educators and others on an everyday and routine basis.

Here is a fragment from a farewell speech by a junior high school teacher to her "homeroom" students:

> I will miss you. And I will think about you, how you are doing. I will miss the good discussions we have shared during class. I will miss the thoughtful and also the embarrassing questions in health and sex education classes. I will miss the letters about novels. The poems you have written. And yes, I will miss even the arguments we have had about why it is a good thing in this day and age to study old-fashioned grammar.
>
> Our homeroom has sometimes been like a home. We have been like a family. And, of course, families have their difficulties and differences. I have admired how you, the students, have looked after one another, how you have shown sensitivity to personal vulnerabilities and strengths.
>
> Like in any home, squabbles did abound. Yet there were many of those special moments that will leave their traces—you know, those are the moments that an insight occurred, that a discovery came to mind, that a spontaneous chuckle, giggle, or laughter broke up the class. Also the moments of a knowing look, a rolling of the eyes, or a quick clearing of the throat, and the occasional happening of a tear to the eye.
>
> I want to say to the parents how lucky they are for having such wonderful sons and daughters. You have been special to me, and I will carry you forever in my heart.

In private conversation with the above teacher she expressed apprehensions: she was worried about passing her students on to others, to senior high school teachers. Not uncommonly, teachers worry about particular students. The same teacher said,

> For example, there is Michael and Alex. Michael and Alex visit me several times a day for chats between classes, during classes, and at the end of the day. They never leave without saying good-bye. I do a lot of listening. Everyday I know what is going on in their lives. These are kids who thrive on personal contact. And now that they are leaving, I wonder: Who will take my place? Will there be some teacher in that large impersonal high school with whom they can talk?

It is because a teacher feels addressed by the "faces" of particular students, about whom he or she worries, that the teacher can remain sensitive to the sometimes "faceless" multitude of all the other students for whom the teacher is responsible. The point is that this deeper sense of care-as-worry is the source for understanding and nurturing the more derivative varieties of care for the faces of the faceless that are theorized and called for in our research literature and professional practices. This is as true for the teaching profession as it is for the nursing, counseling, medical, social work, and other health science and care staff.

Only by remaining attuned to our sense of unique responsibility can we insert into our professional ethical practices the general responsibility of caring in all its various modalities that our vocations require. This is true for many professional practitioners. For the cynics and the pragmatically minded, care-as-worry may still be an unrealistic or a "heavy" idea.

A cynic might say that care-as-worrying seems a burdening responsibility. But so it is a burden. It may not always be pleasant or delightful, but, as Levinas says, it is good: "It's the experience of the good, the meaning of the good, of goodness. Only goodness is good" (1995, p. 61).

Chapter Six

Pedagogical Tact

People-Sense and Child-Sense

Some people seem to possess a keen and sensitive insight into human nature. "People-sense" is a kind of empathic sensibility and wisdom about people and how they tend to feel, act, or react in specific situations. It is an instant kind of understanding or knowing of how a particular person's actions may relate to motives, intentions, emotions, feelings, and moods. It senses the meaning and significance of human frailties, strengths, difficulties, inclinations, and life circumstances. People-sense may account for the fact that some people who possess this dispositional sensibility tend to get along better with others or that people with people-sense tend to be specially respected and regarded; they tend to be sought out by individuals who have personal problems. People-sense is a desirable disposition in psychologists, teachers, physicians, nurses, clergy, but it is not always found in such professionals.

I coin the term *people-sense* because it is more succinct and to the point than an awkward phrase such as "being a good judge of character" or "having insight into human nature." In addition, the notion of people-sense may support the proposition that the term child-sense similarly implies the ability to understand children or young people in a pedagogical manner. Thus, I coin the term *child-sense* to refer to the pedagogical sense (sensibility) of perceptive insights into the child's world, being, experiences, and emotions. The practice of pedagogy relies on child-sense.

Child-sense means sensing or knowing how young people experience things, what they think about, how they think, how they look at the world, how they act, and, most importantly, how each child is a unique person. A teacher who does not understand the inner life of a child does not know who the child is that he or she is teaching. Moreover, the concept of pedagogy not only implies this special child-sense but also includes an animating

---

Pedagogical Tact: Knowing What to Do When You Don't Know What to Do, by Max van Manen, 77–106. © 2015 Taylor & Francis. All rights reserved.

ethos. A pedagogue is a person (parent, teacher, counselor, administrator, etc.) who carries caring responsibilities for children, who understands young people in a personal or professional manner, and who has a special commitment and interest in children's well-being and their growth toward personal maturity and adulthood.

Of course, teaching as pedagogical interaction with children requires not only child-sense but also a complex knowledge base, an improvisational ability, a virtue-like normativity, and an active pedagogical thoughtfulness that differs from the reflective wisdom (*phronesis*) of other practitioners: this is pedagogical tact. The classroom life of teachers is difficult especially because it is inherently ethical and improvisational, and tact constantly hinges on the significance of what happens in the moment. The famous scholar Herbart once argued that pedagogical incidents are really insignificant because there are so many of them, and each act in itself is rather inconsequential. He suggested that it is the overall objective that is of prime relevance; however, in actuality it may be the numerous small moments that, in their singularity and their aggregate, determine the latent implications of pedagogy for the unfolding lives of young people. And, hopefully, this living in the immediacy of the moment is mediated by pedagogical thoughtfulness and tact.

Obviously pedagogy does not consist of a determinate system of rules or values that would be applied by any single person in the same manner to particular situations. Although many of us may share certain values and knowledge perspectives, the way these are actually embodied and expressed is always unique. In this sense there are many personal pedagogies. Every mother and every father is unique. Just so, professional practitioners such as classroom teachers are not replaceable individuals; each person is unique in the sense that he or she possesses a unique knowledge base, a personal history, a uniquely personal style, a personal emotional makeup, an individual set of values, and a unique thoughtfulness and tact for understanding and interpreting particular situations and experiences.

The Nature of Pedagogical Tact

What is pedagogical tact? It may seem that pedagogical tact is an elusive and slippery notion. In the English language there have been only few presentations and discussions of the notion of pedagogical tact (van Manen, 1984, 1986, 1991, 1994, 1997, 2002; Metz, 1995; Juuso and Laine, 2004). What does tactful acting look like when we see it? Indeed, there is no manual, blueprint, or technology to tact. But we can say that pedagogical tact (1) manifests itself in everyday life as instant action; (2) forms a way of acting that is first of all dependent on an intuitive sensibility and sensitivity—in other words, a feeling-understanding; (3) is sensitive to the uniqueness of the child or young person; (4) is sensitive to the particularities and context of the situation; and (5) is unique also to the personal character of the teacher, the mother, the father, the psychologist, and to their personal pedagogies (interpretive sensibilities, attentiveness, existential values, life meanings, ways of standing in life, ontotheologies, etc.).

How or where can we see pedagogical tact at work? Naturally these are also difficult questions. It may not always be easy to tell genuine tactful actions from artificial, pretentious, feigned, and false forms of behavior that do not seem motivated by an authentic interest in children's welfare. Children often can tell the difference quite accurately between teachers who are "real" and caring and those who are "fake" and not truly interested in the children's welfare. Pedagogical tact manifests itself primarily as a mindful orientation in our being and acting with children. This is much less a manifestation of certain observable behaviors than a way of actively standing in relationships. Nevertheless, there are ways of describing how tact manifests itself as a showing in our pedagogical being and acting. Depending on the situation, pedagogical tact shows itself as subtle influence, as holding back, as openness to the child's experience, as attunement to subjectivity, as situational confidence, as improvisational gift, and so on—for a more detailed discussion see *The Tact of Teaching* (van Manen, 1991).

What does pedagogical tact do? Pedagogical tact does what is right or good for the child. But how do we know what is the right or good thing to do? If one cannot go up to the abstract level of moral or critical theory to answer this question in a general manner, then one needs to go down to the concrete level of everyday experience to observe what tact does in specific situations or particular circumstances. We know from our experience of living with children what kinds of actions occur in the sphere of pedagogical tact. Pedagogical tact preserves a child's space, protects what is vulnerable, prevents hurt, makes whole what is broken, strengthens what is good, enhances what is unique, and sponsors personal growth.

How does pedagogical tact do what it does? Pedagogical tact does what it does by exercising a certain perceptive sensitivity as well as practicing an active, expressive, and caring concern for the child. Pedagogical tact relies on our ability to "see" and "hear" (sense) what the needs are of children and also what the possibilities are of these children or of any particular child. This means that pedagogical tact can only do its work when the eyes and ears are used for searching in a caring, open, and receptive manner what is the potential of a child, what this or that child can become—in other words, what is the "essence" or "excellence" of this child. This, then, requires a perceiving and listening that is oriented to the otherness of the child and uses a multiplicity of perspectives, considerations, and vantage points to try to gain a vision and pedagogical understanding of a child. It is important to contrast the openness of this sensitive capacity of tact to the inclination to see and hear only what one wants to see and hear about a child. The latter orientation leads to inflexible judging, stereotyping, classifying—to seeing only the external behaviors of children and not their inner lives and their personal intents and projects.

Personal Pedagogies

Just like each child is unique, so, of course, is every teacher a unique person. However, the educational systems tend to regard and treat teachers as if their performances can be standardized. For the organizational bureaucracy, every teacher is replaceable, just like every soldier in the army is replaceable. The language of the educational management systems tends to rationalize the task of teaching in terms of time economies, standardized subject matter curricula, measurable learning outcomes, school productivity, subject matter scheduling, and so forth.

But each teacher is unique. Teachers have unique personalities and emotional make-ups. Some teachers prefer to teach younger children, whereas others are more intrigued with older children or adolescents. Some teachers have an artistic flair, while others are more businesslike in their approaches. And, of course, the teacher's style and way of being is conditioned also by the subject matter he or she teaches. Language arts teachers may get to know their students well because they are involved in the students' writing activities, science teachers may get to know more logical aspects of their students, and ditto for teachers of other subject matter specialties.

So every teacher has a unique pedagogical personality and style. Students know that some teachers are empathic, while others are more aloof. And it is no doubt true that some teachers are actually rather pedagogically insensitive to the subjectivities of their students. Other teachers seem to know what goes on in the lives of many of their students, even if they teach a large class or several large classes. No doubt some teachers possess a more sensitive kind of pedagogical thoughtfulness and have a greater understanding of individual students.

This is all noticeable when, in meetings, teachers give their views and debrief certain students who may pose special challenges. Teachers may have very different experiences with these students, and even similar experiences with students may be interpreted and valued quite differently by individual teachers. In this sense we may say that each teacher embodies a personal pedagogy—a personal way of understanding and dealing with individual students and classes of students as a whole.

Indeed, all teachers know how a single student may sometimes influence the general quality and atmosphere of a certain class of students. And it is also true that the contingent makeup and conglomerate of students in classrooms may give a whole class its unique character or personality. The whole classroom possesses a "collective personality" depending, of course, in part on the age, gender mix, and social makeup of the group of students in it. These are issues that the administrative educational bureaucracy of the central office knows little or nothing about. But for teachers, these are the pedagogical realities that determine the nature and quality of their educational tasks and responsibilities.

The Immediacy of the Moment

Pedagogical perceptiveness relies in part on a kind of tacit or intuitive knowledge that the teacher may learn from personal experience or through apprenticeship from a more experienced teacher. Most human activities involve tacit or intuitive complexities that constitute a kind of body knowledge or body skill. For example, a medical doctor or nurse confronted with a person who presents certain symptoms may intuitively sense what is wrong with the patient on the basis of such tacit understandings, even though the symptoms may not have been that easy to pinpoint or identify. Similarly, a teacher who senses that a child has certain difficulties in dealing with a learning or comprehension problem may not be able to determine exactly on what clues the perceptive understanding was based. The tacit or intuitive nature of our relational and body knowledge is learned in subtle ways by attuning ourselves to the concrete particulars of situations.

Often, knowing what to do occurs in the very act of doing it. It is as if we are touched by a genie, but only if we are open and sensitive to such a moment. As suggested above, the improvisational demands of teaching may be described as Kairos moments, when we must make use of the moment as it presents itself to us.

As indicated in chapter 4, Kairos is the god of the fleeting moment. He is whimsical, rebellious, and creative. He is bald except for long forelocks of hair growing from his forehead or around his face. He holds a razor, or else scales balanced on the sharp edge of a knife, illustrating the fleeting instant of a moment when Kairos may appear and disappear. He is double-winged, indicating that a Kairos moment is fleeting, evanescent, propitious, and serendipitous. Kairos time is the moment of the now—the instant of the now. In such a Kairos moment, time seems to stand still. We are in timeless time.

Of course, as teachers, our actions are always governed by certain intentionalities—for example, we are busy at restoring order, or we are involved explaining a difficult concept, or we are trying to create a productive atmosphere at the beginning of a lesson. And yet, as I suggested earlier, the reflective component in our immediate interaction with others is usually constrained. When a child acts disruptively in class, the teacher usually does not have time to reflect on the situation in order to decide on the best thing to do. A teacher who pauses and deliberates at some length about alternatives and about what action to take with respect to a difficult student's rude comment may already be interpreted as hesitant, wishy-washy, or spineless. As a teacher, you simply have to do something, even if your action consists of ignoring or pretending that you did not notice the rude remark.

When, during a lesson, a student asks a question that shows misunderstanding, then the teacher does not have the luxury to consult a teaching text in order to deal with this question in the way that is just right for this child (a teaching text would not likely be able to provide advice like this anyway). The same is true for parents and other adults who have pedagogical responsibilities. When the child falls and hurts himself or herself or when a child protests the parent's reminder that it is bedtime, then there is no opportunity to sit back to figure out what to do in this situation. In Kairos moments, where tact is required, there is no chance to reflect in a deliberative or planning manner. Tactful acting is always Kairotic: contingent, immediate, situational, improvisational. And tact as a form of human interacting means that we are in a thinkingly active manner in a situation: emotionally, responsively, thoughtfully. Practical instant acting is driven by inner ontology rather than deliberative epistemology.

To the extent that the educator or parent has internalized pedagogical insights and emotional sensitivities, the tact will display a personal pedagogy. We all hopefully have developed unique personal pedagogies that are ethically and emotionally sensitive to concrete realities. This tact manifests itself in our very being and behavior.

The sensitive eye of tact mirrors back its caring glance. Tact does what it does by using the eyes, speech, silence, gestures, and so forth as resources to mediate its caring work. Again, by using the eye as an example, we compare the analytical and detached glance that coolly observes and judges from above, as it were, with the sympathetic glance that establishes contact and searches for pedagogical understanding in a dialogical relation with children.

The eye that is only observant of the behavior of children objectifies, whereas the tactful eye subjectifies. The tactful eye makes contact, makes personal relationship possible. We know the difference in these two types of glances when we think about occasions when, in our interaction with another person, we gained the feeling that the other person was not really conversing with us but was studying us, as it were. In the latter case the other person is not looking at me but instead looking at my body, my hands, my face, my legs—the other is "looking me over" and thus "overlooking me" who *is* my body. The objective glance cannot mediate my tactful action, and similarly the objective ear cannot ask the mouth to mediate the thoughtful response of its hearing in tactful speech. If I cannot hear the undertones of the inner life in the child's speaking, then I cannot produce tactful speech myself. Just like tact can be mediated through speech, so it can be mediated through silence, through the eyes, through gesture, through atmosphere, and through example.

The glance can express the soul's capacity for a pedagogical relationship. To cultivate pedagogical thoughtfulness and tact, one needs to be able to see this glance and act on one's understanding of it. In other words, pedagogical thoughtfulness and tact are not simply a set of external skills to be acquired in a workshop. A living knowledge of teaching is not just head stuff requiring intellectual work; it requires authentic body-work. True pedagogy requires an attentive attunement of one's whole being to the child's experience of the world.

We may want to be encouraging to an unsympathetic youngster who needs encouragement. We may say the "right" words, but our glance betrays our true feelings. Through a glance we are immediately known to each other—a sobering realization. A glance cannot be manipulated in the same way as words can be shaped to suit our purposes.

And yet there is a practical implication in our understanding of the nature of a glance. On the one hand, we can learn to sharpen our acuity of "seeing." On the other hand, we need to realize that we cannot easily—if at all—cover over our own glance. From minute to minute children and teachers are involved in reading from the face of the other what is disquieting, moving, boring, interesting, or disrupting. Children automatically check what we say with our mouth against what we say with our eyes. If the mouth and the eyes contradict each other, they are more likely to believe the eyes than the mouth. Of course, the physiognomy of the mouth, rather than just the words, is expressive of the person. If you really want to know how someone feels, watch his or her mouth rather than merely listening to the mouth.

Imagine that we have just observed a rowdy classroom. Here is a classic example of a beginning teacher who does not know how to effect "discipline" in a classroom, helplessly facing taunting students, defiant looks in their eyes. Now observe another teacher. One admonishing glance in response to a smart remark from a student is enough for this teacher to settle the same class down to work. How can one teacher be so ineffective while another has only to look at the class to establish authority? Could one learn how to handle a class of students with a glance? Could one write a "how to" book to help others learn? Not likely. To treat the glance as a mere teaching technique is to treat the knowledge of the glance as a set of rigid principles. An effective teacher can be effective with a glance because the teacher *is* the glance. The glance is already the teacher's way of understanding and living the classroom situation.

Of course, it is entirely possible that the glance of an "effective" teacher is effective only in silencing a class into intimidation, fear, or oppression. Such authority is not genuine pedagogical authority. Such discipline is not true pedagogical discipline. So we need to be aware how we, as teachers, are known by our children as we are captured in turn by their glance.

The Pedagogical Meaning of Discipline

To cultivate our pedagogical thoughtfulness and tact we need to reflect on the significance of discipline. Discipline is not just the measure of order in our classroom. Discipline is the measure of our own orientation to order. Or, rather, discipline is a way of talking about what matters to a person, how a person is oriented and stands in life. The roots of the word "discipline" refer to following, learning, and teaching. A disciple is one who can follow a great teacher or a great example. The word *docere* (to lecture) is also related to discipline.

A disciplined person is prepared to learn and to be influenced toward "order." So the teacher needs discipline as much as the student does. Without discipline, a willingness to learn, there is no point in the idea or existence of school. So to create discipline in students or in oneself is to create conditions for real learning. That is why it is often said that true discipline in the classroom cannot be separated from what is being taught or learned; indeed, the pedagogical meaning of "discipline" has little to do with the application of punishment or with authoritarian rule.

In *The Star Thrower* Loren Eiseley (1979) recounts an experience that is about the difference that discipline makes. Eiseley is walking at an ocean beach. There are people collecting shells and starfish that the receding waters have strewn along the shoreline. As he walks past the boiling pots of the shell collectors and the starfish gatherers, Eiseley notices a lone figure in the far distance. A man is gazing fixedly at something in the sand. Eventually he stoops and flings an object beyond the breaking surf.

When Eiseley finally gets near, he sees the man stoop again. In a pool of sand and silt a starfish has thrust its arms up stiffly and is holding its body away from the stifling mud. With a quick yet gentle movement the man picks it up and spins it far out into the sea. "It may live," he says to Eiseley. Eiseley is a bit embarrassed. He notices that no other people have ventured so far down the beach. "Do you collect?" he asks. And while gesturing at the threatened life lying on the shore, the man says softly, "Only like this. And only for the living."

What Eiseley points out with this story is that the essence of the discipline of science is not simply collecting and classifying nature for the worldly uses of humans. To be truly disciplined is to be a "thrower," the one who saves and restores, who labors to understand the nature of nature, for the sake of the natural, for the uses of life. The star thrower he describes is possessed by a passion—the passion of a knowledge that is disciplined, that requires obedience and responsibility. Here "obedience" means being able to listen to what speaks or to what is being said. And to be able to hear stars, one must love their nature.

Many teachers intuitively understand that the daily activities of teaching and learning are conditioned by such ineffable factors as the atmosphere of the school and classroom, the relational qualities that pertain amongst students and teachers, and the complex and subtle dimensions of temporality and lived space of the school's hallways, classrooms, offices, and grounds. This knowledge is not only cognitive in the usual sense; it is pathic (as in em-pathic). It is sensed or felt rather than thought or reasoned. Teacher knowledge is pathic to the extent that the act of teaching depends on the teacher's personal presence, relational perceptiveness, tact for knowing what to say and do in contingent situations, and thoughtful routines and practices. Theories of teaching, which concern mostly external forms of knowledge, are of little consequence for our immediate acting.

It is much easier to describe the cognitive than the pathic aspects of our world. The cognitive dimensions are the intellectual, conceptual, rational features of something. For example, we may describe an architectural or physical space, such as a school or church, in terms of its cultural, functional, and dimensional properties and measures. But such spaces also have their atmosphere, sensual, and felt aspects. Moreover, these pathic qualities are not fixed but subject to change like moods of a landscape. In this sense we can speak of the pathic sensibility of a school, a classroom, or any learning environment.

If we wish to study and enhance the pathic dimensions of teaching and educational life, we need a language that can express and communicate these understandings. This language needs to remain oriented to the experiential or lived sensibility of everyday life (see M. van Manen, 1997; 2014). For example, concrete stories that present moments of teaching may provide opportunities for reflecting pedagogically on actions, situations, and relations of teaching. The practical consideration for a teacher is that he or she must believe that there is a pedagogical way of being with children that sets a teacher-child relationship apart from any other kind of adult-child connection.

Although a teacher may be there for the children, he or she is not primarily there to be loved or to be buddy-buddy with children. As a lover is guided by love, as a friend is guided by friendship, so a teacher is guided by pedagogy. A teacher who is a "true" educator always intends to offer his or her actions as an answer to the question what education is or what it means to be guided by pedagogy. Indeed, it is only in real life that the concrete meaning of pedagogy is discernible. In a way a lover's understanding of love is constantly tested in real life. So it is for teachers. The problem is that one usually does not know the test situation beforehand. Tests that are predictable no longer test.

New parents and beginning teachers tend to be amateurish in their thinking and acting. When confronted with a significant moment, they tend to think first, "What does the book say?" And when they then act, the significant moment is often gone. A professional, in contrast, takes the moment first and then thinks about it. A professional can act first because his or her body has been readied by thoughtfulness. Or to say it differently: educators can act pedagogically at significant moments because they are already animated by the spirit of pedagogy formed by past caring reflections.

A woman who finds herself pregnant is a changed woman. She is not changed only locally in her womb; her whole body, her very being is changed. Before, she might have had little interest in children, but now she sees children all around her. Some women say that, to their surprise, they feel, for the first time, the urge to hold a child or to help a child in need. In a sense a mother-to-be is exercising herself, exercising her body, and being exercised by her body for motherhood.

The same is true for teachers. Teachers who are "pedagogically pregnant" exercise their bodies for teaching. A teacher who reads a significant book about children tends to read with teacher eyes. In this way teachers gain thoughtful knowledge of pedagogy that makes tactful acting possible in significant moments.

We learn pedagogical thoughtfulness and tact through the practice of parenting, teaching, and caring for children in other professional practices—but not only through practice. We come to embody tact by means of past experiences coupled with thoughtful reflection on experiences. And we reflectively acquire sensitivities and insights in various ways, such as through literature, film, stories by children, stories about children, and childhood memories.

The question of the viability of the pedagogical relation is less a philosophical problem that we need to solve than it is a practical concern that introduces itself in situations where parents, teachers, and other childcare professionals interact with children or young people. Calling certain relations "pedagogical" does not mean that these adults should think of themselves as leaders of a band who march up front while dictating the route, pace, and program. From the beginning the task of pedagogy was a temporary responsibility of certain adults who stood in a relation of *in loco parentis* to children.

The pedagogically sensitive teacher (and parent) is a supporter along the way—someone who accompanies the child some distance through life, sharing what he or she knows, showing what one can be, and creating the conditions and the spaces for young people to play an active lead in their own becoming. An adult can pedagogically touch or affect the child as a person in a particular and unique way and only for a limited time—but with consequences that are infinite and timeless for the whole person and the community of which he or she is a part.

Confusing the Possible with the Desirable

In education we often confuse what is possible with what is pedagogically desirable. For example, even if it were possible for many children to be able to read by age four, that does not mean that children should be reading at that early age. The understanding and skill required to teach children to read early is not the understanding and skill required for knowing what is appropriate for children. The first kind of knowledge may be the expertise of reading theorists; the second kind of knowledge is pedagogical.

My point is that no matter how challenging it may be to develop theories or models of learning, reading, doing mathematics, and so forth, no learning theories, teaching methods, or reading models will tell us what is pedagogically appropriate for this child or these children in this situation. That is the task of pedagogical theory and practice. Pedagogical theory has to be theory of the unique, of the particular case. Theory of the unique starts with and from the single case, searches for the universal qualities, and returns to the single case.

A child's learning experience usually is astonishingly mercurial and transitional in terms of moods, emotions, energy, and feelings of relationship and selfhood. Those who absorb themselves in their children's experiences of learning to read, write, play music, or participate in any kind of in- or out-of-school activity whatsoever are struck by the staggering variability of delight and rancour, difficulty and ease, confusion and clarity, risk and fear, abandon and stress, confidence and doubt, interest and boredom, perseverance and defeat, and trust and resentment children experience as common everyday occurrences. Parents and teachers may know and understand this reality. But how many curriculum theorists or teaching specialists know what the child's lived experience is like? How many teacher-educators know how a single child learns? Can classroom methodology be responsive if it does not understand the ups and downs of one child's experience? And what must we do? What knowledge must we pursue? What research texts must we produce that are sensitive to the peculiar question of the nature of pedagogy?

From a pedagogical point of view the problem is that contemporary policy perspectives and discourses of education tend to encourage the teacher to focus away from the students they teach and toward learning outcomes, instructional productivity, social improvement, system scores, accountability measures, instructional technologies, and so forth. Yet for many teachers such issues may lie largely outside of their everyday preoccupations.

Current policy approaches to teaching and schooling tend to be based on models and agendas that do not necessarily reflect the experiential priorities of classroom life. The approaches are described in terms of models derived from business, leadership, industrial, market, technology, and politics, and these models have corporatist, managerialist, productionist, consumerist, technocratic, and political agendas. The key items of these agendas are indicated with buzzwords such as "cost effectiveness," "performance evaluation," "achievement levels," and "user satisfaction." Contemporary policy perspectives tend to be results driven, evidence based, and accountability oriented. And yet these orientations, discourses, and perspectives do not necessarily or adequately reflect the ways that teachers and students experience the pedagogical cares and daily practices of teaching.

We need to ask: What are the political, cultural, and social pressures that may be responsible for the changing nature of the task of teaching? Educators who are critical of the emerging ideology of corporatism in our educational institutions argue that we need to ask questions such as: What would it mean if teachers were regarded not as instructional technicians but as ethical persons, as moral agents with their own professional languages? A professionally acknowledged pedagogical language would allow educators to think of their daily practices as ethically grounded and in service of the children and young people as unique and growing persons.

A distinction between the instructional and pedagogical aspects of teaching needs to be made. Making incommensurate distinctions between the instructional and the pedagogical dimension of teaching may be unproductive. However, the main point of this text is that the responsibility of teachers and schools is first of all pedagogical, concerned with the student as a growing and maturing person.

If teaching is indeed a pedagogical profession, then it involves helping, encouraging, admonishing, praising, prodding, and worrying about individual students and classes. At the end of the day, what matters to pedagogically sensitive teachers is that they did provide their students with academically significant and psychologically relevant learning experiences, that there was a good atmosphere in their classes, that students felt safe and successful in their learning activities, that personal difficulties could be worked out, that life that day was satisfying, meaningful, or good for them and their students.

Teachers tend to develop personal relationships with their students. How could they not? They do not care for their students in the abstract; they care for their students as real persons who have names and personalities and with whom they have concrete interactions. In this sense the pedagogical task is a concern with the unique.

By virtue of their daily tasks, teachers tend to be less attentive to the general than to the unique. The teachers' ongoing concerns are less with institutional problems than with personal problems, less with school productivity than with success of their own students, less with system infrastructure than with personal relational concerns, less with political educational issues than with emotional and moral issues, less with the corporate efficacies of their practices than with the interpersonal dimensions of their actions. In this sense the focus of teachers tends to be on what we call here the "pedagogical"—the complexity of relational, personal, moral, and emotional aspects of teachers' everyday acting with children or young people they teach.

Tact Is Not Ruled by Rules—Yet Tact Is Not "Unruly"

Teachers tend to create and cultivate communities of informal life that function as familiar actuality within the confines of technologically rationalized institutional structures such as curricula, educational theories, school administrations, and centrally governed school systems. The pedagogical relation is the concept of a human vitality that captures the normative and qualitative features of this informal life. There are several ways of viewing the nature and function of the informal life of the pedagogical relation. The formal and informal could be seen to relate symbiotically or antagonistically or as a constantly shifting mixture of both.

First, it may be argued that the informal life is not just an undesirable accident that interferes with the systematic and planned processes; the informal relates to the formalized dimension of teaching as the melody of jazz relates to the rhythmic structures and the melodic ground forms that carry the improvisational themes. In other words, pedagogical actions are improvisationally played on top of the rationalized features that are maintained by the necessities of routines, lesson plans, curriculum programs, philosophic foundations, and specific subject-matter methodologies. And yet it sometimes happens that the features of technical rationalizations become so confining that the possibility of maintaining pedagogical relations between teacher and students is completely thwarted by nonpedagogical themes imposed by overly bureaucratized powers and centralized administrative policies.

Second, we can see the practice of pedagogy as constantly being threatened by the dominant powers of the technological rational mind that tries to defeat and destroy the informal, practical knowledge forms. Informal practices always risk being taken over by technocratic rational understanding and made efficient and productive. The pedagogical relation is comparable to a friendship relation: experientially we know what friendship looks like, but we would not want to try to make the concept of friendship measurable. A friend is someone who we value inherently as an end in itself. As soon as you have friends for your health, for your Facebook score, or for your career, you've got some new kind of friendship. People wouldn't even know any longer what real friendship is (Dreyfus in Flyvbjerg, 1991, p. 7). Still, this is not to say that having a good friend or having a wonderful parent or having an understanding teacher is not good for you. But the goodness of this good is not measurable in a quantifiable sense.

So we stand in danger of losing our informal understanding of pedagogy and of what it means to teach or educate children in a pedagogical manner. Dreyfus gives the example of friendship as an instance of an informal practice that necessarily must remain outside the bounds of the technocratic rational frame. It would seem ridiculous to try to develop a "science" of friendship and try to discover more effective techniques or strategies for behaving as a more productive or efficient friend. And yet that is what is constantly being done with pedagogy, even though the pedagogical relation stands much closer to the relation of friendship than to the relation of the production and control of goods. It is impossible to develop a technology of the qualities, characteristics, and attitudes that mark a good teacher. And this is partly due to the fact that every person is unique. One teacher may know uniquely how to deal with the uniqueness of a particular student, whereas another teacher might approach the student in a differently unique manner.

And yet social practices that are by their very nature communicative, such as pedagogy, fall under the sway of the strange liaison between technological and critical rationality. For example, friendship too is becoming increasingly rationalized. The more "friends" a user of online social media can count as followers, the higher his or her reputation. And more frequently than before people seem to make friends not because of the inherent quality of the experience of friendship but because they hope that being friends and playing golf with the boss will get them ahead in life. Moreover, psychologists are proposing that friendship is healthy for a more relaxed and longer life. Love and marriage too are likewise thought to add years to one's life.

In spite of decades of research into teaching, ever-changing philosophies of education, and countless experiments with instructional methodologies and curricular programs, it seems that the actual reality of teaching and learning continues to defy effective rationalization. It could be argued that, in fact, the more one tries to rationalize educational processes and the tighter the structures of management and evaluation become, the less impressive are the consequences. In the effort to gain more effective control over the curriculum and over the way teachers actualize the programs in classrooms in order to promote greater accountable productivity of schools, the educational leadership increasingly seems to adopt more totalizing perspectives that force teachers to think of their own actions as rationally grounded and rationally executed in a technical sense. All this happens at the cost of the teachers' personal pedagogical sensibilities.

Some modern critics argue that we can no longer practice pedagogy because we no longer know why we should educate the child—we no longer share a set of public values, a concept of the meaning of maturity (adulthood), a consensual practice of disciplinary measures to control children. In opposition to such critiques, I would argue that such social conditions—to the extent that they are true—make pedagogy not only a higher priority; they also make pedagogy possible in the first place.

In the caricature of a totally closed society where all norms and roles are socially determined and fixed, there would be no place or call for pedagogy; pedagogical discretion or tact would become unnecessary or otherwise certainly outlawed. Similarly, in a society where there exists an agreed upon notion of maturity, one needs no longer to be sensitive to the uniqueness and possibilities of the individual child. Education would simply be a matter of preparing each child for his or her fixed station in life. And in a society where young people are controlled by oppressive measures and punishment, there would be no need for pedagogical tact and thoughtfulness either. In short, pedagogy is only meaningful in a society that is relatively open, democratic, and prudent toward the needs of children. So what is the promise that pedagogical relations can continue to govern the informal life of teachers and students?

On the negative side there is the possibility that a greater interest among North American educators in the meaning of pedagogy and the significance of the pedagogical relation is being preempted by the events that I have discussed: the practice of teaching has become increasingly technologized, discourses of education have grown barren of moral content, and Continental theories of pedagogy have turned self-destructive and subject to increasingly totalizing rational frameworks. As a result, we stand in danger of losing the meaning of pedagogy and of the pedagogical relation in schools and life altogether.

On the positive side we see that teachers continue to create spaces for the informal life of the pedagogical relations in classrooms. Informal practices are sustained in spite of—or maybe partly because of—their rationalized institutionalized context. It would be wrong-headed to try to develop technical frameworks or instrumental theories that would aim at bringing about more effective pedagogical relations. However, it would seem possible that marginal spaces can be created in which pedagogical relations have a chance to magically emerge and exist, if only for awhile. In my view creating these spaces is a question of political will and of professional wisdom.

Politically it means that the organizing impulse of educational institutions must remain democratic and pedagogical. Professionally it means that we must admit that the heart of education, the pedagogical relation, cannot scientifically be researched and taught within the present broad technical-rational framework. But rather than putting teachers' colleges and universities out of work, we need to develop informal languages to recognize the essentially informal nature of pedagogical life. In this book I do this by offering a view of teaching as the thoughtful practice of pedagogical tact. And tact is characterized by a set of features that show that it is impenetrable to instrumental rationality and resistant to nihilistic critical reason.

Tact is not just a cognitive facility but rather a mindful body skill (van Manen, 1991). Tactfulness is a kind of pedagogical fitness, the ability to deal instantly with unexpected situations. For example, it can be readily shown that tact is improvisational, morally responsive, and sensitive to the subjectivity of the other. Tact is also unpredictable, uncontrollable in a technical sense; tact is not subject to rules and yet tact is not "unruly" or arbitrary. Tact is governed by a moral intuitiveness that cannot be indiscriminately taught, yet it can be stimulated and strengthened in individuals who are sensitive to its aims.

Pedagogical Understanding

Pedagogical situations and moments tend to be improvisational. No matter how well teachers have planned their lessons or how enthusiastic they are about the subject matter, the interactive situation in the classroom is such that teachers must constantly remain aware of how it is for the students. (In junior and senior high school, for example, you only see the students so many minutes every day or two, and so it is easy to slip into a mode of technical teacher-centered, content-centered thinking and acting that completely ignores the students.) Yet this awareness of the subjectivity of the students is for many teachers more a thoughtfulness than a calculating or deliberative reflectivity, which would put one out of touch with the students because that would create a distance that accompanies any manipulative interpersonal relation between teacher and students. As the teacher interacts with the students, he or she must maintain an authentic presence and personal relationship with them.

The following incident illustrates the subtle nature and the fragile character of the pedagogical relation between teacher and student. At the end of the grade nine school year the students say farewell to their teachers. Next fall they will move on to other high schools. As is customary, some students surprise their teachers with a small gift as a token of their appreciation and as a keepsake to hold memories alive. Marian had been an outstanding student throughout the year. She received top honors in the academic program and was the student with the most and highest awards for accomplishments and service to the school and the community. On the last day of school she brought a present for only one of all her teachers, Mrs. Jensen, with a personal note attached to the inside cover of the gift book:

> Dear Mrs. Jensen, although throughout the year I had feelings that I was not your idea of a great student and that I was not one of the many students that you shared meaningful smiles and glances with, I nonetheless want to thank you. I realize that you care about your students and want them to succeed. I greatly respect you for that and also because it seems like you love your job. You deserve more credit than this, but alas, I am at a loss for words.

Mrs. Jensen, who had been Marian's language arts teacher for the past year, was somewhat taken aback and strangely moved. The student's words caused her to reflect about her teaching style and her way of relating to students. As a teacher she had often been drawn to Marian's sensitive intelligence, her many talents, creativity, and devotion to her studies. But the teacher was never quite sure just how to develop a more personal relation with Marian in class. Perhaps the teacher thought that because of Marian's outstanding work and accomplishments, she did not require or value the small prods and meaningful smiles and glances. Mrs Jensen sensed a kind of reserve in Marian that she felt she should not overstep. But she knew now that she had been wrong and that she should have realized that as a teacher, she needed to risk more and not be afraid of being rebuffed or perhaps in going too far in seeking closer teacher-student relations. So the teacher responded with a thank-you card and a letter:

> I truly regret that we both feel that somehow we were not able to develop a more satisfying relation. I feel this as a genuine loss that cannot be recovered. Teaching is only important to me to the extent that I feel that I can touch the lives of others in a significant way. But with some students I sometimes feel a hesitation that causes me to hold back. I certainly am not perfect as a teacher. And yet your kind gesture and your thoughtful reflections have broken through my mistaken sensing of reticence in a way that I find very valuable.
>
> Thank you for giving me such a fascinating and useful book of stories about words. I feel honored that you put such thought in this farewell gift. It will remind me of these reflections, and I will continue thinking of Marian as a highly gifted and sensitive person with whom some meaningful "smiles" were exchanged by means of these notes—even though it was only at the very conclusion of the school year. I wish you continued success in all that you set out to do. I would be very happy if you were to stay in touch.

The relationship between teacher and student is quite a complex one. It is significant that Marian would offer this teacher a gift and personal letter in the first place. Only a teacher who really meant something to her—with all the shortcomings that may be—deserves this kind of thoughtfulness. Perhaps the teacher showed a skewed "respect" for Marian's exceptional brightness by treating her inadvertently somewhat more cautiously than she had most students in the class. However, this little exchange of notes points to a richness in relational experiences that are so ambiguous and confusing that Marian says, "I am at a loss for words." There was also the quality of the overall dynamic of the class that is too difficult to describe in a few lines. It probably would have been more satisfying if Mrs. Jensen and Marian could have been comfortable with a closer or more personal relation, but in another sense the relation and pedagogical moments in class were no less charged with personal significance and personal dynamics. The letters show, I think, that a positive pedagogical relation may be characterized by certain intensities that can take different forms, even though they may not have been perfect.

In contrast, there are many other teachers who tend to be more aloof, formal, distant, impersonal, overly mechanized, relying on proven management routines, resorting to the recitation method and frequent testing. Such teachers may not be sensitive to the contingent nature of pedagogical moments. They may feel that they are there only to "teach the curriculum"—assuming that what has been taught must have been caught. Such teachers tend to rule the students by means of the four fears of classroom discipline: the fear of failure, the fear of ridicule, the fear of rejection, and the fear of punishment.

However, for teachers who are pedagogically sensitive, life in classrooms is not unlike life at home. One teacher explains how so much of teaching is like "fighting with children; you 'fight' about matters that you deem good for them." Of course, this is not real fighting, like fighting to defeat some threat or for what you may feel is rightfully yours. When you "fight" with your kids at home or with your students at school, it means you are coaxing, inspiring, retorting, ignoring, urging, bargaining, devoting, encouraging, joking, jousting, cheering, cajoling, animating, daring, sparring, pushing, pleading, retreating, persuading, or sometimes just playing dumb. You do this at home, for example, when you try to get your child to practice music, to reflect on their actions, or to clean up a messy bedroom; and you do this at school when you insist on your students giving proper care to their studies, to think for themselves, or generally when you try to influence your students in positive directions. The precarious factor, perhaps, about "fighting" with your kids is that as a parent or teacher, you are not allowed to pull power in the negative sense and thus disable the child. The use of oppressive influence or repressive force in demanding blind obedience or in disregarding the child's view is antithetical to pedagogy. It violates the child and the pedagogical intent to support the young person's growth toward self-responsible maturity.

The teacher who spoke of parenting and teaching as if it were some sort of "fighting" also confessed that she finds this "fighting" extremely tiring and sometimes frustrating. And that there are situations where this pedagogical "fighting" turns into real conflict—real fighting. This may happen with a student with whom you no longer seem to have the proper relationship, a pedagogical relation. The problem is that with such a child you may no longer "fight" in the positive sense because you really have done the inexcusable: you have given up. Giving up on a student makes us experience failure—we know that a true teacher never really gives up. But as a professional educator you have to admit that there are situations where you have reached your pedagogical limit—for example, because you feel that you must save your resources and sanity to continue doing right by the other students. Sometimes the situation of a particular student and a particular teacher is such that there is no longer room or opportunity for a pedagogical relation.

Strangely perhaps, these images of teaching are largely inconsistent with the textbook scheme of the competent teacher as a reflective cool-headed decision maker. In such schemes pedagogical experiences are rationalized: logically and psychologically analyzed, interpreted, reconstructed, and governed by a technical rational framework that is meant to bring the relations of teaching and learning within the reach of effective management. Whatever cannot be so rationalized is then delegated to that common but mysterious realm of "the art of teaching." But what the notion of "teaching as art" misses is an understanding that teaching is not primarily an aesthetic but a pedagogical activity. In the real world, pedagogical relations tend to be driven by intuitive, emotive, immediate, informal, local, or unsystematic forms of knowledge. This is not to deny that educational researchers have not attempted to study teachers' thought processes and practical cognitions of the daily reality of the classroom. The problem is that the totalizing nature of technocratic rationality that pervades official educational discourses is such that this kind of immediate, local knowledge of teachers either gets pushed to the margins or translated back into the self-legitimating discourses of official instructional theory.

There is constant pressure to interpret pedagogical actions in directions that are more rationalized than what teachers experience in their pedagogical relations with their students. Theorists tend to elevate knowledge of teacher-practitioners into worthiness by fitting it into the frames of acceptable research rationalities. These theoretical rationalizations are formulations such as "research into teacher thinking," "action research," "deliberative reflective practices," "collaborative research between academics and practitioners," and the proposition that teachers operate on the basis of "internal teacher theories" of which they themselves may be unaware. The interest in teacher stories, classroom ethnographies, narratives, and so-called constructionist approaches also may be attempts to gain a systematic hold of the slippery knowledges—pedagogical and nonpedagogical—that structure the reality of teachers and students.

When issues arise with respect to pedagogical knowledge, this is the common case of the "difficult student." Teachers commonly experience difficulties with some students who make the atmosphere in class unbearable for the teacher and most other students. Such a student may be seen as negative, impertinent, hostile, and agitating. The student's parents may complain that things are no better at home and that they have little influence on him or her. The school counselor also may not be able to turn the "difficult" student around or improve the situation. Some teachers seem to have come to a silent understanding that they won't bother the "difficult" student with lessons or press with homework as long as the student keeps quiet at the back of the classroom. It would seem that such teachers have found nonpedagogical solutions to their pedagogical problem.

The teacher who remains pedagogically interested in "problem" students differs from the others in that he or she maintains a sense of responsibility for the personal being and becoming of the student. The teacher tends to perceive the student in personal terms and realize that the student may be as difficult for himself or herself as for others. Every day the teacher mobilizes in his or her own way the kind of personal understandings and own style of relating and behaving that enables him or her to do the best possible for the student.

Of course, this teacher may also come to the point of exasperation and wish that the student were no longer in his or her class. Like love and hate in marriage, and like generosity and greed in charity, the pedagogical and the nonpedagogical in the classroom easily unseat each other in the commotions of daily life. A parent may always be able to say to a child, "When you act like that, I do not like you, although I still love you." This is where the pedagogical relation of parenting and teaching may indeed differ. A child may eventually forget a long-term bad relation with a teacher, but a child may never be able to come terms with—and thus make forgettable—a bad relation with a parent.

At the point of real conflict and real antagonism in the teacher-child relation, the teacher may try some kind of "behavioral program" or "discipline strategy" at the suggestion of the principal. Typically such a program may help the teacher "manage" the situation in a manner less draining on his or her energy, but it also tends to work at the cost of the functioning informality of the marginal practices that normally sustain the teacher-student relation. Things no longer are being addressed at a particular, local, personal level but are now dealt with by generalized procedure—for example, after one warning the student is automatically expelled to work in isolation in the library.

Stories of the "problem child" or the "difficult student" should make us wonder. They are remarkable in that they speak to the fragile and intense personal relations that many teachers—but not all—maintain with their students, even though not all relations are smooth. After all, it is in the nature of growing up that one should not expect pedagogical relations to be without problems or difficulties. It happens that teachers are physically afraid of some student in their classes, but such pedagogical predicaments are rarely talked about.

> I had told the students that they had 15 minutes to review their notes for a quiz. The class had been quietly pouring over their work when Jack sauntered into the class, late. He slouched over to his desk, straddled his seat, dropped his books with a thud, and leaned his chair back toward Gavin, who sat in the desk behind him: "What's up? Do we have a test?"
> I watched the scene with some aggravation. Jack was a known troublemaker, rude to his teachers, and mean to his fellow students. In spite of his surliness, he had gained a sort of forced respect from the other kids. It was clear that they half-admired and half-feared him. They would never deny him anything, but they certainly didn't want him as a friend either.
> Gavin glanced at me nervously, then at Jack, and nodded his head slightly.

I managed to find my voice: "Jack, come here and get your test. Please don't bother Gavin, he's trying to concentrate." I hated myself at that very moment. I hated the insipid tone of my voice. I hated the way I treated Jack so deferentially in spite of his rudeness and show of disrespect. I knew I was guilty of playing a double standard between him and the other kids, but I didn't seem to know what else to do.

I picked up a test and motioned the boy forward with a nod. He sauntered to the front of the class and reached out to receive the exam. For a moment we stood, facing each other, holding on to either side of the paper. I struggled unsuccessfully to suppress the slight tremor in my hand and then looked at him straight. His eyes held mine for a moment before a slow, mocking grin spread across his face as he pulled the paper from my weak grasp.

It is sometimes hard for a teacher to hide their discomfort with some students. And yet, these situations are not unusual. Few teachers will talk about these ambiguous experiences.

The dynamic informal life of teaching is the active expression of the pedagogical relation between teacher and students. The more that the processes of teaching are being formalized into behaviors that correspond to management skills, instructional strategies, and technically rationalized understandings and procedures, the more the pedagogical relation itself is sapped of its vitality. Thus, the notion of the pedagogical relation may help us better understand the nonrational and pathic dimensions of teaching. In listening to a young person—or to anyone, for that matter—it is wise to try to listen not only for his or her words but also and especially for his or her experience. Ask: What really is this experience?

The Pedagogy of Teaching

To be tactful with another person, one must "hear," "feel," and "respect" the uniqueness of this person. Whereas the English term "tactful" means the quality or being full of tact, the German word *Taktgefühl* has the additional connotation of having a feeling (*Gefühl*) for tactfulness. There is a hint here that the quality of tact is somewhat like talent (see Muth, 1962). We often think of talent as a fortuitous gift—either you are or you are not blessed with a "feel" or talent for the violin, the canvas, or the stage. But, of course, talent must be recognized, developed, nurtured, and disciplined. Similarly, pedagogical tact, although a gift in some sense, needs to be prepared and practiced as a special "feel" for acting tactfully.

While thinking about processes of teaching, it is helpful to avoid confusing tact with tactic. A tactic is a method for accomplishing an end. There is a calculating, planning meaning to tactic, whereas tact is essentially situational. In fact, tactic and tact are etymologically unrelated. Tactic is derived from early Greek, where it referred to military science, the strategic talents of a general in moving his troops in battle.

Someone who approaches teaching by way of tactics thinks of maneuvers, stratagems, or masterminding a program of directives and objectives. To be good at tactics means that one is good at getting an organization to execute some plan of action. Thus, tactics also connote superintendency and supervision. The tactics of teaching are strategies, schemata, techniques, and means that one draws up like a master plan, scenario, outline, blueprint, timetable, schedule, or design for the preparatory processes of teaching. However, in the interactional sphere of teaching it is often the unsteady, unstable, variable moment that requires tactful action of a sort that is essentially unplannable. And yet this unstable moment is not an accident of teaching but rather belongs to teaching essentially.

It may be helpful to distinguish tact from associated behaviors such as "diplomacy," "address," "poise," "savoir faire," or "finesse." These are terms often provided as synonyms of tact. For example, a diplomat is "diplomatic" for the purpose of manipulating perceptions for political ends. This does not necessarily mean that a diplomatic person would lie or be deceitful, but although diplomacy may not involve telling untruths, it may involve withholding truths that should actually be told. A diplomat is ultimately motivated by self-interest or by the interest of the party the diplomat is representing. Tact, in contrast, is always in the service of the person toward whom the tact is directed. Thus, tact avoids the political motivation and conciliation of "diplomacy."

I distinguish four ontologies of practice—ways of pedagogic being—with which the educator needs to be invested:

1. **Pedagogical sensitivity:** A tactful educator is sensitive to the life of students. This sensitivity is sparked by clues such as gestures, demeanor, expression, and body language. Tact involves the ability to see immediately through motives or cause-and-effect relations. A tactful teacher is able to read, as it were, the inner life of the young person.
2. **Pedagogical sense:** Tact consists of making sense or interpreting the psychological and social significance of the features of this inner life. Thus, tact is the sense of interpreting, for example, the meaning and significance of shyness, frustration, interest, difficulty, tenderness, humor, discipline, and so forth.
3. **Pedagogical sensibility:** An educator with tact has the fine ethical and emotional sensibility to discern standards, limits, and balance that makes it possible to know almost automatically how far to enter into a situation and what distance to keep in individual circumstances. It is an essential feature of pedagogical intentionality that teachers and parents always expect more and more from children. Yet most parents and teachers realize that they should not have expectations

that, when challenged, children cannot manage to live up to. So tact consists in the sensibility of knowing how much to expect in expecting too much. Similarly, teachers often must get close to children, such as when challenging them, sparking an interest, or setting a tone in a class. Paradoxically, they must know how far to go in by going in too far.

4. **Pedagogical acting:** Tact is the enactive moment of saying or doing the right or appropriate thing to do on the basis of perceptive pedagogical understanding of children's nature and circumstances. This active practice of pedagogy in everyday life means that the teacher must constantly distinguish actively between what is good and what is not good for a child or a group of children.

A teacher of English describes a classroom incident with a confrontational student:

> Daniel dresses in provocative attire, street style. His profile is strikingly noble: sultry lips, shaved head, cool and stylish gestures, and proud eyes. Daniel stands out in our small junior high school. It is the first day of class, and I explain my Reading Room program. Daniel wanders into class, positions himself directly in front of me, and proclaims, "I don't do reading."
>
> "Really?" I reply, "Reading Room should be an unusual experience for you then." As the students begin to read, the class quiets down. Silence replaces the chatter and scuffling of the grade eight class.
>
> I notice that Daniel doesn't have a book. He sits sagging in his chair, drumming his index finger on his desk. I peruse the bookcase and select a few novels. I am not expecting miracles. Quietly I approach his desk, bend down, and tentatively whisper, "Uh, Daniel, why don't you choose the least offensive book ... see if, uh, you can read a few pages before the class is over."
>
> He raises his haughty eyes, and with a throw of the head dismisses, me benignly, sighing, "I'll see."
>
> But I leave the carefully picked titles on his desk. Daniel is still hanging back in his seat. He casually spins the books around with his hand, seemingly indifferent. I turn away.
>
> A few minutes later, out of the corner of my eye, I see that Daniel has picked up Carol Matas's novel *The Freak*.
>
> "Yes, I hooked him!" Now the book has to reel him in. I am hopeful: Daniel may turn into a reader yet.

What is happening here? A teacher sees a student who intentionally acts to be recognized as different. The student provokes the teacher's authority. But the teacher refuses to resort to power. She is sensitive to Daniel's sense of self. Her description is light and humorous but also respectful. And she has the wisdom to interpret the significance of the sense of self for Daniel's self-identity. She respects the persona that the student is creating; she understands Daniel's desire to be seen and recognized. The teacher seems to sense just how near to approach the student and how to keep a proper distance. And in this understanding lies her enaction of tact. She nudges Daniel to pick up a book and give it a try. The power of the pedagogical nudge is profoundly underestimated and rarely if ever discussed in the educational literature. To nudge a student can mean to subtly provide an incentive that is a gentle push—or perhaps a pull—to get a student over an obstacle.

But how does this teacher know what to say? How does she know just what distance to keep? No theoretical knowledge, no specific techniques or general rules of how to act tactfully can be found. And yet in the active understanding of what is at stake in this concrete classroom situation, it is possible for the teacher to practice and cultivate thoughtfulness and tact.

Pedagogical thoughtfulness and tact are closely related notions. Someone who is generally thoughtful is more likely to demonstrate tact in a particular circumstance than a person who is relatively thoughtless. Pedagogical thoughtfulness seems to be a reflective capacity. It is formed by careful reflection on past experiences. And now, in the immediacy of having to act in this moment, there is an emphasis on "sensing" what is significant in the concrete situation. Pedagogical thoughtfulness and tact depend on the cultivated ability to perceive and listen to young people. But tact in teaching is not a mere skill; rather, it can be described as "improvisational preparedness." Even so, there are no guarantees, and Daniel's teacher knows this.

> Daniel and I have developed a good teacher-student relationship. This is somewhat remarkable because he could not get along with his science and math teachers due to "difficult behavior." Therefore, Daniel is often in the library working on math or science correspondence school work, and he overhears what I am saying to Louise, our library technician. So we tend to include Daniel in our conversations. Sometimes he even comments on the successes or failures of my English classes.
>
> Daniel is a fast and bright learner, and he does not hesitate to insult his slower fellow students. Occasionally, in class, he will throw a comment: "I don't really need to do this work. I guess other people in this class need the practice." He may then dramatically drop his proud sculptured head to his desk and seemingly take a nap. Afterwards I talk with Daniel about considerateness.
>
> Daniel knows that I expect him to do all his assignments and to participate with insightful comments in class discussions, and he usually is serious about his work. Just last week he spoke to me before class, "You know, I had trouble with two of the questions."
>
> "Not a problem, Daniel," I replied. "We will discuss them in class." When I began the literature interpretation lesson, I mentioned to the grade nine students: "I know many of these questions are tough; inferences are not always

obvious. Daniel was saying a few minutes ago that two questions in particular were difficult for him. How many of you have had a similar experience with some of these questions?"

I began the discussion with enthusiasm.

Within ten minutes Daniel had initiated a disruptive scenario where he was creating a general stir, grinning, cat-calling, and ridiculing another student whose face had turned red. My so-called passion for what I was teaching quickly evaporated.

I stopped the class. There was tension in the air. I glared at Daniel and, with an edge to my voice, demanded, "Stop now. Whatever you are doing I don't like it! I sense that someone is a victim here."

I continued the lesson with a loss of purpose. I felt disappointed, even betrayed. As the class left the room, I said to Daniel, "This wasn't a good class."

He retaliated, "Yeah, I know!"

It was not until several days later that I finally realized what I had done.

It seems banal to say that an inappropriate word or a thoughtless remark can unwittingly cause a rupture in the relational quality that the teacher maintains with his or her various students and classes. In turn, this change in the relational climate can profoundly alter a teacher's feeling of confidence in his or her pedagogical ability and knowledge of the subject.

In this second story of Daniel we see again how to act tactfully means in a particular situation to be sensitive and pick up what goes on with a child and to understand the child's experience. It requires that one can make sense of the pedagogical meaning and significance of what is going on. Next one has to know sensibly how and what to do in a manner that is discretionary. And tact means that one actually acts in the situation in a pedagogically appropriate manner. To act tactfully implies all this, and yet tactful action is instantaneous.

The sensitive attitude, the sense-making understanding, the discretionary sensibility, and the act itself are not separate stages in a rationalized process. Somehow sensitivity, insight, and feeling are instantly acted out. They are realized in a mode of acting that is tensed with thoughtfulness or thinking attentiveness. Tact is a kind of active ethical intelligence governed by insight while relying on feeling. And yet, as we see in the second story of Daniel, sometimes we know only afterward what we should have done in a certain situation. In this situation the teacher realizes that she had nudged too strongly. The point is that even failing to act tactfully but reflecting on it afterward will prepare us for what to say or do next time—when we don't know what to say or do.

The etymology of the Latin *tactus* contains terms such as "touch," "thoughtfulness," "effect." Tact is associated with physical touch, tactile or material things that you can touch or feel with your body. And yet tact carries also the ambiguous sense of a nonphysical influence or effect of one human being on another. Tact possesses the mindful quality of reflection, perceptiveness, thoughtfulness. In tactful action the adult orients concretely and thoughtfully to the child. Often tact involves a holding back, a passing over something, which is nevertheless experienced as influence by the person to whom the tactful action is directed. So the onto-epistemological relation between thoughtfulness and tact is such that thoughtfulness kinesthetically incarnates itself in tactful action. Tact is the active embodiment, the body-work of thoughtfulness.

It helps to make the distinction between thoughtfulness and tact. But we should see that thoughtfulness and tact go hand in hand; they are each others' complement. Without thoughtfulness, no tact, and without tact, thoughtfulness is at best a mere internal event. Thoughtfulness is the process and product of self-reflective reflection on the life of human experience. In a sense tact is less a form of knowledge than it is a way of acting. It is the sensitive application of thoughtfulness in action. Tact is the effect one has on another person, even if the tact consists, as it often does, in holding back, waiting.

Tact is not simply some kind of mediator between theory and practice; it possesses its own epistemological, ontological, and axiological structure based on a certain kind of reflection or, better, on an active intentionality of thoughtfulness. Thus, the essence of tact is that it cannot be separated or divided into theory and practice so that the issue of the relation between knowledge and action would be turned into a technical problem of application in the preparation of teachers with instructional skills or competencies. In this sense pedagogical tact overcomes the theory-practice split and retains a wonderful essential quality of ambiguity.

Thoughtfulness and tact are not identical to skills and habits, yet they are not unlike this constellation of body skills and habits that have become our second nature and determine to an extent who we are, who we have become, and what we are able to understand, perceive, and do. Indeed, the word "skill" is related to the term *skilja*, which refers to the ability to discriminate, to distinguish, to separate between things that make a difference. Etymologically skill means "to have understanding," "to make a difference." And so the notion of body skill is an unexpected ally in our exploration of the nature of thoughtful pedagogical perceptiveness.

When I teach a group of children and notice that some of them experience a certain shyness, exuberance, frustration, animation, boredom, wonderment, curiosity, puzzlement, confusion, or sense of insight, then what I "see" is less given by a "technical instructional skill" that I may have learned in a teacher-effectiveness course than by a more embodied "orientational pedagogical skill" that I have acquired in a more experiential-reflective manner. However, this skill of perceptiveness—of sensing, for example, what a situation means for a child—is something I cannot practice in the same way that I may be able to practice a skill such as lesson planning, classroom management, or even storytelling.

To Live Is to Touch and to Be Touched

Tact derives etymologically from the Latin *tactus,* meaning touch, from *tangere,* to touch. Related terms are "intact," meaning untouched, uninjured, and "tactile" refers to touch, which means to handle or feel something with the intent to appreciate or understand it in more than merely an intellectual manner. We should notice that touch can also imply violation or harm, as in the expression "I never touched the child." We speak of "a touchy subject," "a touching scene." Something is "touching" when it is capable of arousing emotions of tenderness.

Tactful means full of touch, and it also means to be able to have an effect. It is interesting to cite some of the synonyms of tact while bringing these qualities in relation to what it means to be a good parent or a good educator: to be tactful is to be thoughtful, sensitive, perceptive, discreet, prudent, judicious, sagacious, perspicacious, gracious, considerate, cautious, careful. Would any of these notions speak badly of an educator? In contrast, someone who is tactless is considered to be hasty, rash, indiscreet, imprudent, unwise, inept, insensitive, mindless, ineffective, and awkward. In general to be tactless means to be disrespectful, ill-considered, blundering, clumsy, thoughtless, inconsiderate, and stupid.

To teach is to touch and to be touched. The pedagogy of teaching is sensitive because it consists of double reversible crossings. In the interaction with children or young people there is eye contact: I see the child, and the child experiences himself or herself as seen; simultaneously the child sees me, and I experience myself as seen and know that my being seen is seen. It is important to ask: What kind of eye contact is this? Is it encouraging? Trusting? Admiring? The same is true in the tactile touching of hands. I take the child by the hand, and now I feel the child's hand and my own hand. I sense that my touch is sensed: I touch the other, and in this touch I experience being touched by the other and simultaneously I feel or sense myself in this touch.

It is what happens, as in the famous example of Merleau-Ponty (1964) when he describes the left and right hand touching each other: I touch my left hand with my right hand, and I sense my left hand with my right hand while my left hand feels the touch of the right hand, but simultaneously the right hand feels itself touching and being touched by the left hand. This is the principle of reversibility of sensing and the sensed. I look at a gnarly tree and then have the uncanny sensation that this tree stares back at me. This may sound somewhat odd or confusing, but it is an important pedagogical insight: to help children grow up is a constant dynamic and reversible process of touching and being touched. We touch each other with our eyes, our voices, our hands, our presence and absence; these are transitivities of significance from one to the other.

Tact is the touch of contact. Most of us have an appreciation for the value of tact in social life. Often the word "tact" is used in situations where we are stuck in some sense. Someone will then say to us "Well, yes, I guess this situation requires tact." Saying this, however, is as much as a confession that one is quite at their wits' end as to what exactly to advice what to do. In this context "tact" is a bit of a magical term that promises a solution without giving insight into the solution.

But as adults, we do not have a right to expect from children pedagogical tact. Pedagogical tact is an expression of the responsibility we are charged with in protecting, educating, and helping children grow. Children are not charged with the pedagogical responsibility of protecting and helping their parents or teachers grow and develop. Children are not there primarily for us; we are there primarily for them. This does not mean, of course, that children do not teach us and do not show us new ways and possibilities of experiencing and being in the world.

In general, tact implies sensitivity, a sensitive and mindful or aesthetic perception. Tact is defined as a keen sense of what to do or say in order to maintain good relations with others or avoid offense. But the essence of tact does not inhere in the simple desire or ability to get on well with others or to establish good social relations. Tact has interpersonal and normative properties that appear especially suited to bring into relation to our pedagogical acting with children. We speak of tact as an instant knowing what to do, an improvisational skill and grace in dealing with others. Someone who shows tact somehow seems to have the Kairos gift or ability to act quickly, surely, confidently, and in an appropriate manner with quite complex or delicate circumstances. It is important to state at the outset that tact does not necessarily connote a soft, meek, or acquiescent sensitivity. One can be sensitive and strong. A tactful person must be strong, as tact may require frankness, directness, and candor when the situation calls for it. Tactful acting is always sincere and truthful, never deceitful or misleading.

It is perhaps somewhat surprising that the notion of tact has not been of any systematic interest and study for educational thinkers in the English language. The person who introduced the notion of tact or tactfulness into educational discourse is the German educator Johann Friedrich Herbart. In 1802, during his first lecture on education, Herbart told his audience that "The real question whether someone is a good or a bad educator is simply this: how has this person developed a sense of tact?" Herbart posited that tact occupies a special place in practical educational acting. The main points of his speech pertaining to tact were that (a) "tact inserts itself between theory and praxis," (b) tact manifests itself in everyday life in the process of "making instant judgments and quick decision," (c) tact forms a way of acting that is "first of all dependent on *Gefühl* [feeling or sensitivity] and only more remotely on convictions" derived from theory and so forth; (d) tact is sensitive to "the uniqueness of the situation," and (e) tact is "the immediate ruler of praxis" (see Appendix B for a detailed examination of Herbart's text).

In spite of this early fluid conceptualization, Herbart's later writings and especially that of his followers assumed a more instrumental relation between educational knowledge and practical acting. Even in the above paraphrases from Herbart's speech there is evident a somewhat mechanistic conceptualization of the mediating role of tact between theory and practice. Rather than seeing tact as a device for converting theory into practice, we may see tact as a concept that can help us overcome the problematic separation of theory from practice. And rather than understand tact as a process of making instant "decisions," we may reconceive tact as an oriented mindfulness that permits us to act thoughtfully in our living with children and young people.

In Germany the notion of tact has occasionally resurfaced in the discourse about the nature of pedagogical practice. But in the English-language community a more technocratic and pragmatic rationality has governed theories of education and educational competence. The notion of tact has never been systematically studied, and references to tact in English texts about teaching are rare and sporadic.

One reference is by William James in a lecture he presented in 1892 in which he mentions "tact" almost in the same breath as he speaks of Herbart. James discusses the relation between psychology and pedagogy, which in the case of the great system builder, Herbart, were developed side by side. In no way, however, says James, was Herbart's pedagogy derived from psychology. Pedagogy cannot be derived from psychology. To know psychology is absolutely no guarantee that we shall be good teachers, argues James:

> To advance to that result, we must have an additional endowment altogether, a happy tact and ingenuity to tell us what definite things to say and do when the pupil is before us. That ingenuity in meeting and pursuing the pupil, that tact for the concrete situation, though they are the alpha and omega of the teacher's art, are things to which psychology cannot help us in the least. (James, 1962, p. 29)

James provides one brief example of what he understands by tact. He makes a suggestion of how a tactful teacher can foster an early sense of scholarship in young people by working into the school task of learning the impulse characteristic of almost every child: the desire to collect things. "Almost all children collect something," James says. "A tactful teacher may get them to take pleasure in collecting books; in keeping a neat and orderly collection of notes; in starting, when they are mature enough, a card catalogue; in preserving every drawing or map which they may make" (1962, p. 29). James's example suggests that the teacher should be sensitive to the natural inclinations of the child and somehow connect these inclinations to the school curriculum.

We should note that there is more involved here than the more commonly agreed upon challenge for teachers to motivate their students and to make things relevant to them. But what exactly is involved in that ingenuity or tactfulness of which James speaks? He professes that this fundamental question lies outside the domain of the psychologist. After thus indicating that psychology has little or nothing directly to say to pedagogy, James, in the remainder of his *Talks to Teachers,* makes no more mention of the notion of tact.

The important point for us here is that James reminds us that it is tact that is the operative notion that defines what a teacher does in a pedagogical moment. Tact is the pedagogical ingenuity that makes it possible for the educator to transform an unproductive, nonpromising, or even harmful situation into a pedagogically positive event.

Pedagogical thoughtfulness and tact do not, of course, describe everything teachers, whether they are educators or parents, know, be, or do. There are many routine and more technical aspects to teaching and even to parenting. Teachers must know how to plan lessons, fill out report cards, or make effective use of media; parents must be able to change diapers, keep house, and prepare nutritious meals. It is also important to realize that teaching and parenting would be impossible tasks if they were not embedded in routines and habituated dimensions of living, childcare, and teaching. We may even suggest that pedagogical tact (improvisational action) is constantly supported by the routines and habits of living, just as the improvisational melodies in jazz are carried by the "takt" or beat of rhythm. But, still, the real stuff of teaching—and also of parenting—happens in the thick of life itself when and where one must know with a certain confidence just what to say or do (or what not to say or do) in situations with children. Therefore, pedagogical thoughtfulness and tact may be seen to constitute the essence or excellence of pedagogy. We might say that thoughtfulness constitutes the interior aspect and tactfulness the exterior aspect of pedagogy: thoughtfulness constitutes the interior (mindful) aspect and tactfulness the exterior (action) aspect of pedagogy.

CHAPTER SEVEN

Pedagogical Con-tact

The term *contact* derives from *contingere*, which means to touch closely: connectedness, in-touchness. The Latin preposition *con* often has the effect of augmenting the term to which it is attached. In other words, con-tact carries the related meaning of tact but in enhanced, intensified form: it refers to a close human relation, intimacy, connectedness. When a teacher is "in touch," has "close contact" with his or her students, then that implies that the teacher's actions are governed by a tactful sensitivity.

This image of tact as a special contact or relation between people is especially relevant for education and also for other childcare practices such as pediatrics, as shown by Michael A. van Manen in his study of the technics of touch (2012). However, there is an outstanding distinction to be made between general social tact in the interaction between adults, on the one hand, and the more specific form of pedagogical tact in the interaction between adults and children, on the other. And this distinction harkens back to the nature and structure of pedagogical relations. General tact in the lives of adults is symmetrical, whereas pedagogical tact is asymmetrical. Among adults we expect tactful behavior to be reciprocal, in keeping with the nature and circumstances of the situation. And similarly we teach children to practice general social tact toward other children and adults. To be tactful in a general sense means that we respect the dignity and subjectivity of the other person and try to be open and sensitive to the intellectual and emotional life of other people, whether they be young or old.

A Chinese teacher explains how teachers in her culture are less likely to open themselves to their students. Many Chinese teachers don't know how to make contact. I ask her to give an example and describe a moment in her own teaching when she experiences difficulty in making contact with her students in her teaching. She responds with this story:

> I clearly remember this particular moment when I walked into my class with a smile on my face. I looked forward to discussing with the students a captivating

---

Pedagogical Tact: Knowing What to Do When You Don't Know What to Do, by Max van Manen, 107–137.
© 2015 Taylor & Francis. All rights reserved.

story by a famous author. However, as soon as I faced the students and started to introduce the lesson, the same thing happened that always happened. The students all turned their faces down and started writing notes. All I saw were fifty heads of black hair. As I continued analyzing the novel, I did not see a single face, not a single pair of eyes looking at me. I knew that the students were listening to me, but their attention was passive. They simply jotted down notes to later memorize and then reproduce on the test or exam. I felt very unhappy with this inattentive attentiveness. I so wished to have real contact with my students; I wanted to touch them and make sure that the story really meant something to their lives. But even when I asked questions or tried to involve the students in a discussion, they answered politely and dutifully but without a real spark of interest. They merely wrote down the question in case it would appear on the test...

But that day something strange happened. As I was discussing the themes of the story that the students had read, I casually mentioned how my boyfriend disagreed with me about the meaning of the book. I said, "Last night I discussed the story with my boyfriend. But my boyfriend thinks that the book is not about sacrifice at all but really about betrayal. So he and I started arguing about the meaning of the story and about the meaning of sacrifice and betrayal." The strange thing is that when I uttered those words, an unbelievable thing happened: suddenly fifty black heads of hair turned upward, and fifty faces looked at me with expectation, interest, and curiosity.

For a moment I was taken aback with suddenly seeing all these eyes and faces facing me. But then my confusion turned into elation. And I felt that I had to clarify further my disagreement with my boyfriend. But in the instant of the moment I also realized that I had made real contact with my students. I felt totally thrilled.

The young Chinese teacher who told me this story was so impressed with the contact she suddenly had experienced with her students that she wanted to study how she could understand better the personal dimension of teaching. I suggested that she should begin her study with the story she told me. Of course, not only did she experience eye contact with her students; her students also experienced eye contact with their teacher. Eye contact between teachers and students is probably the most common kind of contact that characterize the pedagogical relation. And yet we rarely reflect on the meaning and significance of this contact.

In everyday life as well, face-to-face or eye contact, *oculesics*, is one of the most intimate kinds of in-touchness we may experience with another person. Of course, the eyes can express very different relational qualities: the eyes can be warm and inviting, wondering and inquisitive, friendly and open, but also hostile and cold, distant and reserved. Through a glance of the eyes we can express and experience an interest in the person we pass or with whom we interact. Generally we tend to express through our eyes more authentically how we feel and regard the other than we do through our words (see van Manen, 1991).

Eye contact may be experienced differently in different cultural settings. For example, men and women in some religious communities tend to lower their eyes and try not to focus on the face of the opposite sex after the initial first eye contact. Lowering the eyes avoids potential unwanted desires; glances to those of the opposite sex, young or adult, are prohibited. This means that eye contact between any man and woman is allowed only for a second or two, except, of course, among spouses, family members, and relatives. In everyday life there is an implicit general rule that says that only "clean eye contact" is allowed. Clean eye contact means no "adultery of the eyes" and no glances of desire. This relation of normativity of *oculesics* is so corporeally habituated that in schools too such students tend to lower their glances when teachers talk with them. And the teacher may not realize that this modesty in eye contact is not a sign of indifference or disrespect.

Regardless of the cultural context, a phenomenology of contact makes us aware that the experience of contact is always a deepening or intensifying experience. That is why the topic of contact has such important potential in education, although it is rarely if ever mentioned in the research. Teachers who are blessed with pedagogical sensitivity seem able to "touch" students with their eyes in a tactful manner. Their students feel that the teacher has contact with them. Pedagogically sensitive teachers can touch the students with the subject or knowledge they teach them. The learning of knowledge with such a teacher deepens and becomes more personally integrated in the identity of the student. Contact with a person who matters to us has consequences for the way we see ourselves. In other words, a relation with an other makes possible a relation to self, and this is a condition for an emerging sense of self-identity. We see this when, for example, a student who has been touched by a language teacher says, "I write poetry, I am a writer, I am a poet."

The experience of contact is that moment when, in a manner of speaking, a soul touches a soul. Making contact sounds like an active occurrence, but it may also be a passive instance when someone looks at me in a certain way and I feel that I made contact with this person—that moment may feel like a spark. We recognize such moments when we meet a new person and feel instantly that we have contact with that person. The strange thing is that contact may happen not only when we speak with another but also through the eyes and gestures that we meet in the other person.

We meet a stranger and may feel strangely touched by this person. Afterward we say things such as "I have good contact with her" or "with him I have contact." With one friend we experience contact when we talk together. With another person we may experience contact when we do things such as go for a walk. With yet another friend you can feel contact because you trust to tell this friend your secrets. Contact happens when I touch something or I am being touched by something that matters to this person, this friend, this teacher. Therefore, making contact or experiencing contact with someone or something that matters is always a meaningful action or an ethical response.

Young people crave the feeling of belonging. We can see this in the popularity of mobile or smart phones and the wide usage of social networking sites, text messaging and other digital communication devices. For some students, to be without a mobile phone and not able to text message with friends is a terrible predicament. It would seem even more terrible when a young person has no contact with the friends around them.

Of course, contact is not only an issue in the social lives of young people. The reason to address the topic of the pedagogy of contact is that education is increasingly falling within the sphere of instrumentalism, technologism, economism, corporatism, and managerialism. It is difficult nowadays to think of teaching and learning without immediately being concerned with effectiveness, efficiencies, outcomes and the instrumentalities, methods, and technologies of the curriculum.

Usually when we read about "contact" in education, it refers to "teaching contact hours" that students will receive. Ironically contact has become a commodity or a product to be negotiated in educational institutions. Another—but sad—reference to contact in teaching is when we read or hear about teachers physically touching students inappropriately. This kind of contact marks sexual or physical abuse. The political refrain for teachers has become "Teach, don't touch!" I want to advocate the opposite: "To teach *is* to touch!" But, of course, I mean that teachers touch students pedagogically. The teacher touches the student with his or her voice, eyes, gestures, and presence. To say it more pointedly: a real teacher touches the students with his or her being and mind. Contact is in-touchness.

Governments are concerned with youth violence and criminality, but the great irony is that we do not seem to want to acknowledge that we have created an educational environment that is toxic for many young people. Just as we discovered that the plastic in baby bottles is toxic to children, so the chemistry in the technology of media and teaching has become toxic for our students. Even well-meaning and competent teachers can become toxic teachers in a world where we become impotent and insensitive to the pedagogy of contact in teaching and learning. Toxic contact that children and young people experience may leave damaging consequences for the child's being and becoming.

In an article entitled "Contact" the philosopher Alphonso Lingis (2005) describes a simple moment when someone calls to us in the street. "Hey you!" And Lingis asks, "Isn't it quite striking... that I feel these words coming straight at me, finding me, taking a hold on me?" He says, somehow these words seem to penetrate whatever role I am enacting and makes contact with the "real me," the "core me." In this wonderfully simple phenomenological observation, Lingis makes us reflectively aware of how powerfully a word or the calling of one's name can be experienced as a demand, as an appeal—as contact.

A grandfather says,

> When I visit my grandson, who is still a young toddler, he may be playing on the floor or having a bath. When he looks up, his face may be indifferent or inquisitive, as if he seems to wonder for a moment: Who is this person? But then he sees me, and there is this big smile. In this smile he opens himself to me, and my smile does the same to him.

Isn't it remarkable how a smile can open a space where people make contact? Buytendijk (1998) describes smiling as a moment, an encounter where someone "enters the threshold of my inner life and whose own inner life reveals itself to me." He says, "The first smile of a baby is not just an expression; it is also a response to the person or object toward which our heart has affectionately opened."

> The child reveals his or her human nature through smiling . . . the child who is caught in the stream of unselfconsciousness, but then overcomes it by the ontic participation in the awakening awareness of a felt security. Something awakens in the child from a slumber, like a bird wakens in the morning, welling up from his or her deep innerliness and radiating as a recollection of this origin and as a sign of a certain destiny. (Buytendijk, 1998, p. 23)

You may feel that you can have contact with some people, like your friends, but that it is difficult to have contact with some other people. Some of us have better contact with our mother than our father or the other way around. With some people we feel that we can talk; with others we cannot. Even more importantly, with some people we have such good contact that we can be together without having to talk or to smile. We feel comfortable and pleasant merely by being in each other's company. This too is the intouchness of contact. It may be experienced as the contact of the familial, of togetherness of living together. It is the most elemental kind of contact that we may find with a friend, at home with the family, and in the togetherness of a classroom.

Modes of Contact

The pedagogical contact between teacher and student tends to be experienced as "close and personal." This may be especially the case for very young children and their teachers and even for some graduate students and their professors. In good educational environments personal contact between teacher and students is possible, but we have to distinguish the various modalities of pedagogical contact that may or may not occur at different times in schools and classrooms.

Here I distinguish five modes of contact: familial, deferential, valuing, responsive, and elective. These are modes of contact that are commonly engaged by adults who possess pedagogical sensitivity. Each mode of contact is characterized by certain affects, and these affects, in turn, translate into the pedagogical practices of care, respect, worth, responsibility, and electivity.

Familial contact is what exists between parents and other adult family members and their children. But this kind of contact can also occur between teachers and students. Familial contact is the relation that sparks care, as in the relation between Judith Minty and her son in Chapter 5. The child experiences security, safety, closeness, and being worried about.

The term "family" refers to a form of contact or closeness that is the unity of living together. The pedagogy of familial contact creates trust and is conditioned by trust. It is not uncommon to hear a teacher talk of her students as "my children" and her class as her family. Only if children feel secure and safe at school will they dare to risk themselves and extend themselves. Even when the students have gone to the family at home, they may still be tied to the familial unity of the school and classroom through homework and memories of the day.

But what happens when this basic atmosphere of trust is lacking or is undermined? Here is a story a senior professor at Hong Kong University told:

> I don't remember much from my childhood, but there is one event that I still distinctly remember from grade one. It has stayed with me all my life, for more than fifty years.
>
> It was the end of the school year, and the teacher had handed out rewards for all the students who had done well that year. Many students received prizes, and the teacher gave me a sweet stuffed bear. When I came home, I showed the bear to my father and told him that the teacher had given it to me because I had done such good work.
>
> But my father did not smile. He remained quiet. Then he said, "Son, you received this prize because you are number six in your class." And he looked at me, and then he inquired softly, "Do you remember what student was the first one to get up? Now THAT student is number one."
>
> I looked into my father's face and felt very strange. It seemed he was no longer seeing me with love in his eyes.
>
> From then on my prize was not sweet any longer. That day I had gained a whole different understanding of school and learning.

In this anecdote the love of the parent for this child is no longer felt by the child to be unconditional. The father's love, it seems, is now dependent on the child's performance at school. And if things do not go very well at school and if the teacher does not create a pedagogical atmosphere of trust, then the unity of familial contact is obstructed and the child lives in the constant shadow of the danger of experiencing a lack of familial care both in the classroom and perhaps also at home.

Deferential contact occurs when the child feels that he or she is respected. It is a form of relation that sparks respect, and the child knows that he or she has the right to fairness and equal treatment.

Mona, who is now a thirty-five-year-old teacher herself, recalls a seemingly trivial incident with her grade twelve science teacher. After the lesson, as she was one of the last students to walk out of the classroom, the teacher called her, "Mona!" Mona stopped, "Yes?" "Mona, I just want you to know that I really respect the way you are, and I am very honored that you are a student in my class." Mona recalls,

> That was the nicest thing that happened to me in high school. I was very messed up, and most teachers paid no attention to me, an aboriginal girl with an alcoholic mother and father. They looked down on me. For them I was a lost cause. But my science teacher was friendly and fair. No teacher had ever said something like that to me, and that year I learned to love science. In his class I could learn to respect myself.

What I find compelling about so many student or teacher stories is that they are so uncompelling. They don't concern life-and-death issues, and they are not glamorous or exotic stories. So often the events seem trite in the eyes of teachers. And yet I do not doubt that the experiences that students and teachers tell may have profound latent consequences for their personality. Often teachers do not realize that acting inattentively has created an atmosphere that endures and that leaves latent residues of self-doubt, insecurity, feelings of inferiority, even self-hatred. An act that the teacher considers totally trivial can establish for this student an unshakeable atmosphere of oppression that is damaging to the self.

Valuing contact occurs when the child experiences his or her worth. Valuing contact is a relation that sparks esteem. Typically, in valuing contact the child experiences a sense of achievement, success, feeling valuable, and being capable.

Sometimes teachers may be exquisitely aware that some students they teach are unusual in that they are extremely smart, highly sensitive, artistically talented, or have an unusual background in music or sports. But, of course, many students are not so talented, and so their worth is easily ignored. And yet they too need to be seen and valued. Here is a story by a student:

> I put the finishing touches on my art project. As I cast an appraisive glance at my creation, I am overwhelmed with relief at finally completing the piece. And I am aware of a growing sensation that faintly resembles pride. This is pretty good! I turn expectantly to the art teacher, who is slowly making her rounds through the classroom. I am anxious to show her my finished work. She ambles over to my table and nods distractedly. "Nice," she says, and that is that. She then turns her attention to others at my table who are intently working on much more intricate and more beautiful pieces than mine.

"Nice?" A lump rises in my throat and a flush of embarrassment rushes through me. I am so taken aback at her response. I was at the point of asking her for suggestions but was secretly hoping she would first say something positive about my work. I had not expected her utter disinterest.

I let go of my breath and sink back in my chair. All of sudden I am filled with frustration and disappointment at her curt comment. I want to throw a tantrum and cry at the same time. The vague nod with which she responded to my efforts stings in its dismissal. Her gesture leaves me conflicted and sullen. The fact that my teacher does not "value" my hard work and modest accomplishments leaves me deflated and helpless... what more can I do?

As if at a great distance, I watch her talking to my friends at my table—like I am missing out on something, like I am unworthy of my teacher's attention. I feel completely out of touch with my teacher and with my friends.

Interestingly, many adults also crave the kind of contact wherein they experience being recognized for something they did or achieved. In many work- or hobby-related activities people like to be valued for what they accomplish. Indeed, many university professors are very sensitive to being recognized for a worthwhile research article or book they have written.

Responsive contact occurs when we experience our uniqueness and singularity in our encounter or relation with another. For the adult this may be the moment when he or she experiences the child's otherness, mystery, and "face." The child experiences his or her uniqueness—this is the experience of being a "who," not just a "what." For example, in a moment of responsive contact the teacher sees and is stirred by the depth, the mystery, or the vulnerability of the child. Responsive contact is a relation that sparks feelings of responsiveness and responsibility.

As the students walk into the classroom, the teacher sits at her desk, collecting the homework assignments. Mat slips by the teacher's desk.
"Do you have your writing assignment, Mat?"
"Yes, I handed it in."
"No, you did not," the teacher says.
"Yes, I put it with the others already."
"Well, the papers are all right here in this pile. Identify yours please."
Mat does not move and looks sheepish.
"You did not do your assignment, did you?" the teacher says directly while looking him in the eyes. Mat shrugs his shoulders and nods slightly.
The teacher sees a boy who acts with indifference, passive defiance. She is annoyed and watches him with displeasure.
"Well, I am really concerned about your lack of responsibility and your blatant lying. I want to see you after class."
After class Mat is quite willing to chat. And he smiles when the teacher says that he has developed a really effective skill: "You are a pro! You are just excellent at avoiding work." Mat confesses that in class he always feels bored, and

after school he does not like to do homework: "I can't see the point. When I get home, then, I just don't feel like doing school stuff. So I go on my computer, or I play my guitar, or bike in the woods. Next year I may quit, look for a job, or do whatever."

While Mat talks about his biking and music, the teacher regards him. She looks directly into Mat's face and suddenly is struck by what she sees: an awkward-looking youngster whose depth of emotions seems quite unfathomable. This youngster is so much more complex than the student she saw at the beginning of the lesson. How strange that she can now wonder: Who is this person? She feels moved because not only does she see him as if for the first time; she also sees his vulnerability. Here is a big boy with complex emotions who, like a young child, still seems caught up in the present and for the present, without regard for things that lie ahead. She now feels responsible for helping Mat to start thinking not only of the present but also of the future—his studies and plans in life.

What is going on in this story? What is happening to the teacher? When Mat goes home after the talk, he has promised his teacher that he will try to make a better effort. But teachers know that most promises like this are rather short-lived. After a couple of days good intentions tend to be forgotten. Yet the teacher feels she had made contact with Mat, and in this contact they have experienced in-touchness. She may now have a deeper understanding of Mat, and she has a deeper understanding with Mat. They have talked about personal things—Mat's desires and interests. And the teacher knows that Mat knows that she has really "seen" him.

Yet promises will be forgotten. So what is the good of having had a talk? A teacher would say that teacher-student talk is pedagogically good if it provides opportunities for further contact, for seeing this child or this young person, and for a personal relation to develop. A good talk creates a shared history. A good talk leaves a memory of affect. Students who experience responsive contact with a teacher may be less likely to simply drop out of school.

Pedagogical contact means both that the teacher is "in touch" with the student and that the teacher "touches" the student in a manner that is experienced as encouraging and respectful. When later in the week the class reads a story about biking in the woods, the teacher glances at Mat. She gives him a quiet wink, and he smiles back—the moral spark of contact. The teacher says that she is "suturing" small moments of in-touchness into the pedagogical relation she has with him. So the good of the talk was that, in the days and weeks to come, at the appropriate time, the teacher can exchange a meaningful look—a look that has special significance just for Mat—a prompt to reflect on how his teacher sees him and cares for him, his being, becoming, and growth. Not only does Mat feel seen; the teacher also has a unique and complex experience of contact and recognition.

Elective contact is perhaps more rare because it sparks "falling" for the child. The child experiences feeling elected, being "chosen." To fall for a child is not unlike falling in love—not romantically, of course, but pedagogically, as the teacher in Chapter 2 falls for the child, Ciske the Rat. This is pedagogical love or care for a child who has captured the teacher's care.

> Stefan is a student in Ms. Anderson's grade nine English class. She often tells stories about him to her colleagues. Perhaps it is in part because she does not seem to have Stefan figured out. And yet, as a teacher, she is quite fascinated with him. Or perhaps she is so preoccupied with this young person because he is somewhat of a problem and a puzzle to her. He refuses to be pinned down by her teacher language. As his teacher, she is convinced that Stefan is very intelligent, amongst the brightest of the students she has taught. And yet he is often unwilling to participate in class. He frequently poses the strangest questions that will leave her stymied. In his writing assignments he digresses into dark reflections. At other times he challenges the purpose and nature of her assignments. He complains, (but only in writing) that he does not intend to do writing exercises in which he is not interested. Instead, he may write a remarkably evocative poem. Yet this same brilliant student hardly ever speaks up in class. Unlike other students, he never comes around for a chat. He appears withdrawn and even indifferent. He rarely addresses the teacher directly in class. But quite regularly he will share in his writings some story and private reflections about things happening in his life or at home. Yes, the teacher admits that she has "fallen" for this young person. She wants to understand him, acknowledge him, help him realize his promise as a poet and author. She regards Stefan with wonder and awe.

Pedagogically falling for a child is to become fascinated with this young person. This may be the child who is especially puzzling, captivating, and intriguing and who demands our special care and affection.

We must not see contact as simply making a connection with students. On the one hand, students know when or whether they have good contact with a teacher. On the other hand, contact is not so easily visible to the untrained eye; rather, the existence of contact between teacher and students is felt like a supportive classroom atmosphere. It is the pedagogical atmosphere of comfort in the knowledge that the teacher sees and recognizes you. Falling for the other is a form of contact wherein we experience simultaneously a touching of the other and the untouchability of the other.

The philosopher Levinas points out that love is ultimately oriented neither to the person nor to the unique qualities of the loved one. Rather, love is oriented to the riddle of the Other, with what always eludes us, remains ungraspable, making us one and yet separate in even the most intimate moment. Love is the recognition of what is simultaneously recognizable and unrecognizable in the other: his or her *incognito*. In a pedagogical context we may also have the experience of recognizing the unrecognizable in a student.

The various kinds of contact that I discuss are probably never quite so clearly distinguishable in our everyday life. And yet we come to experience contact in its various aspects. Perhaps falling for a child is the most complex and subtle way in which we experience contact: to be touched by a child or young person. To have fallen for a child means that the child has taken us hostage, in the sense of Levinas. Indeed, we would hope that every child has a parent or a teacher who has fallen for this young person. A teacher who has fallen for a child has a special interest in this child for the sake of the child. This interest is motivated by the love of care, worry, and fascination with the subjectivity and enigma that may be discerned in every child. This may be a child of worry, a child of promise, a child of hope, a child of puzzlement.

Children who do not have meaningful pedagogical contact with a caring adult are in reality invisible. Such child is not seen. Ironically it is exactly in this age of social media that children become invisible. They are invisible because the educational systems are only interested in learning outcomes, not the children themselves. And they are invisible because parents (and their children) are addictively distracted by their mobile devices. They become blind to their children's lives. But in the conduct of pedagogical contact the child becomes visible again—more accurately what becomes visible is the inner invisibility of the child.

Meaningful Learning

Through our words, gestures, and actions we teach our students subject-matter content and skills, and we ready them for tests and examinations. This is the curriculum or *Didaktik*, of teaching and learning. And through the tonalities of our words, through the affects of our gestures, through the sensuousness of our presence, and through the sensitivities of our perceptions, we practice our teacherly tact and thoughtfulness. This is the pedagogy, the relational and ethical dimension of education. Through pedagogical sensitivity and tact we make contact with the talents and intelligences, vulnerabilities and fears, happiness and hopes—the inner lives of the children and young people we teach. Only through genuine contact can teachers open up the spheres of pedagogical encounters.

We not only teach students knowledge and skills; more importantly, perhaps, we teach them to recognize who they are and what they are. We teach them about themselves, to reflect on their own selves, and how we regard them. Educators rarely reflect on the fact that meaningful learning is always infected with the relational and situational particulars of the moment in which the learning takes place. Whatever we learn is always affected by the contextual details of the living situation and relation in which the learning occurs. And, at times, a teacher's action or a learning event may carry meaning that cannot be grasped in the here and now. Such moments have latency: the meaning of this situation or event can only partly and gradually be discerned, and even this partial meaning may not reveal itself until later.

> It was early in September. The first school term had just started. As our new science teacher walked into the classroom, a bright beam of sunlight reflecting from an upper window had landed on the front wall of the classroom. The teacher took immediate notice of it. He slowly walked into the room, gazing at the beam of light. The teacher stood still at the front, folded his arms, and regarded the phenomenon with a wondering kind of smile. The upper sunbeam drew a sharp long triangle, like a huge finger pointing at something. The science teacher proceeded with a lesson about reflection and prisms.
>
> After a few minutes the sunbeam suddenly disappeared as if someone had turned off the light. The teacher pointed out that the next time we saw the sunbeam, in the spring, the course would be in its final stage and we would be reviewing what we had learned during the year for our science test.
>
> "In this class we go by cosmic time," he announced quietly. A smile played around the corners of his mouth and his eyes. I was transfixed. Some kids laughed knowingly. I did not quite understand what he meant, but it sounded intriguing, like almost everything he said and did in class.
>
> The year went by fast. Science became my favorite subject. Nearly everybody in class enjoyed the lessons and assignments during the year.
>
> It was quite a shock when one day we were greeted in the science room by an incredibly brilliant beam of light, plunging as if by magic from the upper light boxes. It descended in a blazing brightness in exactly the same location on the wall. It made me think of a giant exclamation mark, a secret sign. As if it were bringing us a mysterious message.
>
> When the teacher came into the room, he looked enigmatically at the sunbeam's reflection on the board. We could not help but smile with him. It was as if we were in conspiracy with our teacher about its magical appearance. Then he nodded his head quietly; he reached into his desk and, without saying a word, he began to distribute the study review notes.
>
> I felt sort of sad, as if I was about to finish a good book.

This story was told by a fifty-year-old teacher who recalled the event from his own childhood. "It was because of this inspiring science teacher that I chose to study science at the university and became a teacher of science myself," he says. What the story shows us is that inspiring teachers may make pedagogical contact with their students through their subject matter. There is an ontology of mimesis at work in the way that subjects such as math, science, literature, language, or art are embodied by the teachers who do not just teach a subject but *are* their subject and *exemplify* the subject they teach in their being.

When we have a conversation, then we understand the speaking of the other person immediately and directly rather than through intellectual interpretation. The story also shows us that such events have latency that may carry pedagogical significance for the unfolding of a student's future. It is in hindsight that this science teacher realizes some of the latent meanings and significance of his experiences in that high school science class.

From a pedagogical point of view, learning is not like storing information on a digital storage device; learning means that whatever is learned becomes part of the personal being of the student. It is important to reflect on the nature and kinds of contact we are able to establish with the students we teach.

Children who are very young learn through their bodies how they are regarded. Their bodies are attuned to contact and sensitive to the atmosphere of the school and classroom in which they live with their teachers and other students. The pedagogical significance of the various modes of contact lies in this caring quality of in-touchness and living together, in the atmosphere of trust, respect, worth, unicity, and pedagogical eros. Only in such atmospheres do children experience themselves as cared for, worried about, deserving of respect, regarded as worthy, unique, feeling loved, recognized—and, yes, interested, caring, and motivated to learn about the world in which they live and that lives in them.

Pedagogical Relation

The concept of the pedagogical relation has been considered critical and fundamental in educational thought because it was meant to arbitrate over the question of whether the experience of pedagogy—parenting, teaching, childcare—is a primordial human experience and thus constituting pedagogy as an independent discipline for study or whether it is merely an aspect of general processes of socialization whereby young people are initiated into the social order and cultural lifeworld that surrounds them. Wilhelm Dilthey was the first to propose that a "science of pedagogy" could only find its real starting point by studying the relation between the educator and his or her children (Dilthey, 1988). Dilthey's student Nohl has elaborated the notion of the pedagogical relation in Germany during the 1930s.

Nohl (1967) described the pedagogical relation as an intensely experienced relation, characterized by three aspects. First, the pedagogical relation is a very personal relation animated by a special quality that spontaneously emerges between adult and child and that can be neither managed or trained nor reduced to any other human interaction. Second, the pedagogical relation is an intentional relation wherein the intent of the teacher is always determined in a double direction: by caring for a child as he or she is and by caring for a child for what he or she may become. Third, the pedagogical relation is an oriented relation, which means that the adult must constantly be able to interpret and understand the present situation and experiences of the child and anticipate the moments when the child in fuller self-responsibility can increasingly participate in the culture.

Of course, these dimensions of the pedagogical relation are valid for every adult-child relation: at home, in the neighborhood, at school, and so forth. For the school student the pedagogical relation with the teacher is more than a means to an end—to become educated and grown up; the relation is an event that has significance in and of itself. Nohl suggested that our relation to a real teacher, someone in whose presence we experience real growth and personal becoming, is possibly more profound and more consequential than the experience of relations of friendship, love, and so forth. We may always feel indebted for the rest of our lives to a real teacher, even though the stuff we learned from this person may have lost its relevance. In part, this may be due to the fact that what we "received" from a great teacher is less a particular body of knowledge or set of skills than the way in which this subject matter was (re)presented or embodied in the person of this teacher and his or her enthusiasm, self-discipline, dedication, interests, personal power, commitment, and so forth:

> In the pedagogical relation—in the experience of being a father, a mother, a teacher—a part of our life finds its fulfillment. The pedagogical relation is not merely a means toward an end, it finds its meaning in its own existence; it is a passion with its own pains and pleasures. Similarly, for the child the pedagogical relation is a part of life itself, and not merely a means for growing up—for that the pedagogical relation lasts too long, and how many do not experience that aim! Among the few relationships granted to us during our lives, such as friendship, love, and fellowship in the workplace, perhaps the relationship to a real teacher is the most basic one, one which fulfills and shapes our being most strongly. (Nohl, 1967, p. 132)

This description of the pedagogical relation may make intelligible why classroom teachers so easily speak of teaching in terms that are reminiscent of family life: teacher-student relations also tend to be personal, intentional, and interpretive. Bollnow (1989) suggests that the notion of pedagogical relation is so taken for granted (in the German educational culture) that it is perhaps better to use the phrase "pedagogical atmosphere" for describing the conditions and qualities that characterize the lifeworlds of educators, parents, and children. Perhaps it is helpful to point out that the notion of relation and relationship should not just be seen as something functional that connects two or more people.

Almost from birth, mother and father interact with the child in a manner that differs from other human relations: the parent constantly presumes abilities and behaviors in the child (such as language and intentionalities) as if they are already present but that still need to be realized. For example, the mother engages the child in motherese speech as if the child already possesses language competence; the parent may interpret the child's crying in a manner (for example, being hungry, in pain, annoyed, frightened) as if the child intended this interpretation. In short, it appears that the pedagogical relation is a relation *sui generis*, which means that the pedagogical relation resists being reduced to other human relations (Spiecker, 1982).

Relation is not just a connection that exists *between* people but is also something that encapsulates and surrounds people. To be in relation is to be in each other's sphere, to travel in each other's landscape. Pedagogically a rich relation means to experience the other's otherness: their uniqueness and singularity. This is true for the child and the adult—the mother, father, teacher, grand parent, aunt, uncle, childcare professional, and so on. Indeed, the etymology of the term "relation" includes "a carrying back, returning." To "relate," therefore, also means "to bring back, return" (OED, online). Relationships of parents with their children are something that they continually return to. In this sense too, a pedagogical relation can be conceptualized as a sphere—a world—in which the people experience their singularity and identity in various emotional, physical, cognitive, and pathic modalities.

The pedagogy of teaching must take place within a relation of symmetry of respect between young and old and an asymmetry of the relational responsibility that the teacher carries for the students. How these relational symmetries and asymmetries are realized and experienced is the pedagogical challenge. In situations where we feel "called" by the child's vulnerability, or by the child's need for our self-forgetful attentiveness, the adult-child relation is more accurately described as a non-relational relation. The philosopher Emmanuel Levinas has pointed out that when the "other" makes a claim on us, then we temporarily transcend our self-centered way of being in the world. I am just there for the child and thus the polarity and two-sidedness of the relation is suspended.

Still, as children are growing up and sometimes run into difficulties, it is important for adults to realize that even young children do not want to be ignored or talked down to. A sensitive pedagogical relation treats the child with love and respect at a level of equality of human dignity. But it is true that some adults—parents, teachers, psychologists, social workers—are more able to deal with children who show anger, rebellion, or uncooperativeness. They are able to keep an attitude that sees the child as equal, even though the adult is charged with unequal—more—responsibility. Thus, there always exists a dynamic tension of symmetry and asymmetry in the pedagogical relation.

Finally, the process of teaching should not be confused with parenting. But the fact that so many family responsibilities have been delegated to the school seems to be an implicit affirmation of the close links between the pedagogy of teaching and the pedagogy of parenting. Parent and teachers are both, but in different ways, involved in living with and bringing up children and young people (van Manen, 1991).

There exists a broad range of psychological evidence that shows that the pedagogical relation between the parent and the child is marked by affectivities of attachment, typical anticipatory behaviors, and conceptualizations on the part of the parent. Without the development of healthy attachments and relational affectivities, the young person is apt to run into social and psychological difficulties.

The Reflexive Nature of Pedagogy

It is a well-known principle of inquiry that the object of our study is always contaminated by the frame of our observational stance. In the literature of research on teaching, this is easily demonstrated. If our outlook as a researcher is outcomes or results based, then everything the teacher does seems to have consequences for the effectiveness of the classroom. If we regard teachers as rational actors, then we may see teachers primarily making decisions from one moment to the next. If we are preoccupied with the issue of reflective teaching, then we will see teachers operating at various levels of reflectivity in their classrooms. If we look for the presence of moral values in teaching, then everything the teacher does seems to have moral significance. Our interpretive frame seems to account for our perceptiveness as well as our blindness.

Because we have to accept that what we see is a function of our stance, this poses a self-reflective or hermeneutic constraint on our understanding. As the philosopher Grondin (1994) points out, the contemporary situation is such that we not only know that all knowledge and understanding is interpretive but also that we are reflexively aware of this condition. So it is not just our task to interpret what we see; we are also challenged to provide interpretive acknowledgment that our understandings are indeed interpretive. Therefore, it is not good enough to simply admit that the accounts we provide are interpretations. The condition of reflexivity adds a level of self-consciousness to our interpretive act: they become exemplary of the forms of life that engenders these particular interpretations. This famous citation of Heidegger's description of the meaning of teaching stands in the service of learning what thinking is:

> True. Teaching is even more difficult than learning. We know that; but we rarely think about it. And why is teaching more difficult than learning? Not because the teacher must have a larger store of information, and have it always ready. Teaching is more difficult than learning because what teaching calls for is this: to let learn. The real teacher, in fact, lets nothing else be learned than—learning. His conduct, therefore, often produces the impression that we suddenly understand merely the procurement of useful information. The teacher is ahead of his apprentices in this alone, that he has still far more to learn than they—he has to learn to let them learn. The teacher must be capable of being more teachable

than the apprentices. The teacher is far less assured of his ground than those who learn are of theirs. If the relation between the teacher and the taught is genuine, therefore, there is never a place in it for the authority of the know-it-all or the authoritative sway of the official. It still is an exalted matter, then, to become a teacher.... That nobody wants any longer to become a teacher today, when all things are downgraded and graded from below (for instance, from business), is presumably because the matter is exalted, because of its altitude. And presumably this disinclination is linked to that most thought-provoking matter which gives us to think. We must keep our eyes fixed firmly on the true relation between teacher and taught—if indeed learning is to arise. (Heidegger, 1972, pp. 15, 16)

And, of course, Heidegger uses the word "learn" in a more fundamental and authentic manner than in the phrase "learning outcomes." Learning in this more fundamental sense is what we mean when we call someone "learned." In this sense too, learning refers to what a person makes of him or herself.

Teaching and the way we teach can be regarded as showing our living recommendation for what teaching is (or should be). Whether we like it or not, in all our educational actions we set examples for what it is to be a teacher. This is where the principle of reflexivity is important: we know that everything—literally every little thing we do or don't do—in our interactions with children has significance. Why? Because as teachers we stand in relations of influence to our students. And we are reflexively aware of this influence. We stand in relations of influence to our children, and we cannot claim ignorance of this fact.

We know that we cannot *not* influence our children. So the question is not whether we should or should not influence our children—we always do. And this influence is osmotically derived from our entire being: the way we are, feel, act, understand, as well as our reflexive awareness of our interpretive being. In other words, we are not only responsible for what we *do*; we are also responsible for what we *know* and how this knowledge gives us a *view* of the world and a *mode of being* in the world.

The question is not even primarily whether I should influence my students this way or that way. The question is whether whatever I do is appropriate for this or that child or for these young people. Indeed, the practice of pedagogy may be defined as constantly distinguishing more appropriate from less appropriate ways of being and interacting with young people. We can only be pedagogically sensitive and perceptive if we develop our understanding of how the youngsters we teach experience things, including our influence. Strangely, this pedagogical question of how students experience their relations with teachers is seldom asked.

The Paradoxical Nature of Pedagogy

The pedagogic lifeworld is full of tensions and contradictions. The child wants to do something himself or herself, but the parent feels responsible to assist or restrain the child in order to avoid a dangerous or undesirable situation. A new parent or teacher has vowed never to say "no" to a child but finds it impossible to live up to the resolution. A mother or father struggles with the tension between what one would like to be (able to do) and what one is (capable of) at present. A child longs to have a father, but no one assumes the responsibility. Supper is on the table, but the child would rather eat junk food.

These are examples of the endless contradictions, conflicts, polarities, tensions, and oppositions that beset the reality of the pedagogical experience. Most parents or teachers know from experience the challenges that these antinomies pose to everyday practical acting and living with children.

The notion of antinomies is so fundamental to pedagogic life (or to life in general, for that matter) that Schleiermacher (1983) used a discussion of pedagogical antinomies as a starting point for elaborating his thoughts on education in his seminal *Vorlesung* (lecture) of 1826. Pedagogical antinomies do not only challenge us in the practice of daily living; they also require of us a reflective response. No theory or practice of pedagogy can be satisfying if it does not know how to offer a perspective on the various antinomies of daily life.

Starting with Schleiermacher and Dilthey, many authors of pedagogy have addressed the question of pedagogical antinomies at the level of ontology and praxis. By identifying and clarifying the meaning of the fundamental structural antinomies of the pedagogic lifeworld, one hopes to provide a basis for a more thoughtful pedagogical living. Schleiermacher points at two grounding antinomies: (1) the polarity of individual versus social or universal ends of pedagogical acting and (2) the duality of the positive and the negative, the Good and the Bad, in the process of encouraging, stimulating, restraining, and disciplining the child. For Schleiermacher, the project of pedagogy involves these two contrasting but necessary tasks: to help the child in his or her uniquely individual becoming and to place this personalistic process in the service of great universal values. We see with him a working out of the dialectic of *Natur* and *Vernunft*, life and moral reason. Each individual, according to Schleiermacher, is called upon to find his or her way of participating in the moral environment of the whole community. This charge is deeply ethical, almost theological. The parent or educator needs to be oriented to awaken the Good while discouraging undesirable impulses in children growing up.

The grounding antinomies explicated by Schleiermacher have been a stimulation for a further detailed probing of the antinomous dimension of the pedagogic lifeworld. For example, this interest gave rise to the famous German pedagogue Litt's *Führen oder Wachsenlassen* (*Leading or Letting go*) that discusses the dialectic of giving active direction to a child's life while being sensitive to the requirements of letting go or holding back.

Litt (1925/1967) saw these conflicting tendencies to be the expression of two types of guardianship on the part of parents and educators: the desire to supervise and protect children and safeguard the life and quality of the culture and the desire to give the child free rein and permit the child's becoming of a unique personal life. Litt's work is characterized by the endeavor to always reflect on the welding together of two contradictory notions in order to expose the need to come to terms with polarities in everyday life and at the level of values and systematic thought.

Hintjes (1981) identifies three main types of antinomies that recur in the works of pedagogical authors: the antinomy of the subjective and the objective culture-world; the antinomy of freedom and control or freedom and constraint; and the antinomy of the real and the ideal. Nohl and his contemporaries thought that the exercise of pedagogic responsibility required that the adult actively would know how to come to a resolve of the many contradictions and tensions that are implicated in living with children. However, "resolve" for them did not necessarily mean that one comes to a "solution" or a cancellation of the antinomies.

The antinomies of freedom versus control, autonomy versus dependency are inevitable characteristics of the pedagogical lifeworld. Some contradictions and/or tensions may be resolved, but others remain, and these are now better understood at increasingly reflective levels. Nohl understood the process of reflection as a hermeneutic clarification and understanding (*verstehen*) of the inherent tensions and polarities that are characteristic of the pedagogical life sphere. It was expected of the professional educator to think through these antinomies (reflectively) in order to ready him or herself to be able to deal with the antinomies practically. Nohl (1967) talked in this context of a "praxis-theory-praxis" cycle. Praxis leads to reflection that readies for praxis, and so forth.

For example, the experience of freedom is opposed to control or discipline and yet requires (self-)control or discipline to transpose itself into a higher form of freedom and vice versa for the experience of discipline. Many pedagogies are dealing with the issue whether one should care for the child through arrangements of dependency or let the child be independent. From the point of view of pedagogical antinomies, this conflict between dependence versus independence is a false dichotomy, and a construct of binary thinking. Children who are kept totally dependent do not thrive, but children who are given total freedom do not thrive either. Independency and dependency, freedom and control, constantly must be brought into a certain harmony, relative to the child's age and maturity. Children can only become independent through dependence. The question therefore is not dependence or independence but rather what kind of dependence the child needs in certain situations for the sake of growing independent. No human person is probably totally independent; even adults maintain relations of dependence with their life partner, lover, relatives, friends, and communities. In our experience these antinomies are intermingled and not really separable.

Pedagogical Atmosphere

Obviously is it not possible to act always consistently in a pedagogical manner with children, and there is no point paining oneself with blame. There are days when we may feel depressed or just not in the mood, and the last thing we feel like doing is facing a class of students. Or we simply have bad days and cannot help but make mistakes or fail in our pedagogical responsibilities. Other times we think we do what is best, and we discover to our dismay that we did wrong, that we misjudged, that we fell short, or that we acted in ignorance. Indeed, we cannot avoid making mistakes and doing wrong with the children we parent, teach, or care for. Neither parenting nor teaching is a technical enterprise; rather, the pedagogical dimension of teaching—and parenting too—is thoroughly moral, emotional, and relational and shaped by mood, tone, or atmosphere.

Every home, every classroom, every school contains a certain atmosphere. The question is not whether there should be a pervasive atmosphere in the school but rather what kind of atmosphere is proper for it, worthy of it. "Atmosphere," as the word suggests, is a sphere that envelopes and affects everything. The atmosphere in a church will hold a transcendent quality. A cabaret or bar may exude erotic sensuality. Tall spacious architectures induce feelings of awe. Even entire cities hold specific pervasive moods, noted especially by travelers.

Just so, homes and places of work have "atmosphere." Even small objects in them help to create special feelings and moods. This chair belonged to Grandpa, and under that lamp Grandma used to do her crafts. Both lamp and chair hold the warmth and love of parents for their children and grandchildren. The sense of mood or atmosphere is a profound part of our existence. Through it we know the character of the world around us. Atmosphere or mood is a way of knowing and being in the world.

Schools too have atmosphere. Parents feel something of a school's mood during a parent-teacher interview. For a young child the school can have the feel of an alien and threatening place, or it can create an atmosphere that shelters the child and inspires him or her with security and confidence.

But the pervasive mood of a place, its atmosphere, is a complex phenomenon. A place that is experienced as threatening and intimidating by one child holds adventure and challenge to another. The mood of a place also depends on the disposition or frame of mind we bring to it. Yet it is true as well that the mood of a landscape, for example, or the beauty of evening light, can bring to us a stillness and sense of peace we did not know before.

Atmosphere belongs to all aspects of human existence: to things (a spiritual painting, a cozy chair), to space (a peaceful landscape, a happy beach), to events (a festive graduation, a solemn speech), to time (a happy harvest, a thankful ending). Or, better still, for each specific object or quality, atmosphere or mood is the way human beings experience the world.

Therefore, the recognition of the concept of atmosphere is pedagogically a positive phenomenon. Parents and teachers should understand the power of atmosphere to contribute to the general sense of being and to the positive well-being of the child. A sensitive teacher is able to create or foster an atmosphere that is productive for certain kinds of living and learning. Teachers may not all agree on what specific qualities a school should hold, but no teacher will deny that school is a special place and that therefore children should experience its corporeal, temporal, and spatial dimensions in a positive manner, pedagogically speaking.

Most teachers intuitively know this and therefore "dress up" the walls of classrooms with colorful displays and interesting materials. Yet even so, walls plastered with pictures, announcements of obligatory assemblies, or other brightly colored materials may only create an atmosphere of inauthenticity, of mere business or shallow commitments. Some teachers seem to need to impress their colleagues and parents more than to edify the minds of the children who sit in their rooms all day. Classroom environments that contain too many competing colors, displays, and materials can actually hinder learning and prevent the establishment of an atmosphere of quiet work or focused attentiveness. Better perhaps to clean up before we continue with something new, to gather and put away the books used during the previous lesson.

So a teacher has to learn to become sensitive to the ways children experience the complexity of elements that contribute to the atmosphere of the school and classroom. The school is special in the same sense that the home is special: it is a place where we provide children with time and space to explore the world without becoming part of it. On the one hand, school is a protective enclave, a shield against various realities for which children are not ready yet. On the other hand, it is a place where the private and personal space of home is expanded to take in larger public or community space. In this sense the school mediates between home and the larger world.

As we walk into a classroom we like to feel that the atmosphere, even the sheer physical space, is sensitive to the need for intimacy, security, and shelter as well as to the enticing call of a big world of public life and mysterious impersonal forces. When we enter a classroom, we soon have a sense of what pedagogy is practiced there. The atmosphere tells what vision the teacher has about what is a good space for children.

The lived space of the classroom, its textural and spiritual qualities, first should remind us of what schools are for. School is a place where children explore aspects of the human world. An elementary classroom speaks of the ways children come to know their world: mathematically, socially, historically, musically, literally, aesthetically, and so forth. Rooms in secondary schools may take on an atmosphere suited to individual subjects. A biology room is different from an art room, for example.

When a student enters an art class, her orientation shifts radically from the biology room she has just left. There the teacher discussed the structure and function of the human hand. She observed evolutionary characteristics in the hand bones of a primate, an Australopithecus, and a Homo sapiens. She noted how the straightening of the fingers became more pronounced over time and how the last phalanx of the thumb broadened and lengthened—how useful an opposable thumb and its related musculature!

However, when she walks into the art appreciation class, she notices a marvelous replica of Rodin's sculpture of the *Praying Hands* on the teacher's desk. Some students chuckle when they see it, as if caught by surprise. Sensitive fingers, extended upward in a devoted plea, transcend their instrumental function. How miraculously expressed is their earth-bound spirituality. How different is the atmosphere in this classroom.

Two different worlds, each with its own values, feelings, beliefs. How inappropriate it would be to attach terms like saddle joint, abductor pollicis, and the evolution of the last phalanx of the pollex to Rodin's hands. How can one familiar hand be part of two such different realities? As I write this I look at my hands. Such strange objects. I reminisce on a poem by Rainer Maria Rilke. He recalled once how, in reaching under the table, he saw his own hand groping, and for a moment it seemed that this "thing" had a life of its own. It seemed a foreign object, something in a different world, acting on its own mysterious impulses. I recall the images of this sensitive poet, for they left an indelible impression on my mind. I try to remember the exact words, but my eyes glance at the preceding paragraph, and instantly I am back in the classrooms and marvel once more at the shifts of mood that come when hands are set in different atmospheres.

Carefully we create an atmosphere in our home when we choose the color on the wall, the nature and arrangement of the furnishings, the placing of all the little things we grow so accustomed to that we get to see them only when they are missing. So teachers carefully, sensitively arrange their classrooms.

Some displays speak to children about the tasks the school demands. They bring to mind that life requires a certain order. There is a time for everything. School is a place where one learns to mediate between lived time and clock time, leisure time and time on task, time for scheduling and completing things, personal time and collective time, beginning time and the sigh of ending.

Other aspects of the classroom bring to the student lived aspects of the world that home and neighborhood may lack. An urban classroom should remind children that all is not concrete and plastic; there are organic materials as well—wool, cloth, earth, clay, and plants. In this way the school balances the otherwise impoverished world of the child.

Displays and furnishing in the classroom may also serve to reinterpret the significance of past learnings. First Lucy studies spiders in class. Then she finds a little spider at home in the corner of her bedroom. She discusses with her father what she should do with the little creature. Capture and release it outside her window? Leave it there? Better leave it. The next day it has settled near the light fixture on the ceiling. Better leave the window ajar just a bit, enough to provide the spider with the option of staying or going. In school Lucy now scrutinizes once again the pictures and drawings of spiders on display, for the little leggy friend at home has taught her to look at the pictures with renewed interest. Old questions acquire new meanings, and new questions emerge: What does a spider see? Would he see me? Is he a he or a she?

Atmosphere is the way in which space is lived and experienced. But atmosphere is also the way a teacher is present to children and the way children are present to themselves and to the teacher. Mood is set by bodily gesture and tone of voice. When the teacher reads Oscar Wilde's story *The Happy Prince*, a mood of spiritual beauty and sensitivity interweaves with the mood of storytelling itself. The teacher's voice breaks a little toward the end, and it deepens the catharsis for quite a few of the children. How can love sacrifice itself so beautifully and yet so sadly for the little swallow?

When the teacher slowly closes the book, there is silence in the room. Even those children who were not really touched by the story refrain from talking for a moment. This silence has mood as well. It is not just an absence of sound or voices; it has a tonal quality all its own. In the stillness of the book that closes, the story lingers and charges the silence with contemplation. It is the silence of reflection, of reckoning. This silence has a different atmosphere from the silence that reigns when every child is working individually at a math text.

Presentative and Representative Contact

Mollenhauer (1986) points out that children in earlier cultures learned skills, knowledge, and values in a direct or "presentative" fashion from their elders by directly participating in the lives of their parents and others in their communities. Young people were expected to live and work alongside the adults (farmer, craftsperson, miller) who presented them with the knowledge and from whom they learned to make a living. In most contemporary societies children are expected to go to school, where the knowledge and skills have been packed in textbooks, electronic media, and activities of the school curriculum. So Mollenhauer (1986) termed the earlier pedagogies of informal relation between adults and children presentative, whereas the more contemporary formal schooling pedagogies tend to be representative. The school selects and structures from the culture the knowledge that it deems worthwhile passing on to the young. This knowledge is represented in the school curriculum. In contemporary terms we can distinguish between curriculum content and teaching or didactic content. First, there is the mandated and prescribed curriculum content selected from the larger culture (disciplinary and nondisciplinary content); second, there is the content that the teacher selects from the curriculum (using didactic criteria of relevance, teachability, etc.).

The school curriculum is a structured complex of teaching-learning goals and materials that is supposed to represent selective elements of the culture. But what is represented is therefore detached from ordinary living. The representations may be experienced as meaningless and alienating to children who do not experience the presentative realities and meanings of the representations. The school has become the in-between sphere between home (the private) and the outside world (the public).

So experientially we can make a distinction between presentation and representation, between presenting something and representing something, between presentative languages and representative discourses. A presentative mode of experiencing something is immediate or direct, whereas a representative mode of experiencing is mediated or indirect. For example, for young people to be actively involved in political protest is a different experience from reading about political protests in history textbooks. Directly experiencing something involves a different kind of learning from that of indirectly getting to know about the matter.

The important point that Mollenhauer failed to make is that the ways the teacher embodies the representations that he or she teaches are in themselves also experienced as situated presentative pedagogies. There is a living sensibility to the subtleties of the pedagogical relations, situations, and (inter)actions of teacher-student experiences. We become aware of this presentative pedagogical reality when we compare the shared atmosphere of a class discussion with the shared atmosphere of an online discussion or when we compare the presence of a physical, face-to-face, personal telling of a story with the presence of listening to the teller of a story on a podcast.

But in doing so the school creates its own secondary presentative school realities: the school pedagogy is a reality of presentative contact with the secondary reality of representative meanings embodied in the programs and media of the curriculum. The presentative and representative, the immediate and mediated forms of contact in teaching and learning, parenting and growing up has become complex in the new technological environment in which we live. In contemporary contexts the experiences of travel, television, the Internet, digital devices, and constantly changing social networking technologies may blur the distinctions between presentation and representation, between participating in events directly or indirectly, between real and virtual experiences, immediate or mediated realities, and so forth.

How Do Children Experience our Presence?

It is surprising how perceptive young people are about the inconsistencies between what we say or do and what we are. Just as a true lover cannot be fooled for long by a partner's pretending, so a child cannot be misled by a teacher's fake enthusiasm or false expertise. A teacher who does not know what he or she is talking about (whether aware of it or not) is soon unmasked as one who should not be taken too seriously. "Teacher so-and-so isn't real," young people say.

A young and insecure teacher who desperately tries to feign an air of self-confidence soon gives away his or her real state of being. Children will quickly sense it in an awkward gesture, a false pose, a look in the eyes. So much that happens between teachers and students transpires through the face and eyes. A powerful teacher is a man or woman who has a powerful presence. Let us explore what it means to be present as teacher to some child or adult. It is sometimes said that we know a person by his or her deeds. But it may be easier to observe and describe what we *do* than what we *are*.

If a teacher competently adheres to a set of curriculum objectives but in a deeper sense does not know where he or she is going, if a teacher discusses poems but is unable to poetize life, if a teacher talks about responsibility but does not live a responsible life, if a teacher constantly assigns grades but fails to make perfection the standard of his or her own striving, if a teacher works hard at being liked by his students but then forgets what teaching really is, if a teacher knows many jokes to amuse students but lacks a true sense of the joy of being, if a teacher shows an eloquent command of language but produces mostly empty chatter, if a teacher effectively individualizes the curriculum but fails to really know children, if a teacher gives evidence of knowing the world but does not take responsibility for it, if a teacher is able to cite important educational aims and goals but is unable to live a deep sense of hope for each child, if a teacher integrates his or her subject with others but lacks a vision of the whole, if a teacher asks students many questions but does not truly know how to be addressed by a question, if a teacher acts with authority but does not know what authorizes him or her pedagogically, if a teacher . . . one could almost go on forever . . . then the observable teacher behavior, what that teacher is doing overtly, is a profound contradiction of the way he or she exists in the world or, better, in the school, in this classroom, with these young people. Or maybe we should say that when a teacher fails to be what ostensibly he or she does, then that teacher is really an absence, is not at all genuinely present to those students.

We may be physically present to children while something essential is absent in our presence. Similarly, we may be physically absent from children while in a different sense they remain present in our lives after school and we remain present to them. This happens to a child doing homework who feels the teacher looking over his or her shoulder. Or to a teacher preoccupied with something that happened during the day who cannot put a particular child out of his or her mind.

Whether we like it or not, adults cannot help being examples to children, either positive or negative examples. Children are experiencing adults as examples when they ask, "How come you always tell me to do this but you never do it yourself?" Or, "Why do you care so much about my report card but you never take any interest in my work?" Or, "Why do we have money for a new car but not for airplane tickets for visiting Grandma?"

When an adult turns from merely being an example of behaviors children imitate to being a real example, living the great values he or she tells children to uphold, then that adult assumes pedagogical significance in children's lives. The adult is no longer just an entertaining parent, a mere teacher of skills or information, a shallow television hero, a popular sports figure— he or she has become a pedagogically significant adult. What a thoughtful parent or teacher does is offer the young person a vision of what kind of life is worth living and what image of adulthood is worth aiming for.

Of course, the imitation may not always go in a manner that we would immediately regard as pedagogical. In life such moments may be somewhat messy or awkward but then turn positive, as this young university performance violin student recounts:

> The world-renowned violinist was coming through town as part of a crosscountry tour. The Music Department was buzzing with excitement because he had agreed to do an hour-long master class at the university before his concert. Three of us were asked to perform for him in Convocation Hall. News of the master class spread through the city's musical community like wildfire, and when the day arrived, the hall was completely filled with string teachers, symphony members, and pretty much anyone who knew a thing about this famous musician. This audience was composed of the city's most critical and knowledgeable musicians. I was the first one to perform. Stage fright had never been much of a problem for me, but the thought of a miniature lesson from one of the world's most famous violinists combined with the presence of a house full of critical musicians and teachers watching transformed me into a nervous novice.
>
> I figured I would just play as well as I could. All week I had been listening to the platinum Sony recordings in a pitiful attempt to match his rich sound. "Maybe if I played like him, he wouldn't be hard on me," I thought. Dressed in my tuxedo, I looked more like a groom in a wedding processional than a violinist awaiting a lesson from a master teacher. The doors opened, and one of my professors emerged. Behind her were members of the media and

a little man dressed in dirty black sweatpants with a matching hoody. Is this the famous master?

Our lesson began. I put my bow to the string and started into the piece. It is customary at a master class for the teacher to allow the student to finish playing before offering criticism. Well, a world famous master is above customs. He stopped me after a mere ten seconds. "Catch, then release!" he interrupted. Bewildered and confused, I paused for a moment, and then started the piece again. This time after five seconds he stopped me and in a slightly more frustrated tone said again, "Catch, then release!" This went on for a few more times, and I was beginning to become totally flustered. Each time I tried, his voice would become slightly louder, and more impatient. I simply did not know what he wanted. People in the audience were starting to giggle and whisper. I attempted the passage one more time, and then the most amazing thing happened.

He opened his own violin case, took out his beautiful Antonio Stradivarious, and showed what he wanted. The sound he created was magical. It filled the entire hall, and for a few seconds the whole auditorium was silent with awe. As I watched him, I instantly knew what he meant. He didn't have to say another word. I put the bow to the strings just as he showed me, and although my sound was pale in comparison to his, I knew I got it. He smiled, winked, and tapped me on my shoulder with his bow. "Go practice," he said. And that was that. A few months later I received a phone call inviting me to come and study with the famous violinist in his summer music school.

But for the next few weeks I couldn't go anywhere with my violin without people jokingly saying, "Hey Mark, 'catch then release!'" I smiled, I had indeed learned something invaluable from the great master, but it was something more consequential than "catch then release." I had learned the power of showing over saying.

Indeed, this imitational process (mimesis) is the meaning of learning. In early English to "learn" meant to teach or to let learn as well as to learn. It would then be correct to say that someone could "learn" someone to learn something. In the Dutch language "to learn" (*leren*) is still used interchangeably for teaching and learning. "Teacher" is *leraar*; "student" is *leerling*. Etymologically to learn means to follow the traces, tracks, or footprints of one who has gone before. In this sense the teacher or parent who is able to "let learn" therefore must be an even better learner than the child who is being "let learn."

The Pedagogy of Being (What We Teach)

We cannot be all things to all children. So when I call myself a math teacher or a teacher of literature or history or science, I declare that I have available a vocational range of pedagogical possibilities and responsibilities. So what is it like to teach children literature or history? To be a teacher of history or literature may mean that I can tell many stories or talk endlessly about poetry and the works of great poets. Obviously to know a particular subject means that I know something in that domain of human knowledge. But to know something does not mean to know just anything about something. To know something is to know what that something is in the way it speaks to us, in the way it relates to us and we to it.

To know a subject does not only mean to know it well and to know it seriously in the fundamental questions it poses. To know a subject also means to hold this knowledge in a way that shows that it is loved and respected for what it is and the way it lets itself be known. We learn about the subjects contained in a school curriculum. It is also true that the subjects let us learn something about them. It is in this letting us know that subject matter becomes a true subject: a subject that makes relationships possible. Our responsiveness, our "listening" to the subject, constitutes the very essence of the relationship between student and subject matter. Water (H_2O) is its chemical and physical properties, of course. But it is also the cooling (or uncomfortable) rain on our body, the habitat of fish and fowl, a necessity for the growth of our food, an opportunity for profit, a reason for war, a cascade of beauty, a confirmation of religious grace.

This listening attentiveness to things is often an interpretive act of meaning. And once we accept that every act of interpretation is a relational act of attentiveness and caring, then we admit to a surprising conclusion: we should be just as accountable for what we *know* as for what we *do*. We may speak of a morality of knowledge, an ethics of epistemology. For example, knowing a rare species of animal as a result of studying it with a camera is ethically a very different kind of knowledge than knowing that animal species as a result of hunting and shooting it to kill. There are some kinds of knowledge that may not benefit us as persons and that may not benefit our natural environment or humanity at large. Sometimes it may be better not to know certain things. But just like being unable to forget having seen some horrid images of human cruelty, we cannot forget the unforgettable, we cannot unknow what we know.

Our professional knowledge too has an ethical dimension. A teacher who primarily knows the practice of teaching behaviorally and technologically understands individual students and classes of students differently from a teacher who knows the practice of teaching pedagogically and relationally. And, of course, there exists complex and subtle relations between what we teach and how we teach.

Some people think it does not matter whether teachers know a great deal about the subjects they teach. Good teaching is determined by the *how* (teaching method or style) rather than the *what* (content), or so the thinking goes. The practical reality is that we see physical education teachers in front of English classes, or history teachers teaching science. And yet there is undeniable truth in the statement "you are what you teach." A math teacher is not—or should not be—just somebody who happens to teach math. A real math teacher is a person who embodies math, who lives math, who in a strong sense *is* mathematics. We can often tell whether a teacher is "real" or "fake" by the way this person stylizes what he or she teaches; indeed, a fake is incapable of stylizing what he or she does not embody in the first place. When a person says, "That's not my style," the statement means, "That's not the way I am. That's not me."

The way we stylize subject matter is a tell-tale expression of the way we hold it. We may possess a certain amount of information in literature, math, or science, but only the knowledge we embody has truly become part of our being. A "real" English teacher tends not only to love reading, writing, and carrying poetry under one arm during coffee break; a "real" English teacher cannot help but poetize the world—that is, think deeply about human experience through the incantative power of words.

There is much to be learned from what students say about outstanding teachers they have had. Or from hearing them describe the teachers they learned best from—the ones they would like to be themselves. Certain themes will begin to emerge, themes hidden behind stories and anecdotes that easily lead to generalizations about such teachers being fair, patient, caring, able to communicate, keeping good discipline, having a sense of humor, being interested in and knowing children, knowing what to teach.

The themes behind these generalizations are harder to put into words. At an even deeper level teacher competency has more to do with pedagogical tactfulness, having a sensitivity to what is best for each child, having a sense of each child's life and his or her deep preoccupations. It also includes a sense of the aspects that draw the curricula of mathematics, English, social studies, art, or science to the curriculum of life itself.

When a child tells real-life stories of how he or she wanted to be trusted and believed by a teacher, he or she also touches on that deeper sense of trust and belief without which a teacher is no longer an educator. When students say that teachers should like what they teach and have a sense of humor but that they should "not always try to be funny or tell dumb jokes," then they point in the direction of what it really means to be what you say or do as a teacher: to have a sense of joy and deep commitment to life, to the world, and to the subject matter that draws teacher and students into the world. When students say that teachers should know how to "connect" with students, then they ask for teachers to be present to students as persons and that teachers approach students as persons. When students say that teachers should "know what students need," "help them with homework," "be available to them," and "not hand out work and then walk out the door," that teachers should "have patience" and "not give up on kids," then they have pointed once again to the essence of pedagogical tact: a teacher who gives up on a child, who no longer knows how to have a sense of hope for that child, immediately falls back from being a teacher. When students say "good teachers know how to make you learn," "good teachers know how to make you like math or science or English even though you always hated it," "good teachers are enthusiastic about what they teach," then they refer to another essential aspect of teaching: a good teacher does not just happen to teach math or poetry; a good teacher embodies math or poetry. The pedagogy of being a teacher is that good teachers are what and how they teach.

Virtual Contact

It is relatively easy to understand what it means for teachers to "connect" with their students and to be present and available to them. But how do students experience the "contact with" and "presence of" the teacher when this contact and presence is mediated by new media and technologies? Also, how is the "contact" that students experience with the subject matter they learn shaped by the technologies such as Smart Boards, iPads, computer screens, and screens of smartphones? Although e-learning and online classrooms employ powerful media and technologies, there is no doubt that these lead to altered modes of pedagogical contact. We only have a superficial understanding of the "contact" that the new media afford.

It is well accepted that bodies play very different roles in the teacher's physical presence in a face-to-face classroom versus the virtual presence of bodies in experientially synchronic and/or nonsynchronic relations. Participation in online classrooms may or may not be mediated by face time, but even face-to-face contact mediated by screens has a different quality in the sense that we do not really look the other in the eye. And yet it is only when the looks of our eyes cross that we experience real eye-to-eye contact with the other person.

Even in real-time classrooms it is different to learn a subject that is presented by the teacher through a carefully prepared and structured PowerPoint (or similar slideware or Smart Board technologies), from learning a subject through immediate eye-to-eye contact with a teacher who may be improvisationally talented in telling a compelling story.

In a darkened PowerPoint classroom the pedagogical relation between teacher and student is obviously dramatically altered. Student eyes are drawn by the screen images rather than the teacher's presence. And the knowledge presented through the PowerPoint tends to be converted into "points" that may possess more or less cognitive and logical cohesiveness and that may carry more or less justifiable truth-value for the students. The PowerPoint tends to impose its own predetermined lesson structure that may be less flexible and less open to the contingencies of relevant questions and clarifying conversations (see Adams, 2006, 2012).

Students who have an implicit trust in the knowledge taught by an admired teacher will internalize the subject they learn face-to-face from this teacher in a manner that is likely invested with fascination and motivated interest. But this knowledge internalization will be less charged with affect when it is offered and "delivered" on screens through online media.

It is also true, however, that MOOCs (massive online open courses) that deliver courses through video and related material may be highly motivating and compelling for student participants who are witnessing the presentation by a highly eloquent and/or famous international speaker. In such contexts students may be less likely to interact with the subject matter critically or with a healthy dose of doubt.

Historically and culturally the world contains many possibilities of living and being. Children encounter these worlds through friends, schools, media, neighbors, and the mediation of teachers. And these encounters consist of reversible crossings where bodies ensnare each other. This is the natural process of imitation or mimesis. It is how we have made our own father's, mother's, teacher's, or admired friend's gestures and ways of being our own:

> Mimesis is the ensnaring of me by the other, the invasion of me by the other; it is that attitude whereby I assume the gestures, the conducts, the favorite words, the ways of doing things of those whom I confront.... It is a manifestation of a unique system which unites my body, the other's body, and the other himself. (Merleau-Ponty, 1964, p. 145)

In the context of such social conditions, children must find their own uniqueness and identity through personal exploration, choice, and commitment.

The question is: How can we, as teachers or parents, assist in making such conditions and alternatives available? What worlds are worthy of our efforts of presentation and representation? Children cannot just be expected to *discover* a life; they must also be allowed to act, experiment, and create themselves.

Chapter Eight

Pedagogical Regard and Recognition

Every child wants to be "seen" and "regarded." A person who is regarded is being valued, seen, known and also guarded and watched over. Being "recognized" describes situations wherein an interpersonal encounter is experienced as generative: the relation to other and the relation to self; moreover, these two relations interact in such a way that they are formative of identity, subjectivity, consciousness, self-awareness, the development of self, and, generally, the becoming of a person. Children, young people, and even adults cannot flourish without being seen, regarded, known, and recognized by those who matter in their lives. Some forms of "regard" and "being seen" and "being recognized" are conditional for the very possibility of developing a sense of self, being able to handle relationships, and growing up toward a state of healthy (inter)independence, and so forth.

Being recognized is not always positive: there can be false recognition, when teachers or parents try to increase children's self-esteem with empty praise; there can be misidentification, such as when a child is regarded with personal, psychological, or social (gender or racial) bias; or there can be lack of recognition when positive regard is withheld, such as when children desperately try to win their teacher's or parent's approval by trying to perform beyond their best ability in competing for first place on exams and tests. The pedagogy of regard and recognition asks: In what ways and under what conditions can children and young people realize themselves at private, personal, intersubjective, social, and existential levels.

The notion of pedagogical regard or recognition is a pointed example of what constitutes a pedagogical language because it describes emotive and ethical pedagogical situations, relations, and actions. To recognize the importance of pedagogical recognition is to reinstate and place as central the meaning and significance of the emotions in the experiences of learning and in the practice of teaching and parenting.

Pedagogical Tact: Knowing What to Do When You Don't Know What to Do, by Max van Manen, 139–155.
© 2015 Taylor & Francis. All rights reserved.

The stage is tiny. That is my first thought as I slip quietly into the gym of my old school, watching the students parading in noisily. For seven years I had filed into this same gym with my classmates, to sit on the floor amongst the dust motes, waiting for the grade six masters of ceremonies to raise their hands for silence. I have been through this ritual so many times that I can live it through with my eyes closed. But now I am no longer a student here. I am an outsider, a stranger in a place that was once as familiar to me as my own home.

As I sit down, uncomfortably, in a chair between the mother of a former classmate of mine and a man I don't recognize, I try to remind myself why I came here. This is the retirement assembly of Ms. Rose, my beloved and highly respected teacher, who showed me how much I love to write. I really want to see her today, but ... well, I'm beginning to wonder whether it is worth this experience of feeling left out, excluded by those who were once my family.

The assembly rolls by. There are presentations by students, teachers, and parents whose lives have been touched by Ms. Rose. All the while, the retiree sits quietly at the side of the gym, sporty jacket and khaki flood pants contrasting sharply with the standard conservative garb worn by so many school teachers. Presently she stands to make her speech. I see tears in her eyes, tears of a woman about to give up something she loves. I feel about to cry myself as her eyes rove lovingly over the students she taught the year before. But she never even glances my way. Not her fault, of course. How could she know I was back here? But still, I wonder: Does Ms. Rose even remember me from four years ago? Or to her, am I just another face in the crowd?

Finally the assembly is over. I remain seated for a while, struggling to hold back the tears welling up in my eyes. Finally I am the only one left in the room. Why do I feel so depressed? Dejectedly, I get up and head out toward the back doors of the school, the student doors. I can't get used to the idea that, as a visitor, I can use the front door. I step onto the tarmac where all around me there are children playing. Recess. The sun is bright in the sky, and it seems the very picture of a carefree schoolyard on a bright spring day. Everyone is happy. Everyone but me. I begin to walk home across the fresh expanse of the green field, hands in my pockets, feeling very lonely. Then I notice a familiar profile: Ms. Rose, out for a last supervision. Almost against my will, I veer away from the well-worn path leading toward my house and quietly approach her, strangely nervous.

"Ms. Rose?" My voice is small, quiet, timid. She turns, and my heart skips a beat: Will she remember me?

I need not have worried. Immediately she breaks into a broad smile. Her eyes crinkling slightly at the corners deepen the familiar smile lines. Those eyes. I admire them, love them, trust them. Their respect and affection mean the world to me. "Alyssa!" she exclaims, genuinely glad to see me. Her distinctive and familiar voice warms me to the core. "How are you? You are looking wonderful. What are you doing now? Read any good books lately? Or are you just about ready to write one of your own?"

The above story is written by Alyssa, a grade nine student, in response to a request to describe an instant of a moment of being "seen" and "regarded" at school. What the student describes is not only her desire to be "seen" and "remembered" by a teacher; something else happens in writing this experiential account: Alyssa is expressing in her own words understandings that usually remain tacit, silent. She brings to language several dimensions of school life: the emotional quality of lived space, the temporality of routines and events, the special sense of ceremony, the atmosphere of security and familiarity, the mood of belonging, the feeling of a new unexpected strangeness as well as the corporeal quality of the chairs, the doors, and the "tiny" stage that now remind her of her grown body. These emotive sensibilities too belong to the experience of being seen and known. They bring to awareness an understanding of the self-world relation. Alyssa sees herself in the things she re-cognizes in her old school. As well, the furniture, the walls, the rooms, and the hallways "see" her—she is "regarded" by the things that belonged to her bodily being in the school. But in being seen, she also recognizes how she has changed and how she is different now.

The notion of "being seen" derives its ethical and political significance from Hegel's phenomenology of recognition (1977). The human person comes into being and is formed through recognition of what lies outside of ourselves and through being seen by someone or something. Recognition is to come to oneself through what is other (*Im Andern zu sich selber kommen*). One can only become a self-aware and a full human being through processes of being seen and being known by what is external to the self—that is, in relation to what is other and what is different from the self. The notion of being regarded and being recognized can give us rich insights into the complex and subtle phenomenon of becoming and learning, especially in present-day contexts in which learning is sometimes narrowly identified with cognitive gain and measurable outcomes (see Saevi, 2015).

Pedagogical reflection on the experience of "being seen" shows how the notion of self, other, and relation are inextricably entwined in learning as meaningful formative growth (the German word for this is *Bildung*)—the relational appropriation of "other" and "difference" into self and sameness. Herein lies the pedagogical power of experiencing oneself being seen and known: formative learning occurs in relational context—in relations to self and other.

Pedagogical seeing and recognition of the student is arguably the most consequential but also the most undervalued and unexplored phenomenon in the study of education. Why has the value of "regard" and "recognition" received so little attention in educational circles? Perhaps this question is more pressing now than it was a few decades ago. Have children not always needed recognition, felt to be seen, to be known? No doubt this is true. Being seen by others makes us visible and confirms our very existence and worth. But being seen and known may have been less problematic in earlier times. One derived one's sense of self from one's family, neighborhood, church, and other institutional and social structures. In present-day times being seen and known plays into the experiential processes of communicative technologies of social networks and through social contact by means of mobile media. Thus, feeling that one is seen and known is technologically mediated and shapes the experience and the formation of identity in new and different ways.

It is not surprising perhaps that many stories that students tell have to do with approval, being noticed, feeling special. Giving encouragement and positive feedback is one of the most common gestures expected from teachers in classrooms. It means that we prize, value, and esteem someone for something. Moreover, supportive commendation is supposed to build self-esteem in students. But obviously giving praise is not without danger.

Pedagogical Aspects of Being Seen and Being Known

It is important that teachers understand the positive as well as the possible negative consequences of praising students. A compliment should be meaningful and should not be granted indiscriminately because, if given too readily and too freely it may lose its significance. Yet many students no doubt deserve commendation for a variety of reasons. And on occasion it is possible that only one student or only a few students stand out for their accomplishments. For this very reason compliments create dilemmas. Teachers would like to recognize all students, especially if they make good efforts, but the practice of praising everyone equally in all instances is self-defeating. And sometimes teachers want to praise a single student, but they may not always realize that such acclaim may create difficult situations for the student. This is how a high school student describes such a situation:

> Mr. Jackson made a big production of his disappointment. He went on and on, exclaiming his amazement at the mistakes people had made on the science test. "My God, did I do such a poor job at explaining this stuff to you people? I know there is nothing wrong with your brains. And, you Wendy. . . ? Ken. . . ? What happened?"
> It was obvious that he did not really expect an answer. And nobody tried. The class was completely quiet. None dared to crack a joke. Most kids got a failing or near-failing mark. Only two or three students barely made over 60 percent. Again Mr. Jackson blew his cool, uttering his disgust while he walked around the room, demonstratively placing each paper in front of its owner, as if he could not quite believe it, as if he wanted to verify each case. Most students sort of looked sheepishly. I feared my turn, feeling already ashamed. A sense of doom seemed to be hovering over the class. I tried to tell myself inwardly that this was not the end of the world. I would do better next time. When the teacher finally reached my desk, he stopped and suddenly changed his tone of voice.

The shift was so dramatic that I am sure everyone in class startled. All eyes were on me. But the teacher's face lit up, and I heard him say, with an air of approval: "Oh, thank God, there is one amongst you who has caught on. It goes to show that there is still hope . . ."

He waved my test paper above his head, like a silly flag, before he placed it solemnly in my hand. "Good for you, Sarah, not a single mistake. A perfect mark!"

I scarcely could maintain my composure. I had expected the worst and was awarded the best. I did not need a mirror to know that my face was blushing red. The class was still strangely silent. No one uttered a word while the teacher walked back to the front of the room.

I kept my face turned down, staring at my test paper. I could not completely suppress a faint smile. Was it relief? Vanity? Embarrassment? I dared not look at my friends. I did not trust my eyes.

Why did I feel so stupid when I was supposed to feel smart?

This looks like a story of humiliation (of the whole class) and praise (of a single student). The teacher singles out a student for recognition, but the student feels confused. What seems a positive gesture on the part of the teacher—to compliment a student on good work—has potentially ambivalent significance. The pedagogical question is: Did the teacher act appropriately? What is the experience of recognition?

To receive recognition literally means to be known. Someone who recognizes me thereby acknowledges my existence, my very being. This is not the same as fleetingly noticing people who one passes in a busy street. Recognition is inextricably intertwined with selfhood and personal identity. And self-identity is the realization of the tension between the being of self and the becoming of self, between who we are and who and what we might become. And that is how recognition plays such a powerful role in teaching and learning.

Recognition and the feeling it produces—a positive sense of self—are public phenomena. It is something that unfolds in the space of relationships. Although a teacher may compliment a student privately, the compliment is more strongly felt when it is conferred in public, in the presence of others. Why? The others are implicated or witness to the feeling of pride that follows from praise.

But a problem with giving recognition is that it may lead to feelings of inequality. Recognition seems to assign special value and special status to the person. And so a student who accepts the praise thereby may feel that he or she is making a claim to superiority. Of course, such gestures could easily be regarded again as a sign of vanity, for which one should feel shame.

Blushing is a way of showing embarrassment. But by showing embarrassment, the student reduces inequality and the effects of praise and pride. Thus, we see that in the above anecdote the student's feelings are quite mixed and confused. Sarah seems to feel special and yet also seems to feel embarrassed for feeling special. Teachers need to actively understand such situations. To reiterate: pedagogy is actively distinguishing what is appropriate from what is less appropriate in interacting with children or young people.

There are social and spiritual spheres that can be broadly conceived as the settings for the present-day social and political struggles for recognition. Minorities, ethnic and gender-based groups, and the disadvantaged demand equal recognition and equal treatment. No doubt, there are tensions and contradictions in these demands. For example, theoretically all individuals and groups are to be treated fairly and equally before the law, and yet in actuality this fairness is often compromised. Moreover, individuals and groups sometimes demand to be treated not just as equals but with preferentiality.

Regions of Regard and Relations to the Self

Within pedagogical contexts there are regions of "regard" that sponsor certain pedagogical sensitivities. For example, within the familial region children are hopefully perceived with love and affection. Within the general public sphere they need to be perceived with dignity, equality, fairness, and respect. Within the institutional educational sphere young people are perceived for what they have achieved and what they can do. And within the relational ethical sphere they are hopefully perceived for *who* they are in their uniqueness (rather than only for *what* they are or what they can do). Each mode of "being perceived" sustains a practical relation to self—different experiential relations of recognition to the self: self-confidence, self-respect, self-esteem, and self-identity. These are emotively charged forms of self-realization.

- *Self-confidence* is conditional on being loved and cared for. Experiencing the world as safe, secure, guarded, and, therefore, daring to take risks. Every child needs at least one person for whom he or she is most and unconditionally loved.
- *Self-respect* is conditional on knowing oneself entitled to the same rights, treatment, and standing as others.
- *Self-esteem* is conditional on recognizing one's value in relation to others and, therefore, that one is worth of being believed in. One gains self-esteem by measuring up against the performance of others, by standing out. Self-esteem is a much more complex phenomenon than the tattered notion of self-esteem that has led to questionable pedagogical practices of shallow and "feel-good" praise.

- *Self-identity* is conditional on recognizing that one's "self" is irreducible to anyone else's judgments or categories. One gains a sense of self-as-other by being experienced as a true other (with deference).

Children want to be seen not just for what they are but for who they are in their uniqueness. Self-identity means recognizing the formative potential between being and becoming. It is the openness created in the recognition of the difference that the temporality of past, present, and future makes in our living and evolving self. I am now what I will be tomorrow. Ones sense of self may also be experienced in a manner that is highly meaningful, as this young woman shows:

> By noon I had left the valley and was skiing hard up the headwall. The incline was steep. The snow was crusted over with ice, and I knew I was foolish to be here alone where no other skiers venture. Now I stop for a moment to glance back into the sloping "U" of the glacial valley below. From this angle I can see the upper chutes from where massive avalanches have descended. And here I stand, alone and exposed to the elements. I push on up the last few feet of the slope and stand still on the edge. The mountain peaks rising majestically above me.
>
> I gain a view of the spectacular amphitheater stretching in front of me. The sun beats down on the already-brilliant snow giving the entire setting an unparalleled radiance. I pan the deep steep-walled basin ahead, quite indescribable in its frozen beauty. So intense is the silence, the solitude, that I become keenly aware of myself, my physical being. My bare forearms look oddly out of place, as do the skis, which protrude awkwardly before me. I begin to feel conspicuous in my ungainliness, as though some immensity is silently watching and can hear my wildly-pounding heart. Yet I know there can be no one else in this magnificent place.
>
> As I recommence my ascent to the summit, the rocky crags towering above me blur, and I know that I have had a singular experience; and that I will never again stand in just such a moment, on such a day, in such a place.

A profound sense of self-identity may occur in the experience of depthful awe and wonder when one senses that one is seen by or tied into something immense or cosmic.

The pedagogy of regard and recognition asks: In what ways and under what conditions can students "realize" themselves in the various domains of self-identity—at private, personal, intersubjective, social, and existential levels. These various regions are not structured like stages or hierarchies; they may intersect, overlap, mix, or move in and out of the experiential relational spheres of a person's lifeworld.

Feeling and knowing oneself "being seen and being known" needs to be studied for the way it is deeply implicated in education, learning, personal growth, and for the ways it shapes pedagogical relations between teacher and students. The pedagogical framing or order of the school or educational system can be seen as a fragile structure of complex and graduated relations of social and personal identity.

Being seen is more than being acknowledged. For a young person it means experiencing being seen by the mother, father, or teacher. It means being confirmed as existing, as being a unique person. Not all experiences of being seen have this quality, of course. Lucky is the child who is being seen regularly with pedagogical discernment.

A real teacher knows how to see children—notices a shyness, a certain mood, a feeling of expectation. Real seeing in this sense uses more than eyes. When I see a child for whom I have responsibility, I see the child with my body. In the sensory quality of my gesture, the tilt of my head, a certain bounce in my feet, my body sees the child's manner of starting this day, and the child experiences being seen. So to really see a child at the beginning and completion of each day is to give that child his or her place in specific time and space.

Such a teacher knows that each school day has a specific wholeness, a color, a significance for each child. No school day can be repeated. It may seem a cumbersome ritual to shake each child's hand twice each day, and indeed another teacher might greet each child with a warm smile and comment. But whether the greeting is a physical or a verbal handshake, the teacher who makes the effort touches each child. How easy it is, otherwise, to let days go by without being in touch with certain children. The quiet and "easy" child can remain untouched for quite some time.

Similarly the disturbing behavior of the difficult or "problem" child is often related to the child's need to receive attention. Especially in our large, comprehensive high schools, there are many young people who move from class to class, from school year to school year, without ever really being "seen" by teachers. These are the children no teacher really knows, about whom teachers cannot speak. Some teachers in large educational institutions are responsible for hundreds of youngsters each day. Such contexts breed technocratic acts. Even those teachers who try to interest and inspire students rarely have an opportunity to discover how interest is experienced and lived by their students. Such a teacher is a minister without congregation. Few such teachers ever make real "home" visits with their students.

The important pedagogical theme of "being seen" and "being known" is that the child emancipates the self through the parent/teacher and so forth. The formation of self is not only a self-formative process; it also occurs through the mediation of others who open themselves and give of themselves. Teachers as pedagogues give their students access to the world, and more importantly, they give access to the dialogue that they themselves hold with the world and with what is other. Thus, pedagogically empowered teachers give themselves and give of themselves.

A thoughtful parent or an effective teacher is not necessarily one who can construct or control a child's every possible experience. But a thoughtful educator might be one who can catch a question and deepen it with a quiet gesture. "I have quite a few conversations with Michael about questions that concern and preoccupy him," says his kindergarten teacher. "This morning he asked, 'Where does the earth come from?' So I told him that people have been wondering about that question for a long time, and I offered him some of the stories people have provided as possible answers to it. I wanted to keep the question open for him, not fix it with an answer."

What is a good story to answer a child's question? A good story does not automatically orient the child to the natural order of modern science. The child is not necessarily asking for causal explanations of natural phenomena. "Why do the leaves turn color?" Many answers are possible: "It's nature's way of saying that trees need a rest." "The autumn leaves make the world beautiful before the winter arrives." "See how nice it is to smell and walk through the fallen colored leaves." An appropriate answer for a particular child is a story that belongs to that child. A good story provides an answer that remembers the child's interest in questioning. A tactful educator will keep alive the interest that produced the child's question.

Who Am I?

"Who am I?" Not "*What* am I?" but "*Who* am I?" is a profoundly pedagogical question. The question "Who am I" can be experienced in a complex and ambiguous manner. It is an experience that is "deeper" than the sudden experience of self-consciousness that has to do with the reflexive experience of being an "I." The wonder of the question "Who am I?" presumes the awareness that "I exist" or that "I am here." Many people have looked at themselves in the mirror and experienced the sudden confusing realization of the existential fact of being in the world. The question, "Why am I here?" or "What am I doing here?" are questions that do not really have answers. And therefore, these are experiences of real wonder.

But the question "Who am I?" seems to be a wondering that does need an answer. But what could this answer be? For those who, like me, have been stirred by the compelling music of Supertramp, the same question sounds plaintively and even accusatively in the emotionally arresting lyrics of "The Logical Song," a song about school. It reflects on the modern school that teaches the child to be logical at the cost of what a pedagogically sensitive education might have been.

> When I was young, it seemed that life was so wonderful,
> a miracle, oh it was beautiful, magical....
> But then they send me away to teach me how to be sensible,

> logical, responsible, practical.
> And they showed me a world where I could be so dependable, clinical, intellectual, cynical.

One must play the song at an appropriate volume in the stillness of one's own being to catch its powerful pedagogical condemnation and appeal.

> At night, when all the world's asleep,
> the questions run so deep...
> I know it sounds absurd
> but please tell me who I am,
> who I am, who I am, who I am?

Indeed, the request to tell me "who I am" is absurd. Not only because nobody can give a pedagogically appropriate answer to that question but also because what is most inner is also most secret. Sartre has argued persuasively in his famous inceptual essay "The Transcendence of the Ego" that there is no "I" that can be equated with the self that is somehow at the center of everyday experience. When saying, "I thought that...," then this "I" is never existentially identical with the one who was doing the thinking. When I ask, "Who am I?," the "I" who asks the question is not the same as the "I" who is being questioned. Just so, in "The Logical Song" the "I" is already objectified from the flow of subjectivity. This is the "I" that reflects on itself. It asks: please tell me who I am. And then the plaintive repetition of the chorus line: "Please tell me who I am" that confronts us with the realization that schools were not meant to be institutions where wonder and meaningfulness are banned from the curriculum.

In the poem "Dauer der Kindheit" (Duration of Childhood) Rainer Maria Rilke (2015) also describes this fragile experience of wonder in the child who stares at himself in the mirror, and is confronted by the puzzle of his own name, his own existence. Rilke's poem is more sensitive to the phenomenality of the wondering child than the Supertramp song. The child in Rilke's poem simply wonders: "Who? Who?" But then the parents come home again and disrupt this magical moment of self-discovery. For Rilke, the others (the parents) become the obstacle for the child's searching and coming to himself: "Once more he belongs to them" (1982, pp, 264, 265; 2015).

In *The Self Illusion* Bruce Hood (2012) examines our sense of self-experience and argues that the self is an illusion, which does not mean that the self does not exist but that it is not what we think it is: an individual who somehow inhabits our body. He uses an incident from the puerile movie *Zoolander* as an example of raising the question "Who am I?"

> After his career has faltered, über-male model Derek Zoolander looks at his reflection in the muddy puddle next to the sidewalk and asks himself, "Who

am I?" To answer this he decides that he must embark on a journey home. It's a familiar story of self-discovery—where we seek to find the answer to who we are by following the trail of evidence right back to our childhood.... We think of our self as travelling a path in time from childhood to adulthood, punctuated by life events and the people along the way who have influenced us and shaped who we are. (p. 71)

But who is this self who travels back along the memory narratives of our past? Hood suggests that it is the enigmatic "looking glass self" of the sociologist Charles Horton Cooley, who argued that no self exists apart from the one reflected back to us by others: "Spouse, family, boss, colleagues, lover, adoring fans, and beggar in the street each hold a looking glass up to us every time we interact, and we present a different self" (Hood, 2012, p. 72). But the self reflected back to us by all those from our past and from every time we interact in the present is not a stable self; rather, it is a different self. Furthermore, we cannot really know how others see us. And, in turn, others may think that they know me but they cannot know all the different contexts in which I exist. So, paradoxically, I am not what I think I am and I am not what you think I am; rather, says Hood, "I am what I think that you think I am" (p. 72). However, Hood does not notice that, in his narrative this self as *who* has now slid into the self as *what*. But, of course, the question is not "What am I?" but "Who am I?" And it is the *who* question that is confounding.

Authors who have not forgotten to think mindfully may inspire us. In trying to answer the question "Who Am I?" the famous poet and author E. E. Cummings observed that the question comprises two problems, united by a certain wholly mysterious moment that signifies self-discovery. "Until this mysterious moment," he says, "I am only incidentally a writer: primarily I am the son of my parents and whatever is happening to him. After this moment, the question 'who am I?' is answered by what I write—in other words, I become my writing." But, this is a superficial answer. More essentially the question "Who Am I?" is somehow forever shrouded in mystery. And yet we must try to penetrate this mystery: "And thus," Cummings says, "we arrive at the parents of a longlost personage, who is these parents' child" (1953/2014).

For the child in Rilke's poem, the question "Who am I?" signifies a moment of self-recognition that is wholly mysterious. Cummings too points at the inceptual pedagogical significance of this question that lies at the beginning of our personal existence and yet can never be answered in a conceptual psychological manner—and even less in the manner that the school describes the identities of students in terms of test results, achievement profiles, and learning outcomes. At best the answer can only be evoked in the meaningful encounter with the mystery of the self itself. The fascinating significance of this search for self-identity does not lie in a determinate answer but in the reflexive experience of the wondering of the question itself. If considered sensitively, the question "Who Am I?" lets each of us, as singular persons, experience the truth of our own singularity. In the delicate memories of his father and mother, Cummings adds a pedagogical dimension to his question of self-identity. For him, as a grown-up child, the mystery of the self finds its source in the miraculous events of the lives of his mother and father. Only in this inceptuality, he suggests, can you probe "the mystery which you have been, the mystery which you shall be, and the mystery which you are."

The question "Who am I?" is obviously a very different self-experience from the question of the self that is being "constructed"—rather than pondered—in online blogs and in virtual environments of social networking technologies such as Facebook and Twitter. The constructing of virtual or digital self-presentations may help or hinder in the process of becoming a healthy and reflective self. Just so, the practice of making and sharing snapshot selfies and other digital self-images can confuse or contribute to the realization of a positive and mature sense of self-identity.

The Secret Self

Langeveld shows that the child needs the experience of a special "place" for self-discovery. The "secret place" is the place where the child withdraws from the presence of others. Langeveld sensitively describes what it is like for a child to quietly sit in this place to which the adult does not pay attention. This special space experience does not involve the child in activities such as hide and seek, spying on others, doing mischief, or playing with toys; rather, what we see is that the child just sits there while perhaps gazing dreamily into the distance. What is going on here?

Langeveld describes this space experience as a place of growth. The child may find such space experience under a table, behind a heavy curtain, inside a discarded box, or wherever there is a corner where he or she can hide or withdraw. This is where the child may come to "self-understanding," as it were. As a clinical child psychologist and pedagogue, Langeveld's intention is to show the formative pedagogical value of the experience of the secret place for the growing child. He describes it as "normally an unthreatening place for the young child to withdraw" (1983, p. 13). Langeveld says things like "the actual experience of the secret place is always grounded in a mood of tranquility, peacefulness: It is a place where we can feel sheltered, safe, and close to that with which we are intimate and deeply familiar" (1983, p. 13). He portrays the various modalities in terms of which the secret place may be experienced. Of course, sometimes children may experience certain spaces such as the dark cellar, the spooky attic, the mysterious closet as uncomfortable, as looming danger:

> The phenomenological analysis of the secret place of the child shows us that the distinctions between the outer and inner world melt into a single, unique, personal world. Space, emptiness, and also darkness reside in the same realm where the soul dwells. They unfold in this realm and give form and sense to it by bringing this domain to life. But sometimes this space around us looks at us with hollow eyes of disappointment; here we experience the dialogue with nothingness; we are sucked into the spell of emptiness, and we experience the loss of a sense of self. This is also where we experience fear and anxiety. The mysterious stillness of the curtain, the enigmatic body of the closed door, the deep blackness of the grotto, the stairway, and the spying window which is placed too high to look through, all these lead to the experience of anxiety. They may seem to guard or cover an entry-way or passage. The endless stairway, the curtains which move by themselves, the door which is suspiciously ajar, or the door which slowly opens, the strange silhouette at the windows are all symbols of fear. In them we discover the humanness of our fears. (1983, p. 16)

But during the fourth and fifth year of life the "I" gradually begins to assert itself against the world, the anxieties disappear in degrees. These are the beginnings of the initial developments of a unique human personality in which the first opposition between world and "I" becomes conscious and in which the world is experienced as "other," says Langeveld. Now the secret space becomes invitational:

> The indeterminate place speaks to us, as it were. In a sense, it makes itself available to us. It offers itself, in that it opens itself. It looks at us in spite of the fact and because of the fact that it is empty. This call and this offering of availability are an appeal to the abilities of the child to make the impersonal space into his very own, very special place. And the secrecy of this place is first of all experienced as the secrecy of "my-own-ness." Thus in this void, in this availability, the child encounters the "world." Such an encounter the child may have experienced before in different situations. But this time he or she encounters the world in a more addressable form—everything which can occur in this openness and in this availability, the child must actively fashion or at least actively allow as a possibility. (1983, p. 17)

In spite of quoting these sentences from Langeveld, it is quite inadequate to summarize or paraphrase Langeveld's text, as it is precisely the quality of the entire text that leads one to recognize reflectively what the experience may be like for a child. In the journal article, "The Secret Place in the Life of the Child" we can also observe how Langeveld locates the normative in the phenomenological account of the experience of the secret place. He shows not only what the experience is like; he also shows how it is a pedagogically appropriate experience for the child:

> In the secret place the child can find solitude. This is also a good pedagogical reason to permit the child his secret place ... something positive grows out of the secret place as well, something which springs from the

inner spiritual life of the child. That is why the child may actively long for the secret place.

During all the stages leading to adulthood, the secret place remains an asylum in which the personality can mature; this self-creating process of this standing apart from others, this experiment, this growing self-awareness, this creative peace and absolute intimacy demand it—for they are only possible in alone-ness. (1983, p. 17)

Langeveld proposes that it is inevitable to see how the normative is intimately linked to our understanding of children's experiences because we are always confronted with real-life situations wherein we must act: we must always do what is appropriate in our interactions with children. We could say that a phenomenology of practice sponsors a pedagogical sensitivity that expresses itself in tactfulness on the part of the adult. Often the texts by Langeveld are not only insightful but also evocative. The texts not only analyze and probe the lived experience; they also "speak" to us and they may stir our pedagogical, psychological or professional sensibilities. (For a lengthy discussion about the phenomenology of practice and the language of evocation, see van Manen, 2014, pp. 240–297; see also Tyler, 1986.)

Phenomenological Pedagogy

Phenomenological pedagogy is the term that describes the general perspective taken in this book. Phenomenological pedagogy is an approach to pedagogy that places primal importance on the *experiences* of the children or young people who we teach or for whom we care. Of course, understanding the pedagogical experiences of the parents and teachers is of prime importance as well. However, the first question should always be: How did this child or these children experience this situation or event? As adults we may think that we know what children experience, but we should never simply assume that we do.

If we want to be pedagogically sensitive and available to children, then it is important to know the personal lives of these children. Of course, it is not possible to really "know" all the students we teach, but we can observe many children in informal settings such as at recess time. And sometimes we are drawn into certain situations or predicaments where we must understand the phenomenology and the psychology of the experiences of the students we teach. No doubt all teachers are sometimes drawn into the lives of young people who may experience special difficulties or significant events.

> It is recess time, and I am on playground supervision of our primary-elementary school. The playground is a stretch of concrete, partially shadowed by the old brick inner-city school building. Supervision duty means that I must forego a well-earned cup of coffee and break time. But there are benefits to this

task. Walking back and forth amongst the children across the schoolyard tells me about their lives: their joys, moods, needs, strengths, and conflicts. Some things you just "see" by being there: Who is playing with whom? Why is Carl sauntering there all by himself? Should I strike up a conversation with him? Or does he seem to need some time alone? There is Jeff picking on some little kids again. I glare at him, and Jeff lets go of his victims. Some kids ask me to help untie a knot in a long skipping rope. The boys are into skipping too, and I give some words of encouragement and demonstrate how to do Double Dutch. The kids laugh. Tease. Where did I learn to skip? I joke that I used to be a boxer. Then I proceed with my walk.

Already there are some kids walking beside me. Marie is just content to walk quietly. David strolls along too. He likes to hang around. Hands in his pocket. Deftly kicking little pebbles that lie in his path. But Crystal is chatting away. She pulls my arm, steps half in front of me, and looks into my face. Am I listening? Her voice has a gossipy tone.

"Her parents are always fighting," says Crystal.

I realize that Crystal is talking about Nicole, her best friend and grade six student. I remind myself that Nicole was not at school this morning. She is rarely absent.

"Where is Nicole?" I ask. "Is she sick?" But Crystal ignores my question.

"And Nicole has told me a secret that she and her mom may be running away soon. Please don't tell her that I let you in on the secret." (I promise my oath of honor as a teacher).

"It was really weird," she continues. "Two cars pulled up at the park where we were playing yesterday. The car doors flew open almost at the same time. Nicole's mother was in the one car. Her father in the other. Each was shouting for Nicole to come into their car."

Crystal is silent for a moment. Her face reflects a strange serenity. Both Crystal and Nicole are so much alike: both children of poverty, family violence, and abuse. And both are such fine kids—affectionate, gentle, bright, eager to learn. Flowers grow in the most unlikely places.

"You know, I felt so terrible for her," says Crystal. "I know that Nicole loves her mother so much more than her father, who beats her. She is really scared of him. And he beats her mom too. Anyway, Nicole's mother called her to get into her car. She was yelling really loud. 'Quickly! Come on! Quickly!' But you know, Nicole's father . . . he was cursing and telling her to come with him. And oh, Nicole started balling too. For a moment she just stood there, looking at them, weeping. She was screaming really. . . . Isn't it awful to have to choose between your mother and your father?"

Crystal looks emotionally distressed as she collects yesterday's memory.

"And you know what was so weird?" She halts for a moment as if to add drama: "The car Nicole went into . . . it was her father's car."

This anecdote is experientially rich because it shows us both the experience of the teacher who appears to be pedagogically attentive to the children on the school grounds, and it contains the experience of one of the students who shares a story with the teacher. Now, the sense we (as readers) make of this incident is an expression of our personal pedagogy. How do we understand why Crystal is sharing this secret? And why would Nicole have chosen the father over the mother? Is she fearing that her mother is already in danger of abuse from the father and so the mother cannot offer security and safety? How is the teacher to respond in this situation with Crystal? What should he say? Do? What is it that Crystal needs? And what could the teacher possibly do for Nicole?

The approach is called phenomenological because it requires that we try to grasp the lived or prereflective meanings that lie at the basis of these experiences. For example, in the above story the teacher is challenged to understand what it is like for a child, like Crystal, to share a secret that is a burden for this child and yet she feels she must tell the teacher she trusts. At the same time the teacher is aware of how emotionally complex it must be Crystal to have seen, from a distance, the drama of her friend Nicole to have to choose between a mother and a father whereby the choice is colored by fear: physical fear, fear of abandonment, fear for her mother, and so on. But these phenomenological insights into childhood secrecy, making impossible choices, fear of punishment, fear of insecurity must be interpreted in the context of these real lives of Crystal and Nicole. So phenomenological pedagogy must mobilize two kinds of insights: phenomenological insights into the meanings of certain lived experiences (phenomena), and psychological insights into the concrete life situations of these particular children, Crystal and Nicole. It is in the tension of these insights into experiential realities that the teacher must know what to say, what to do, and how to act tactfully.

In addition to the phenomenological and psychological considerations there are also additional ethical and perhaps ontotheological considerations that need to go into a pedagogical judgement or action. The following story told by a high school student shows the need for a larger ethical perspective as well. It is a story about the results of a classroom test given by a teacher.

> "Have you marked our tests yet?" some kids asked the teacher.
> "Yes, I have finished marking, but I cannot give the tests back. I need to keep them on file. If you like, I'll read the marks you received right now. Does anyone have any objections to that?"
> Immediately some kids urged him on. The class period was almost over. But I was not so sure that I liked him to do that. It could be embarrassing. As I looked around I noticed many others who were against publicizing their marks.
> The teacher too must have sensed the uncertainty because he said, "If you do not like to have your marks read aloud then raise your hand."
> Immediately more than half the class put up their hands. But rather than offering a different solution, the teacher seemed annoyed. He closed his book and said, "Well, it does not matter. You'll see your marks reflected in your grades on your report cards."

Now many kids started to hassle. Some turned against their classmates. Others tried to persuade the teacher to change his mind. Of course, the real smart kids, they enjoy hearing how well they do in front of the others. At first I thought, "Well, all right then." Because I was really eager to hear how well I had done. My marks are usually in the eighties anyway. But as I looked around me I noticed how Jane was really nervous. She is not a top student and always suffers severely from bad test results. I have even seen her cry over her test marks.

For the last time now the teacher repeated if anyone would still object hearing their marks in public. Nobody raised their hands. Nobody... except Jane!

At that very moment I realized how hard it must be for her to become the scapegoat in the eyes of everyone else. So almost without thinking I too put up my hand.

The teacher looked at her and then he looked at me. I felt totally terrible. I hardly heard the boos from all the other kids.

The teacher shrugged his shoulders, closed his book with a bang, and walked out of the room.

In this story a student shows a fine sensitivity that is of pedagogical significance. Although we should not shoulder young people with pedagogical responsibilities, it is clear that sometimes situations unfold where they do take such role, as in families where older children must take care of the younger ones. But this classroom anecdote is also significant in that it shows the potentially destructive aspects of approaches to teaching that emphasize competition for grades, the ranking of students, and the embarrassments that may cause. We have to ask what kinds of qualities this teacher is instilling in his students and what effects such teaching strategies have on the formation of character. And yet it is exactly here where a fellow student empathically enacts a value of self-sacrifice. Experiential stories like this should be part of the preparation of the pedagogical sensibilities in novice teachers. These are the thoughtful pedagogical elements that condition the readiness for tactful teaching.

Chapter Nine

The Phenomenology of Student Experience

The previous chapter ended with reflections on the nature of phenomenological pedagogy and the observation that the critical element of phenomenological pedagogy is that one starts with actual lived-through experience. Now, educators commonly speak of student experiences. Teachers plan student experiences. But do we really know what happens when a student has an experience? For example, do we know what it is like for a student to experience their name? This seems like a simple question, but there may be more to it (van Manen, McClelland, and Plihal, 2007).

In everyday life, in schools and classrooms, teachers call on students, address students by their names, pronounce, mispronounce, or confuse their names, and sometimes forget student names altogether. As adults, we may have had many experiences with naming, misnaming, or name forgetting. We may have heard the story of how we came to be named as we are. The name was chosen before we were born, or parents waited until they saw us and then decided on a name. Or the girls in the family take the mother's name and the boys take the father's name, or perhaps we didn't receive a permanent name until a ritual in adolescence settled a name upon us. Some of us received shortened names or nicknames—honorable or dishonorable, humorous or affectionate. Giving names seems an ordinary and yet a most peculiar act. What occurs when one gives a name? asks Derrida (1995b). What does one give? One does not offer a thing. One delivers nothing. And yet something comes to be. The act of naming seems indeed a wondrous phenomenon.

The stories of who named us and why that particular name was chosen are a link to our origin and take on significant meaning for us. When someone calls us by our name (especially when this someone is a significant person), then we may feel addressed in our singularity. Calling a person by his or her first name may create a sense of intimacy and trust. Sales people of all kinds know well this phenomenological feature of naming. And sometimes we may feel irritated when a sales person adopts a tone of intimacy with our name that seems misplaced. Teachers also know that naming is a crucial aspect of the relation they maintain with students. Many teachers try to memorize their students' names early in the new school term; they realize that it is important to be able to recognize and call their students by their proper name.

Naming is recognition. We are able to recognize aspects of our world by naming them. Not only do we make things recognizable by naming them, but also we make them real somehow. That is why Gusdorf suggests that "to name is to call into existence" (1965, p. 38). And just as we call things into being by naming them, so we ourselves need to be named to exist for others and for ourselves. Things that fall outside of our linguistic reach may stay more indeterminate. And this is also true for proper names of people. The strange thing is that people, even those we think we know, do to some extent remain indeterminate until we remember their names. Somehow, by being able to call them by their name, we seem to be able to reach them and stand in meaningful relation to them. When, as teachers, we call students by name, we point to the singularity of a specific student, and we may take for granted that calling the name calls the student into relation with us.

To be called by my name is to receive recognition, and to receive recognition literally means to be known. Someone who recognizes me thereby acknowledges my existence, my very being. This is not the same as fleetingly noticing people whom one passes in a busy street. To cognize means to know, but to re-cognize is to know again in the sense of becoming part of people's memory. When I recognize someone, I revive my cognitive experience: this person has become part of my experience, my life history. He or she exists for me; this person is now memorable. It is not surprising, therefore, that naming and recognition play such a critical role in people's lives. One's very existence depends on being named and recognized—to be known by others. To paraphrase Descartes: "I am recognized, therefore I exist." The experience of recognition is inextricably intertwined with selfhood, identity, and one's sense of personal being.

In light of these preliminary reflections, it is strange that the pedagogical significance of students' experiences of naming has received virtually no attention. How do students actually experience being called by their names? What it is like for them to be misnamed, nicknamed? Or how do they experience incidents when their names are forgotten altogether? Asking students about their name experiences in school and classrooms does not necessarily yield experiential results. When we ask individual students questions about their name experiences, they may say things such as, "It is important that the teacher knows who you are." "The science teacher still did not know my name by Christmas time!" "I don't like it when a teacher calls me by my last name." Comments such as these suggest that name experiences are important to students and that they are able to tap into these experiences if only we give them the opportunity to do so. But it is important to distinguish between student accounts that offer interpretations, views, or beliefs about name experiences and student accounts that describe as much as is reasonably possible the experiences as lived through. A phenomenological inquiry requires "lived experience" accounts as data for reflection (see van Manen, 1997; 2014). To this end students are prompted to describe their experiential moments themselves. So the phenomenological pedagogical question is, how do we orient to student experiences?

Orienting to Student Experience

Researchers who have taken a narrative or ethnographic approach in their inquiries tend to be sensitive to lived experience—experiences as lived through. By way of example we note a researcher who is aware of the danger of treating experience as a reductive concept, a philosophical idea, or an abstract variable. Karin Dahl (1995), who is interested in students' early reading and writing practices, articulates the importance of focusing on the students' experience: "We need to listen to them, pay attention to what they show us about themselves and their views" (p. 124). Dahl suggests that taking student experience seriously may give teachers more relevant understandings and insights for teaching. "Learning from children's voices allows us to know at a deeper level who children are as learners and, because we have that knowledge, to expand and enrich our sense of what it means to teach" (p. 130). In her ethnographic study Dahl offers descriptions of the child Addie, an "angry girl" in first grade:

> This teacher "called the shots" and Addie was put through her paces with no time for stalling or power plays. Addie would rebel, having tantrums over such requirements as making the letter d correctly or reading a sentence accurately. She wanted it to be her way, whether it was letter formation, word identification, or the decision about the next activity. She acted out and made loud groans in defiance; but the teacher kept the lesson going. It was a battle of wills. These sessions were difficult for both teacher and learner. (p. 128)

Rather than reduce student experience to some variable or general concept, Dahl aims to give us a sense of the reality of the classroom and of Addie's mood or disposition. Yet this description could go further, letting Addie herself tell what it is like for her in this class. Perhaps Dahl believes that a grade one child cannot tell how she feels in a situation. Dahl's description is told from the adult perspective, not Addie's. In addition, the observational account lacks concreteness and specificity. We are told how Addie would rebel in these kinds of situations, but we do not learn how Addie "rebelled" in this specific moment when the observation took place. A more careful look may show that the child's experiences in this situation were actually much more complex and multifaceted. By placing the terms "rebel" and "battle of wills" on Addie's behavior, her actual lived experience disappears from view. What did Addie really experience? And how might this experience be best described? We would have to practice close observation, trying to understand her experience from subtleties of her gestures, physiognomy, utterances, her eyes, and so forth.

What was it about being in the reading recovery room on that day that was important to Addie? Would she rather have been somewhere else? Or somewhere else in the room? How did she experience the teacher's presence? And the researcher's presence? Their gestures, glances, and tone of voice? Their instructions? Their attentiveness, inattentiveness, misattentiveness? Certainly obtaining an account from a child in the primary grades poses special challenges, but the use of observations alone still leaves us considering student experience from the outside. This example from Dahl's work is taken not to criticize her work per se but to illustrate how commonly qualitative methodologies may unwittingly lead researchers to speak on behalf of students rather than letting students speak for themselves.

And even if the researcher lets the students themselves speak, these accounts may still be *about* their experiences. When students are asked to tell about their school, they are likely to respond with comments such as "I have ten friends or so and at the breaks [time] I usually play football.... My school is red, it was green before.... We can play outside, we can draw, we can play with Lego. In natural sciences we get to taste different fruits. In handicraft lessons we can make balls of wool. We usually paint several figures" (Allodi, 2002, pp. 188, 189). When researchers such as Allodi ask students to tell about school experiences, they tend to receive general descriptions *about* experiences rather than descriptive accounts of experiences as they happened, as the children actually *lived* through them.

Naming the Experience of Naming

It is true that even with older children or young people, obtaining students' accounts is not easy. Some researchers feel that they have collected students' experiential accounts by interviewing them or by asking them to write about their experiences. But, as suggested above, what they may have gathered are opinions, perceptions, views, and explanations by the students, not accounts of the experiences themselves. To give an example of what is meant by taking serious a fuller meaning of the notion of student experience, here follow some accounts from students.

The focus here is on the student's experience of the most elemental and basic aspects of classroom life: getting to know and becoming known by

THE PHENOMENOLOGY OF STUDENT EXPERIENCE

the teacher, including being called by one's name. Here is an account told by a grade nine student. The student describes an incident experientially—from the inside out, as it were—by recalling the experience as it happened:

> "Square roots, class!" Mrs. Richards exclaims excitedly. "There's just so many ways to look at them."
> Sitting in math class early on a Monday morning is never a really exciting experience. However, here I am, for I have no other choice. We are taking notes, and as all teachers do, Mrs. Richards is trying to get us actively involved in the discussion. Personally I don't see how anyone could be interested in square root signs (but let's keep that quiet).
> Dutifully I raise my hand to share my insight to her first question.
> Catching my eye, Mrs. Richards calls out, "Yes, Stiffany!"
> I pause for a moment, certain that I have just misunderstood; she probably has just said my name "Stephanie." Glancing around the room, I spy Tiffany, who gives me "the look." It is a "did-she-just-say-what-I-think-she-said?" kind of look. Tiffany is cool, though I don't know her very well.
> After this momentary pause it is evident to everyone in the room what happened just now, and immediately laughter breaks out.
> Mrs. Richards, however, seems to be unaware of her mistake of mingling my name Stephanie with Tiffany's. I desperately try to look as though I have no idea about the sudden uproar and share my thoughts about the square root problem with stifled giggles in between.
> We return to taking notes, but my attention is elsewhere. I must say that I am rather pleased about the slight name confusion and not at all offended.
> Now, whenever I see Tiffany in the halls, we always call one another Stiffany or Stiffy. I find it rather cute and comical. We have become friends. This new nickname seems to have connected me to Tiffany in a simple but significant manner.

What do we see here that we do not see in the account about Addie? When Stephanie relates her actual experience in a descriptive form, it becomes visible for us in a way that it is not visible using other means of description. How would this account differ from the one that Dahl may have written as observer? Would she have caught on about the name confusion? Would she have been able to describe the subtle significance that is involved in naming and misnaming? Of course, we can never know for sure what Stephanie's experience was or completely understand it (that is not the aim of our interest here), but in this type of experiential telling we see hints of what the situation might be like for her. We notice how the misnaming experience seems to have created a bond between Stephanie and Tiffany. The moment Stephanie describes is a simple one, and we see it repeated in various forms in many classrooms every year. Yet in this ordinary moment there may be something worth noting. Even though Stephanie was not offended by being called Stiffany, there must be something slightly amiss in Mrs. Richards blending the names. Both laughter and Stephanie's focus on the episode while the class returned to square roots show us that the mistakenly called name must matter in some way.

Through these experiential accounts we gain a sense of how important names are to students. After all, when a teacher calls a student by name, then something is called into being: the student as unique person. But sometimes the student is prevented from experiencing a sense of personal identity and uniqueness because of a teacher's casual habit or indifference to such sensibilities.

> "Go get 'em, Mac!" he says. I sigh, but leave the bench anyways. What possesses him to give me a nickname? Does a nickname really help anybody anyways? Is Benjamin not short enough for him? He could call me Ben. Or can he not remember? Yes, maybe that is it. Maybe he just cannot remember my name. As I ponder that, I almost miss the puck as it slides down to my end. Quickly I recover and shoot it back down the ice to one of our forwards—a player whose name our coach can spell backward. I am a little upset. After all, this has been going on all season. "Come on, Mac. Keep your head in the game." He must know, though. I mean, how can you coach a hockey team and not know your own players' names? The whistle blows, and I skate back to the bench, trying to think of any other names that our coach has forgotten. There is that one kid he calls Bobby, but I think that is a reference to Bobby Orr. Same with Fuehr, Wayne, and Rocket, all great old-time hockey players. I also suspect he enjoys naming people something they're not. Can there be some fabulous hockey player named Mac? or possibly nicknamed Mac? It doesn't seem very likely to me, for I know a lot about hockey and the players and not once have I heard of a Mac.
>
> So what should I do? What can I do? I have to make him use my proper name. How can I go around as Mac for another year? I walk up to our coach. "Hey Mac." "Sir, my name is Benjamin, remember!" "Well, sure I do," he says. I exhale a sigh of relief that I'd been holding, pleased that is over with and a little embarrassed that this name thing had gotten me all worked up.
>
> "Your shift's up. Now get out there, Mac!"

Benjamin does not mention in this story that his last name is MacPherson. Perhaps he does not realize the physical education teacher is playing on his last name. Or perhaps he does not like to be called by his last name, especially a nickname version of his last name. But what matters is that Benjamin does not like being called Mac.

Naming is a relational experience, but by misnaming the students, the teacher of Stephanie and Tiffany gets it wrong, seemingly without being aware of what goes on with the students. In contrast, Benjamin's coach seems to want to get it wrong. Something about gender could be at play here. The coach is playing *tough*, as is not uncommon in physical education classes, where the relation between coach and players tends to be boisterous. The point is that only through listening to the student do we learn that, indeed, an experience occurred and what the nature is of such experience.

Although the focus in this chapter is not on teachers' experiences of naming students or being named by them, it is worth noting that attending to teachers' experiences can stimulate reflection on students' experiences. Here is an example from a teacher:

> The first few times that I meet my classes I remind myself to look over the class list to make sure I know all the names of the students. As I quickly rehearse the names, I try to connect these names with the persons to whom these names belong. Soon some of these students I will know so well that I no longer have to remember them. I will simply know them. I will have trouble remembering the names of other students for quite some time.
>
> For example, in my grade nine class I have a boy who looks very much like his older brother who was in my class last year. During the first few weeks of school I kept confusing and calling Tim by his brother's name, Don. One day, when this happened again, I could see that Tim was clearly annoyed even though he did not say anything. So spontaneously I made a public apology to him. Of course, I felt embarrassed having to do this, and my confession was somewhat like self-punishment. But I knew it important to let Tim know that he mattered to me. I told him how sorry I was that I kept confusing his brother's name and how I appreciated him for who he was.

Although the teacher may never have reflected on the phenomenological significance of the student's experience of being named—in this case by a wrong name—the teacher does seem to realize that this is not an unimportant matter. The teacher senses how misnaming the student by his brother's name somehow does violence to his sense of self and self-identity—for who he is in his own right. Here follows a student's description of an experience of being connected to a sibling by name:

> "Sally Tilburn?" "Here." The first day of school has finally arrived. Mrs. Larson is taking attendance. My older brother, Ben, attended this school for three years. He set the reputation for me. Let's just say he wasn't exactly the teachers' favorite student. The benches in the hallway saw a lot of Ben throughout his school years. Every teacher I meet and talk to on this crisp September morning makes this connection to Ben. When I confess my name is Sally Tilburn, I can see the glimmer of hope in their eyes. Hope that I am not like my brother. "Tilburn, as in Ben Tilburn?" "Yes," I respond. "Oh . . . I see," Mrs. Larson's voice lowers, no doubt remembering the times she had with Ben a couple years back. Everyone's eyes turn to me. The whole class realizes what type of student Ben must have been just because of the disapproving look on Mrs. Larson's face and the awkwardness it creates. I glance at her. It seems as though she has no problem remembering who Ben was. Trying to lower my head, I can only imagine what the next few years of school will be like.

How does Mrs. Larsen's association of Ben with Sally influence the possibilities for the relationship between teacher and student? When other students in the class see Mrs. Larsen's disapproving look and then turn their gaze to Sally, what are the possibilities for Sally's relationship with her classmates? When a teacher doesn't use a student's name correctly, then the student may experience immediate and often intense feelings and thoughts.

> Mrs. Smith is in a particularly foul mood this depressing Monday morning. I mean, she always seems to pick on me, but today is especially bad. Science is a dreaded subject for me, but this year has to be the worst, all because of her. I raise my hand to answer her question and am really not expecting what I'm about to hear, for I have been in her class for about eight months already. But in a horribly sharp tone she says, "Yes, Alexandria, what do you have to say?"
>
> For a moment I think about what to reply and then I say, "I'm sorry, Mrs. Smith, but that isn't my name." (I believe that I answered quite appropriately considering the mistake she just made, after having me in her class for over eight months).
>
> "Oh right, well, get on with it, then, Alexis," she answers in a terribly unkind tone.
>
> The class erupts with overflowing laughter. Jeremiah, the class clown, of course, pipes in and yells, "Her name's Alexa." And he repeats, "Alexa!"
>
> Well, that just about makes Mrs. Smith's patience snap in half. "Shush up! All of you!" she exclaims. She is obviously embarrassed. We go on with the lesson, but I can't help but notice the slight rosy tinge on her cheeks for the rest of the period. Should I be happy, or should I not be happy that she got the embarrassment she most certainly deserved?

We can hardly blame teachers for occasionally making mistakes with student names. The act of teaching is inherently improvisational. Teachers must instantly (inter)act in Kairos moments of contingency, and they must often lead their students through a myriad of activities in fast-paced environments where split-second decisions need to be made and students' comments and actions are often unexpected. So it is no surprise that teachers are bound to slip up on students' names now and then. Our discussion here is not to be critical of teachers when this happens but to call attention to students' experiences and to what it means when we try to determine what it is like for a student to have an experience. Even university students may feel sensitive to name confusions in their relations with their teachers:

> Last term I took philosophy from Professor Berg, who I really liked. And he seemed to like me because he often called on me and would say things like, "Frieda really makes an excellent point ...." or "Frieda, what do you think of this issue?" and so on.
>
> Some of my friends would laugh when Professor Berg called me by the name Frieda. But I did not mind so much because he really seemed to respect me. At

the end of the term, after writing the test, I went up to him and said, "I really liked your classes and I think you are such a wonderful teacher. I have learned so much from your philosophy classes. However, I want you to know that I am not Frieda. My name is Jane."

Professor Berg had been smiling as I thanked him but then looked shocked: "Oh, no, I am so sorry!" But I said, "Never mind—you had it partially right. My name is Jane Friedman."

There seems to be a paradox related to Frieda and Alexa: we don't really know a person if we don't know his or her name, but we can know his or her name and not really know him or her. Likewise, we may not know a person's name but have a brief encounter and now know some aspect of the person intimately. Both Jane and Alexa seem to hesitate about correcting the teacher. Perhaps they know intuitively that it can be embarrassing for a person to forget someone's name. And, of course, there is the practical challenge that it is not easy to remember all the names of the people we meet.

Many teachers would agree that the first question educators always need to ask themselves is: What do the students who are in our classes actually *experience*? More importantly, it matters less what we, as educators, *say* that children experience; more crucial is what students themselves say. For example, a teacher may believe that he is caring about a student whom he teaches, but if the student does not *experience* the teacher's act as caring, then the teacher's belief is less relevant than what the student experiences.

How to Gain Access to Student Experience

How, then, can we attempt to come to understand how students themselves experience things? We can ask students to describe specific instances of their experience in as much concrete detail as possible. We can do this by asking students to write anecdotes—short stories about single events. To understand how students experience teachers' use of their names, we may ask them the following:

> Can you recall a name experience? Think of a specific time when a teacher called you by your name or by an incorrect name—or possibly when a teacher seemed to avoid calling you by any name. Tell what happened without explaining or giving opinions about it. Just describe the experience as you lived through it. Recall what was said by the teacher, by you, and by others. How did the teacher act, talk, and use gestures? What was the tone or feeling of the interaction? What did you say, think, feel, do? (This event may have happened recently or several years ago. Do not use real names of teachers or students.)

When working with students, one must show interest in their writing and, in collaboration with the teacher, perhaps even teach them to write vivid experiential accounts. Students are given the following suggestions to increase the narrative power of the anecdote (van Manen, 1999, p. 20; 2014, pp. 249-259). An anecdote:

1. is a very short and simple story
2. usually relates one incident
3. begins close to the central moment of the experience
4. includes important concrete detail
5. often contains several quotes (what was said, done, etc.)
6. closes quickly after the climax or when the incident is passed
7. often has an effective or "punchy" last line.

Depending on the events themselves and how able students are to describe them in detailed, concrete words, the anecdotes will vary in complexity and depth. For example, the following anecdote was written by a school student who recalled an experience she had in the third grade when her class was lining up in the hallway on their way to lunch.

> Ms. Polanski was reminding us to get in two lines. "No pushing, no playing tag." She was coming down the line, but, in truth, I had hardly noticed. I had been daydreaming. Except that I suddenly felt that something brushed my face. I startled a bit and automatically turned my head . . . but then I saw that it was the teacher. She had stopped and now looked at me while continuing to stroke my hair out of my eyes. "Monica!" she said in such a nice voice that I felt completely warmed by her touch. "Monica"—that is all she said. Just my name. Then she kept on walking down the line. I think she was still talking about not leaving the cafeteria until we're excused, but I'm not sure. I just felt so special!

Compared with Stephanie's anecdote presented earlier, Monica's anecdote is simpler and yet also rich with meaning. Anecdotes can be meaningful because when students are asked to write them, it is they who recall experiences that are vivid and hold meaning for them. And it is they who relay what was said, by whom, and in what tone. The student describes how he or she felt and thought and what he or she did in the situation. In some sense the student is enabled to discover his or her own experience by writing it, and furthermore, by writing the experience it becomes real and may entice the student to now reflect on it's meanings.

From the researcher's point of view, students writing their experiences as they lived through them give the researcher access to the subjectivity of classroom life. Lived-experience descriptions, such as the anecdotes in this text, are written experiences that the researcher borrows in order to examine what meanings may inhere in them with respect to a particular phenomenon such as the name experience. The researcher can then interrogate the anecdotes, looking for what, at first reading, might be unseen, probing for deeper understanding of the situation and of the meanings the incident held for the students. For example, in Monica's anecdote we see a situation that may occur in any elementary school any time of the day. There is nothing special about lining up to go to the cafeteria, library, gym, bus, or playground. And we may observe similar gestures in teachers. So what was it about this episode that made it so significant for Monica? What was it about having her name called that led Monica to feel liked? Perhaps it was that the teacher seemed to single out Monica for no apparent reason. A touch and saying the student's name creates a moment of intimacy in the midst of an otherwise ordinary situation. In this moment of pedagogical contact Monica seems to experience being "seen" by her teacher.

However, Monica's description of her experience may also be used to reflect further on the ambiguous nature of experience itself. These reflections should make us aware that we have to be very careful with our theoretical as well as the common-sense understandings of the nature of experience. In other words, the notion of student experience that we have been trying to describe is still too simplistic. When we speak of experiences as data, then what is the nature of these data? What do we refer to when we name something an experience? Or perhaps we may ask: How are experiences experienced? Or are they?

What Is Named When We Speak of "Experience"?

Experiences seem to arise from the living flow of everyday existence. In German language this living sense is retained in the term *Erlebnis*, translated as "lived experience." Gadamer suggests that there are two dimensions of meaning to lived experience: the immediacy of experience and the content of what is experienced (1975, p. 61). Both dimensions have methodological significance for qualitative inquiry. This thought is also expressed in the well-known line from Merleau-Ponty: "The world is not what I think, but what I live through.... If one wants to study the world as lived through, one has to start with a direct description of our experience as it is" (1962, pp. xvi–xvii).

The "contents" of experiences are recognizable in the sense that we can name and describe them, or perhaps they come into being as experiences as we name and describe them. No doubt we could distinguish many more such experiences in the above student accounts. For example, in Monica's description we could distinguish the experience of waiting, of being startled, of the teacher's look, of the touch of the teacher's hand, of hearing one's name spoken in a certain tone of voice, the atmosphere of the cafeteria, and so forth. Every nameable experience seems to acquire an identity that makes it potentially distinguishable from other experiences. We could single out any of these moments we just named and ask, "What is the phenomenological meaning of that experience?" What is the phenomenology of being startled by feeling something touching our face? Next, it is possible to focus more carefully on the nature of touch and ask: How is the experience of being touched or struck by an object different from being touched by a person's hand? What is the phenomenology of the human touch? How is being touched by a friend or a teacher experienced differently from being touched by the hand of stranger?

Indeed, phenomenology always asks those sorts of questions: What is the nature and meaning of this or that experience-as-we-live-through-it? How does this phenomenon present itself as a distinguishable experience? It is often baffling how the meanings of experiences are so much more difficult to determine than the meaning of concepts, which can be studied by examining their use in language. Gadamer explains that all lived experience has a certain immediacy that eludes every determination of its ultimate meaning. Why? Because when we try to recover the contents of our experiences through memory or reflection, we are in some sense always too late. We can never recover experience as it happened in the instant of the moment. Moreover, says Gadamer, everything that is experienced "is experienced by oneself, and part of its meaning is that it belongs to the unity of this self and thus contains an unmistakable and irreplaceable relation to the whole of this one life" (1975, p. 67). Indeed, what belongs to a certain experience cannot be exhausted in what can be said of it or in what can be grasped as its meaning (Jay, 2005).

The phenomenological interest is focused on the *phenomenon* as an aspect of our existence. It tries to grasp the living sense of the moment before we have lifted it up into cognitive, conceptual, or theoretical determination or clarity. Indeed, this conceptual or theoretical clarity would be misleading or at least full of assumptions. We therefore try to come to an understanding of a phenomenon by constantly investigating and questioning these (psychological, personal, cultural, theoretical) assumptions. We ask: What is experienced in that moment before we reflect on it, before we conceptualize it, and before we even name and interpret it? Only through this type of questioning can we come to discern the complex and subtle nature of experience when we speak of *student experience*.

We need to acknowledge that even in naming a student experience we have already lifted it up, so to speak, from the raw reality of human existence. That is why we have to constantly remind ourselves that we are trying to understand not some named concept but the prereflective existent—that raw moment or aspect of existence that we lift up and bring into focus with language. Is experience ultimately a linguistic phenomenon? And how is the body involved in our experience as we live it from moment to moment? Does experience already have meaning before we are consciously aware of it? Or are these experiences more primal phenomena? And how is this prereflective moment already part of our lived experience? The point for us is not that we should try to develop philosophical answers to these questions but that we must remain aware of their openness and reach.

The Pedagogical Significance of Orienting to Student Experience

So what we are learning (coming to understand?) about any experience and the experience of naming in particular is that we need to realize that even by naming an experience, we already do violence to the prereflective nature of experience as we live it from moment to moment. And yet we must try to do the impossible and reflect on the possible meanings of the experiences that we live.

> I am a foreign student who has been in Canada only for a few months. My Chinese name, Huixia Ling Ho, is difficult to pronounce for Canadians. I am also rather quiet in my classes due to my inadequate English skills. All in all that makes me feel rather invisible in class. In one of my classes I am impressed by the teacher's ability to motivate students' participation in class discussions. The teacher learned everyone's name very quickly despite the large class size. He always calls students by their first name. However, he rarely mentions my name. I thought that I did not mind it that much. But one day, when he discussed each group project, calling each student's name as if he appreciated every member's effort, I found myself waiting for my name to be mentioned. At last it was our turn. There were four in our group. I concentrated on the teacher. He began to name the first two individuals in our group. Then, I saw him hesitate for a moment and skip my name to the fourth member. I was unrecognized. I was a bit surprised at myself. I did not expect that I would be so disappointed. I was embarrassed. I was painfully aware of my Chinese name which makes me who I am. I realize that I have become nameless, a nobody in this class.

Huixia, who is a secondary school student, shows remarkable insight into her experience. But we should realize that this awareness is only possible because she has expressed her experience in language (here in written form). She seems to realize that, at the collective level her Chinese name gives her a certain identity, but she also realizes that at the personal level her name refers to her singularity, her uniqueness. On the one hand, it is her uniqueness that is denied by the teacher not including her by her name. By the teacher forgetting or skipping her name, she cannot feel recognized—she feels nameless. On the other hand, her cultural identity is also at stake in the teacher's name forgetting. Huixia seems to experience hurt that is associated with the withholding of recognition at two levels of subjectivity: her universal subjectivity (being Chinese) and her singular subjectivity (being her own unique self).

Even though we seem to be speculating about Huixia's and, earlier, Monica's inner lives, it needs to be pointed out that this is not the intention of phenomenology. As researchers we are not the teachers of these particular students, and we are not really able to "know" Monica or Huixia as their teachers would know them. As phenomenologists we are trying to construct a qualitative text that makes the experience of naming recognizable to readers. In this recognition lies the possibility of becoming more pedagogically sensitive to the experiences of individual students such as Monica, Stephanie, Alexa, Jane, and Huixia. A teacher practitioner must be interested in his or her students' individual experiences as well as in the phenomenology of the naming experience. In concrete classroom situations the phenomenological and the personal understandings merge into a fuller phenomenological pedagogical understanding. That is why this approach was described as phenomenological pedagogy.

From the perspective of professional practitioners, there are always two pedagogical aspects to a phenomenological interest such as the student experience of naming. On the one hand, there is the experience of naming as a human phenomenon, and on the other hand, in actual teaching-learning situations there is the inner experience of this or that particular student. Of course, phenomenology, as a philosophical methodology, cannot help us understand the inner lives of particular students. As researchers, we can only focus on phenomenological understanding. And yet there is always the larger picture of the actual lifeworld where teachers must deal with the socio-psychological lives of real children. At the general level teachers can increase their thoughtfulness by reflecting on the phenomenological meaning and significance of naming, and at the level of everyday thinking and acting the teacher also needs to know pedagogically, as best as possible, how a particular student experiences a specific learning moment or a specific classroom incident. In concrete and practical pedagogical relations and situations these types of understanding—phenomenology and pedagogy—cannot really be separated. They are grasped together and enacted, as pedagogical thoughtfulness and tact, in the present instant of each teaching moment.

CHAPTER TEN
Cyber-Pedagogy

Through cable and wireless connections at home, at work, in the street, and at school, through Wi-Fi networks and wireless hotspots in hotels, coffee shops, and town squares, we are connected to each other and to our own lives. But how do we experience this connection? Social networking technologies such as Facebook, LinkedIn, Twitter, Messaging (and its numerous variations) increasingly seem to seduce their users to stay in touch, keep the happenings of their lives posted, and to reveal their inner thoughts and feelings. Social networks give access to what used to be personal, private, secret, and hidden in the lives of its users, especially the young.

At an early age children are introduced to e-life, life as mediated and lived through electronic screens and digital data. As toddlers they may have played already with the parent's smartphone or media tablet. Televisions have turned interactive. At school teachers are competing for their students' attentiveness with virtual media, Smart Boards, and software-mediated technologies such as PowerPoint. Students are messaging each other on their devices or checking contacts and interests online. Through computer-managed instructional programs teachers can have instant access to students' e-work, and they may be able to exercise electronic supervision of student performances and activities. In other words, a teacher can monitor every move that students make as they touch their keyboards or screens. In a manner of speaking, teachers can "see" what and how their students think as the students interact with their screen.

The Inner Self

The idea that private thoughts and feelings inhabit some kind of inner space or inner self has a curious history in Western cultures, dating back at least to the Greek mythology of Momus, the lesser-known god of mockery and sarcasm, and his conflict with Hephaestus, the divinity of technology, fire, and the crafts. Hephaestus designed, among other things, the thunderbolts

---

Pedagogical Tact: Knowing What to Do When You Don't Know What to Do, by Max van Manen, 171–178.
© 2015 Taylor & Francis. All rights reserved.

for Zeus; he fashioned the invincible armor for Achilles, and he made arrows for Eros, the god of love. In addition, Hephaestus created the first woman after Zeus had ordered that there be a new kind of human being because Prometheus had only included one gender, which was male. And so Hephaestus formed the first woman from clay, whereupon Zeus breathed life into her. The woman's name was Pandora.

The legend tells that one day Hephaestus became involved in a dispute with Athena, who had conceived a dwelling, and Poseidon, who had made a bull. They were arguing about which was the superior creation. So Momus, son of Nyx (goddess of the night or dark), was requested to arbitrate and appraise the creations. Now, Momus was known for his critical skills, and he immediately started to mock the house because it had not been made moveable so as to travel or to be able to avoid living next to bad neighbors, he ridiculed the bull for not having eyes positioned above his horns to let the bull take better aim when he gored something, and he criticized Hephaestus's creation of the woman for not having placed a window or door into her breast so that one could see her secret thoughts and feelings.

Thus, as the god of poets and authors, Momus became the first to express the desire to access what was hidden in the human heart by means of a technology of surveillance. Momus's mockery caused him to be expelled by Zeus from Mount Olympus. It may be noted, in passing, that Momus had also made the mistake of ridiculing Zeus for his infamous insatiable lust for the womanly creatures. But two more incisive observations need to be made with respect to Momus's interest in the hidden nature of the inner life.

First, the popular psychology of everyday life is still very much caught up with Momus's conceptualization of the inner life as a space located inside the human breast or heart that can be opened up, if only there were the empathic technology to do so. To keep a secret is to guard the inner space of the soul from the piercing glance of Momus. Second, it should not be overlooked that Momus was known as the patron of authors and poets, for whom the hidden interiority or the secrecy of innerness constitutes the very focus of their writerly gaze. Literary fiction may indeed be regarded as the narrative explorations of secret interiorities. There is no other form of narrativity or inquiry so well suited to give access to the inner life of the head and the heart: the uniqueness or singularity of the person.

Cyber-Pedagogy and the Search for Self-Identity

Privacy, secrecy, and innerness in young people's lives play a critical role in the development of self-identity, autonomy, intimacy, and the ability of learning to negotiate closeness and distance in social relations (Levering and van Manen, 1996). The experience of privacy and personal secrets is the inevitable collateral of the emergence of inwardness or inner space. To keep

Momus Criticizes the Gods' Creations, Maarten van Heemskerck, 1561, Gemäldegalerie, Berlin

a secret is to hide. What is hidden in personal secrecy is the evanescence of interiority that harbors the singularity or alterity of the person. In learning when and how to keep things inside and when to share, young people learn to confer their sense of identity, independence, uniqueness, and autonomy. Cyber-pedagogy asks the question: Are Momus technologies profoundly altering the quality and nature of social relations and especially the possibility of and need for self-identity, solitude, intimacy, closeness and how does this affect young people? How should adults view and deal with the digital influences in children's lives?

Young people crave intimacy and closeness and desire to belong. And intimacies are cultivated through a fascination with the hidden—the interiorities of self and other. But the hidden can only reveal itself when the exteriorizing of the interiorities of inner life are safeguarded by the private. The point is that it is privacy that is at stake in the various social networking technologies. The Momus effect of these technologies is that they provide direct access to what is most innermost, and simultaneously, they may also have the effect of trivializing and broadly casting the private onto scattered planes of the public.

Social networks invite people to "spend time with their friends," which translates into pressing thumbs or fingers on a mobile handset or computer keyboard. For many young people (and older people as well), ever-changing social networking sites have become the new commons: the place where you hang out, commiserate, and gossip with your friends. What do we mean when we speak of digital intimacies? What do people experience when they wittingly or unwittingly experiment with their identities online? It is in this context that pedagogical questions arise regarding the formative consequences that social networking technologies have on the lives of young people.

Sharing personal information can be unexpectedly risky, in part because sexual predators and pedophiles prey on unsuspecting social network users—for example, pedophiles who write well and know how to use language that belongs to young people, their interests, and cultures. They know how to use language seductively in a manner that stirs and traps young people into a sphere of trust and seeming closeness or intimacy. And sharing personal feelings is precarious when online intimacy is betrayed through false representation of self or through cyber-bullying. The social effects can be devastating to young people who desire intimacy or who crave to be loved or to belong.

So there is risk in the ease with which one may unguardedly or unwittingly spill one's personal information or even innermost feelings with those others in the mutualities of what Giddens called "pure relationships" (1993, p. 2)—relationships of utter emotional equality. Even with strangers, whom we have never met face-to-face, we may experience an uncanny sense of closeness. Through fantasy enhanced by evocative texting and (true or false) images, we may become "virtually enchanted" (Ihde, 2002, p. 82) with someone distant. And we may say things and reveal intimacies that we may not so easily share with people around us. Many young people do not realize—or may not care about at this time in their lives—that whatever they put online can no longer be withdrawn and controlled and may become forever the picking of the treasures, trash, and debris circulating in cyberspace.

Text messaging on mobile phones and other communication technologies tends to be abbreviated, coded, and lacking in depth in a traditional narrative sense. The language of keeping in touch tends to be narratively undifferentiated. With respect to wireless handheld devices, one would suspect that the shallowness of texting through abbreviated messages would not seem to be a favorable recipe for meaningful conversations. And of course, texting is mostly intended for purposes of sending brief messages, making appointments, or simply feeling in touch. Even shallow communication online, ironically, may provide the participants the feeling of a certain kind of depth and certain qualities of intimacy. The more important question is, therefore: What is not just lost but also gained in the way that technology alters the experience of intimacy, social nearness and distance, and personal proximity.

Young people are tuned in to the cultural codes of online communication that is part of their way of texting. A teacher of English discovered that there exist subjective sensibilities to the codes and linguistic habits of texting that quickly betray that privacy is trespassed by a stranger to the code:

> While I personally use alphanumeric shorthand to speed my writing, many of the teens with whom I communicate in the course of my work don't. They use the intuitive text feature of their phones. So when I jokingly grabbed a phone one day and texted something silly to a friend of one of my friend's daughters, the girl laughed at my attempt at humor: "she'll know it's not me because I don't use shorthand like that." And she was right—a text came back, with no alphanumeric abbreviation: "What? Who's using your phone?" And the girl used the apostrophe—something I often don't see even in formal writing.

Acronyms, symbols, and ever-inventive neologisms are used as shorthand, but they can also be used as a secret language in online communication, meant to disguise and share private feelings and inner thoughts. Symbols that represent winks and warnings can be used for letting each other know that someone is watching or that the conversation is under surveillance, thus suggesting exclusive togetherness by covering hidden relations. But this can also be experienced as hiding one's identity and yet aiming to achieve a certain intimacy by wearing virtual burqas: posed pictures that represent false exteriorities and posting words that suggest closeness—they substitute for veils and eyes.

Constant Contact and Digital Intimacy

Young people receive smartphones from their parents so that they can be reachable, safe, and, thus, under parental control when away from home. But, ironically perhaps, these mobile technologies also have the opposite effect of freeing young people from parental surveillance and giving them a certain independence and autonomy because they have more license to roam in a virtual as well as in a real sense. Parents who are using the mobile phone's apps to track the whereabouts and travels of their adolescents may not realize that tech-savvy young people have ways of avoiding tracking and hiding the contents of their messages.

Many youngsters report that throughout the day they are constantly in touch with others through text messaging on their mobile devices—in school and outside of school. They feel "naked" without it. For some young people who are shy or less verbal, text messaging by mobile phone is psychologically an attractive way to communicate with each other exactly because texting does not require engaging in extended conversations, as one may be required to do when talking over the phone. Texting allows one to feel in touch with friends and acquaintances without, it seems, having to be too close: a virtual experience of present absence. The experience of proximity through texting is a distant kind of intimacy. Of course, lack of distance is not equivalent to nearness. Although computer-mediated and wireless technologies overcome physical distance between people, they do not necessarily bring them intimately near to each other. In interviews with young people one young woman said,

> The tendency of constantly checking how your friend is doing and feeling right now, what he or she is having on his sandwich, that your friend has a third coffee by 10:00 a.m., how she hates a certain song on the radio, how he found some moldy food in the refrigerator, the clothes your friend is wearing today, the disagreement she had with her boyfriend, how she feels tired after shopping for groceries—all these trivialities of daily life bore me.

And yet constantly monitoring of how your friend is doing as the day progresses can have a mesmerizing effect that may appeal to some (if only a few) people. In a strange way social networks that encourage constant contact, short messaging, selfies, and photo-pics let you get to "know" your friend in ways that is unexpectedly personal and "intimate," as if you are living with this person. And yet this kind of intimacy is also largely screen-mediated intimacy, enhanced perhaps with snapshots or selfies taken with the built-in camera of the mobile device one is using. Of course, intimacy experienced through texting, Skype, and instant messaging is not a new phenomenon. In online communication we may feel close even though we are physically distant. We may also feel distant even though we are physically near. Ambiguously, closeness is not the same as nearness.

How does digital intimacy differ from nondigital intimacy? On first sight, digital intimacy is obviously different from physically proximal closeness in that it is a distant intimacy—it is intimacy at a distance mediated through texting. But distant intimacy appears to be somewhat of an oxymoron. Does one not need to be close to experience nearness? Yes, but the opposite is true as well: one cannot experience closeness without distance. It also depends on how one understands nearness and distance. Digital intimacy may offer the sensibility of one-to-one closeness, but the one-to-one may be "real" or illusory. Within this binary sphere of intimacy between myself and the screen, you are addressing me, only you and only me (even though many others may be reading your writing and feel the intimacy I feel). But at the moment of reading your posting I may not "know" this or I may not want to know of the presence of these others.

From an experiential phenomenological point of view, contact through mere words or pictures on the screen may provide an uncanny sense of intimacy or closeness. It is only after I remove myself from the digital screen that I may admit to myself that you were not revealing yourself to just me. Wittingly or unwittingly, digital intimacy can be polygamous intimacy. I felt close to you but did not realize that it was not you. Or I may realize that you were not really yourself when you seemed to be showing off and "posturing" to your readers online through your primed postings and personal pictures.

It is also possible that the mediated experience of the other may be preferable over immediate or unmediated presence. For example, when I text or e-mail someone, I may experience an openness that I may not experience when in the physical presence of that person. The fact that I do not feel hindered by the scrutiny of eyes or the vulnerability of physiognomic and physical expressions may allow me to be more vulnerable in my writing. Conversely, in reading the other's writing, I may feel addressed, stirred, or touched by the written words. I experience a depth in the written words that spoken words do not easily possess or do not possess in the same manner.

There are also apps that ironically facilitate face-to-face meetings between strangers of a certain age who happen to be physically nearby and who are willing to meet strangers after a little digital small talk. In this case digital intimacy may grow into an eye-to-eye intimacy. It is when I look the other in the black pupil of the eye that I may really feel connected with the innermost self of the other person who looks me in the black of the pupil of my eye. It is ironic that we may feel most intimate in a face-to-face encounter when we look into the empty black pupil of our friend's or lover's eye, which is exactly the place where, strangely, nothing can be seen (Marion, 2002, p. 115). The point is that face-to-face contact through social media does not let me experience looking the other person straight in the black pupil of their eye. With present software one always looks past one another.

Textual intimacy may benefit from a certain reflectiveness regarding my thoughts that would not be likely when we are in the immediate presence of the other. In writing to the other I can weigh my words, taste their tonalities, feel their evocations with a subtlety and a sense of emotional intimacy that face-to-face contact would not achieve precisely because of the pathic power of the linguistic intimacy of written textual contact. The conversational nature of writing may sometimes draw the person closer to the point toward which the conversation is oriented. When writing to a friend about a topic, a book, or a movie, it may happen that we get so involved in the writing that we temporarily seem to forget that we are writing to someone or that we are writing for others.

It is also possible that the feeling of online intimacy is a self-occupied or even narcissistic intimacy with the self: a kind of reflexive sphere of intimacy, as I may have felt in writing in my personal diary of yesteryear. It is possible for people on the Internet to think they are close, but in the sober light of the next morning the closeness was an illusion or perhaps a simulated intimacy. It could have been an intimacy that consisted of seducing oneself through one's own writing: feeling moved, stirred by our own words, as if they came from the outside. This too may be an unexpected benefit or price, gain or pain from writing online.

The phenomena of secrecy and intimacy stand in a direct relation to each other and to the relationalities in which they are engaged (Thompson, 2008). Intimacy is the occurrence of togetherness when the interiority of secrets or inner intimacies is exteriorized and brought into naked contact with the interiority of a trusted other. Both secrecy and intimacy lay claim to inner space. Sharing a secret is an act of discretion, of tact: to make contact with the other. Relational tact means to touch or be touched by the other. Contact is intimate in-touchness, and intimacy is the relational ambience of exposing, disclosing, making known, revealing what is concealed. To be in intimate contact with the other is to touch the other's secret: his or her uniqueness or singularity.

In the adult sexual context intimacy is what we experience in the relational state of undress with a lover. Taking off our clothes and entrusting the reach and depth of the secrecy of our embodied being to the other means that this other must know how to dwell in this intimate space by being tactfully respectful, receptive, active, and available. By definition, intimacy is selective and exclusive. Properly speaking, intimacy is a binary relation—when one person shares a unique aspect of his or her interiority with another. The question is whether and how digital lifestyles and techno-social relationalities may enrich or erode, deepen or alter such sensibilities, notions, and relations of intimacy.

Chapter Eleven
Pedagogical Knowing and Acting

The challenge of pedagogy is to act sensitively and sensibly in dealing with children and young people. This means to act with proper knowledge and understanding while distinguishing actively right from wrong, good from bad, or ethical from unethical ways of bringing up and educating children and young people. Ethics is concerned with substantive and sensitive considerations of what is appropriate in particular situations in relation to particular children. At heart a pedagogue could be considered an ethicist, one who specializes in questions and concerns that have to do with pedagogical situations, relations, and actions. Pedagogy asks: What is in the best interest of children? And how can we know what is good for children?

What is required of an adult to be able to practice the rational-ethical sensitivity of pedagogy? First, the adult needs to have a reflective sense of what it means to be a humane human in this complex world and how each person is on the way to become a uniquely human person. Second, the adult needs to be oriented to the question of what is in the child's (best) interest. Third, the adult needs to understand his or her responsibilities in helping the child become independent. Fourth, the adult needs to have an active understanding of the pedagogically ethical perspectives that come into play in distinguishing good from less desirable ways of interacting with and educating children. Fifth, the adult must deeply care for the children in his or her care. This care-as-worry is an affect that cannot be forced or coerced onto parents or teachers, but without this caring concern pedagogy is impossible.

And, of course, much more is needed. For example, children should have trust in a teacher. Susan Trenny is a grade ten history teacher, and during a meeting of our teacher research team, of which she was a member, she shared some of the frustrations of a difficult year at school. We had hardly started with discussions of our research topic of pedagogy when Susan commented about the worries and concerns she had experienced with her students:

Pedagogical Tact: Knowing What to Do When You Don't Know What to Do, by Max van Manen, 179–194.
© 2015 Taylor & Francis. All rights reserved.

Another one of my kids died. And now I'm thinking about Lewis. How I got to know him and how I have to remember him. You know, at the beginning of the year . . . his whole autobiography started with: My dad put his thing in my mom's thing and out popped me . . . that was kind of like the beginning of his autobiography . . . and it was just strangely funny . . . in that he talked about how devastating it was when his father drowned. It was full of pain, and I kept it.

So anyway, last weekend I'm on my way to school . . . it is report card time, so I was going for Sunday breakfast, and I promised myself to go into school and do all of my work. And I walk up to a restaurant, and there are the newspaper boxes in the front of the restaurant . . . and I look and there it is—Lewis Left Life—right on the front page. And what had happened was, he and two of his other classmates that I teach, they were really drunk, they had stolen a Jeep, they were driving the wrong way down the Baystreet Bridge, they crashed, they got out, and they started to run. Lewis was trying to run across the frozen river, and he disappeared into the abyss—he drowned.

And so yesterday it all came around. Like I knew it. And that's what's so strange. That it has been a difficult time, teaching those kids and worrying about what's coming—and Lewis was just one of many in that situation.

Like, it was difficult when Sylvia Warren got murdered in Lakeside last fall, and they had the newscast on.

I went home that night, and I got my class list out and phoned. And I said, "Tommy, look, it's Miss Trenny—did you kill that lady?" Because the description fit him so easily . . . and he goes "No, Miss Trenny, but Sonny did . . ." And he says, "But you can't tell anybody."

The laconic manner in which Susan Trenny told us about Tommy and the killing of Sylvia Warren amazed us. Of course, we immediately wanted to know what she did with what Tommy had confided in her. Well, she had asked Tommy how he felt, and he had said that he did not sleep very well. She told him that no wonder he did not sleep well—he could not live like that, and he had to talk with Sonny; he must tell his parents and go to the police and report what had happened. Apparently the death was really an accident rather than a murder. Anyway, that is what happened. Teacher Trenny had nudged Tommy. This is again a fine example of the pedagogy of nudging.

Different ethical perspectives may be helpful in understanding what is at stake in pedagogical actions, experiences, arguments, and judgments (see Appendix A). However, the very extensive literature on ethics is proof of the realization that there are no perspectives and theories that would rationally guide us, unequivocally, to good action and the ability to give unequivocal pedagogical advice. In addition, the different ethical perspectives cannot always be clearly distinguished. Different families and different schools provide us with distinct senses of ethos.

Certain terms of ethics have specific or broad applications. For example, bioethics refers to the applications of ethics to specific ethical problems and controversies brought about by technological and scientific advances in medicine and biology. Professional ethics (e.g., business ethics) is generally concerned with the development and advancement of standards of good practice and codes of conduct in professional disciplines and practices. Feminist ethics applies ethical perspectives to the moral interests and roles of women in society and professional lives.

Basic ethical terms are moral norms, principles, values, and virtues. *Ethos* is a Greek term that referred originally to "habitat" or "place" as well as to a "state of being" expressing the inner source of a place. The communal ethos of a place may be experienced as competitive or cooperative, authoritarian or democratic, risky or safe, and so forth. The ethos of a place may be compared to the pedagogical atmosphere that governs there. The ethos influences and is influenced by the kinds of pedagogical actions and values that one encounters and experiences in a place. So we may define the pedagogical ethos as the totality of beliefs, atmosphere, sensibilities, values, norms, and rules of conduct that a habitat and its people hold or share in their relation to children. We can speak of the ethos of a school, the ethos of a society—meaning the ethical spirit of a place.

The Ethics of Responsibility

Responsibility is the state of being responsible. It derives from the Latin *respondere,* to pledge, promise, reply, or answer. In our moral response to an ethically charged situation we experience our responsibility. Responsibility has three qualifications. First, responsibility assumes that the person who is responsible can freely act or chose. If one is not free, one cannot be held responsible for one's actions. Second, responsibility can be weighed. One can be more or less responsible for an action or for something or someone. Third, there is a temporal dimension to responsibility. Responsibility as accountability has to do with the past. Responsibility as task has to do with future. And responsibility as virtue has to do with presence.

When one is held responsible for a past action, one is regarded as accountable or answerable for that action. Afterward one can be held responsible for what one has done or failed to do in the past—one may have acted responsibly or irresponsibly. Teachers are held accountable for their professional conduct as well as for the effectiveness of their instructional competencies. Responsibility as task describes what one is expected to be able to carry in terms of future obligations, duties, and expectations. And responsibility as virtue relates to the character and being of the person. A virtuously responsible person is known as a person of wisdom, of independent and balanced judgment.

Sometimes a person may carry diminished responsibilities or be completely excused from certain responsibilities. For example, one is held less responsible or not responsible when one is ignorant or confused about the nature and consequences of a certain action, when one is forced to act in a certain manner (i.e., under strain of not being able to chose or act freely), when one is prevented to act properly because of circumstances beyond one's control (e.g., illness, absence), when one is not competent to deal with certain situations, or when one is not knowledgeable about the possible implications of certain actions.

The Embodied and Temporal Nature of Practical Knowledge

I am visiting a school, and I accompany a teacher into her classroom. I cannot help but notice how competently the teacher moves around. While I feel, as a visitor, somewhat strange and awkward in this place, she moves amongst the tables without bumping into them, turns to her own desk, holds the door for students who enter the room, talks to one student then to another while doing this or that, and I notice how she simultaneously tunes in to the gathering class. Then she gets the attention from the whole group and proceeds with the lesson in a confident and easy manner that is only *un*remarkable because it seems to require such little effort. She walks about the room, spurs a student on with a quiet gesture, stops here, interrupts there, responds to some commotion or a question, and so forth.

Obviously this teacher feels at home in this room, in a way that allows her to act with such confidence and self-forgetful ease. Indeed, this teacher is so effective precisely because she can forget herself and completely absorb herself in this situation with her students. If we were to ask the teacher to give an account of every one of her actions, then she would most likely be stymied. Yet it is the totality of all those microsituations—and not just the overall intent and pattern of the lesson—that defines the teaching-learning reality of the classroom. A study of the practice of teaching has to be sensitive to the experiential quality of practical knowledge: the acknowledgment that much of this tact, this instant knowing what to do, ensues from one's body and from the things and the atmosphere of one's world. We might even say that the practical knowledge of teaching resides *in the things* that surround us: the physical dimensions of the classroom that I recognize as my room to which my body is adapted. My practical knowledge "is" my felt sense of the classroom, my feeling of who I am as a teacher, my felt understanding of my students, my felt grasp of the things I teach, the mood that belongs to my world at school, the hallways, the staffroom, and, of course, this classroom.

This practical skill is like a silent knowledge that is implicit in my world and in my actions rather than cognitively explicit or critically reflective. This silent knowledge cannot necessarily be translated back into propositional discourse. Indeed, the ultimate grounds of propositions are not even themselves propositions. The ground of a legitimated belief or justified knowledge claim is not some ultimate ungrounded proposition; rather, it is an ungrounded way of acting (Molander, 1992). The rationalist fear of ungrounded action actually should extend to theories and moral principles as well. Even theories and beliefs cannot finally be grounded in certain basic assumptions or basic truths. Arguments to support a belief, proposition, or theory have to come to an end somewhere. And what we are left with, then again, is not an ungrounded presupposition; it is an ungrounded way of acting.

The way we normally exist and act in our world should not even be conceptualized as a silent knowledge, an implicit knowing, and even less as implicit theories that somehow guide our actions; rather, when we are involved as teachers with our students, then we are part of this classroom, this world, in which we practice what we know as teachers. In other words, our pedagogical practice expresses itself as an active understanding of how we find ourselves here as teachers with certain intentions, feelings, passions, inclinations, attitudes, and preoccupations. And yet this active Kairos understanding is not necessarily reflective or even articulable in a direct conceptual manner. To make this practical knowledge available we may need to employ vocabularies that are attuned to the lived meanings of the forms of life of teaching. This is the task of phenomenological and narrative human science methods.

If teaching is so embodied and so tied into the phenomenology of one's world, then it is no surprise that the experience of practice teaching or internship is so important for the pedagogical preparation of teachers. The student teacher must somehow acquire this knowledge in an imitative and personal relation to the master teacher. By observing and imitating how the teacher animates the students, walks around the room, uses the board, and so forth, the student teacher learns with his or her body, as it were, how to feel confident in this room, with these students. This "confidence" is not some kind of affective quality that makes teaching easier; rather, this confidence *is* the active knowledge itself, the tact of knowing what to do or not to do, what to say or not to say.

Rather than see practice teaching as applied theoretical (university-generated) knowledge, one needs to see that practice possesses its own integrity. Rather than say that implicit theories, such as constructivist knowledge, gives meaning to the actions we perform, it would seem equally valid, if not more accurate, to presume that our actions give meaning to the words we use. Wittgenstein has suggested that ultimately actions are not so much founded upon propositions—rational accounts and principles—but rather upon other actions (Wittgenstein, 1968, 1972). That is why good teachers often have difficulty identifying why things work so well for them (or why they do not work well, for that matter). If teachers are requested to account for their successes or if they are asked to convert their actions into verbal propositions, then they will normally be tempted to reproduce the kinds of abstracted principles or theories they feel are expected of them. What else can they do? It is much more difficult to capture in language the kind of knowledge that inheres in our body and in the things of our world.

At the microlevel there is difficulty determining the boundaries that define a discrete action component and that allow distinguishing the action from its context and from other related actions. For example, a teacher's gesture may carry the meaning of a personal understanding, an encouragement, a secret shared, the exclusion of others, or it can be seen as a confirmation of a problem solved, or it can be seen as part of a larger instructional process or teacherly style, and so forth. Although on first sight any particular action may seem singular in meaning, intent, and structure, action really is multilayered, multidimensional, multirelational, and multiperspectival. The meaning of any teaching act is therefore experienceable and interpretable in a variety of ways. For example, a teacher's joke may be intended to take the edge off a situation, but it could also be a manifestation of the teacher's desire to be liked, to appear chummy, to seem flexible, approachable, to appear clever, and so forth. From their side, students may experience the teacher's humor variously as invitation, as critique, as fakery, as hint, or as secret message.

If my allusion to the practical tact of teaching is indeed in keeping with how thoughtful teachers actually experience their practice, then the requirement that teachers constantly critically reflect on their actions may need reconsideration. Why should we demand that everything one does as a teacher requires critical reflection, reasons, or justifications? Perhaps it is the other way around. It is doubt and distrust in certain practices that should require reasons or justification. Indeed, we sometimes put a misplaced emphasis on critical reflection in teaching. The aim of critical reflection is to create doubt and critique of ongoing actions. But it is obviously not possible to act thoughtfully and self-confidently while doubting oneself at the same time. If teachers were to try to be constantly critically aware of what they were doing and why they were doing these things, they would inevitably become artificial and flounder. It would disturb the ontology of practice that animates teachers' being and everything they do.

Knowing What to Do When You Don't Know What to Do

There are certain qualities that are generally considered to be desirable character traits of adults with pedagogical responsibilities: pedagogical love for the child, respect for the child, being trustworthy and trustful, being dependable (children need continuity in their relations with significant adults), being reliable, believing in the child, and providing encouragement, security, patience, hope, humor, and availability.

> The drone of the school buzzer has announced that school has started. But Mr. Turner, the teacher, is still sorting stuff at his desk, muttering to himself, frustrated. He seems to be looking for something. Some of the kids sitting close are observing his antics with obvious amusement.
> One boy in the front starts to imitate while stealing glances and smiles from his neighbors. Silently he pronounces "F. . . . " He knocks his books on the floor and gathers them with impatient gestures while mouthing swears. The F word is actually heard aloud. Now the teacher has noticed the imprudent imitator. A cloud seems to draw across his face. The tension is momentarily tangible, and some of the kids in the front quickly straighten up. They fake seriousness, innocence. Look away from the teacher. But instead of bursting into anger, the teacher stares at them intently and says with a slow, deliberate drawl. "Well, I don't seem to be able to find the surprise test I was going to give you this morning. What do I do now?"
> The kids who heard him cheer. "No way."
> Now the rest of the class tunes in. "What? A test? What?"
> The teacher remains stone-faced. But his students know him. They are accurate face-readers. They sense that this is only pretense. They risk catcalls, jokes, a flurry of rebellion. Pretense all around.
> All the while the teacher has opened a textbook and moves to the board. He waves his book and starts to write, feigning to suppress a secret smile. What is he up to now? The class turns momentarily silent, intensely watching the words appear from his hand. Suspense. Is this a test after all? But as soon as they recognize the nature of the assignment, books and binders fly open like the flapping wings of a flock of geese taking off. Relief. A pleasant sense of routine seems to settle over the class.

This whole incident did not last for more than a few minutes. But it is undeniable that an intangible atmosphere conducive to working has grown out of this seemingly trivial chaotic classroom moment.

There is recognizable banter in this classroom observation. On the part of the teacher, the scene contains moments of awkwardness and witty repartee, showing that life in classrooms is contingent, that every moment is situation-specific: a Kairos moment. Life in school depends much on the nature of the personalities of the teachers, the individual students, the class as a collective, and the social sphere they shape together. To define the meaning of this relational sphere we use the phrase "pedagogical situation." The pedagogical situation describes what adults and children bring—or fail to bring—to a shared situation so that it acquires the conditions of a situation where education, teaching or learning can take place. Some teachers are able to infuse the quality of a certain sphere into their classes so that each student experiences a personal relation to the teacher and to the subject matter he or she teaches. But it is in the nature of teaching and learning that there are no guarantees.

I have been teaching for more than twenty years at many different grade levels, so I rarely write up my lesson plans in detail. But I want to make sure that the reading of Oscar Wilde's story *The Happy Prince* will accomplish what I intend. I have been asked to fill in for the grade teacher for the day. So I carefully prepare the students by checking and discussing the relevant vocabulary and narrative features that they will encounter in listening to the reading of the story. None of them has read the story before, although some think they might have seen a cartoon version of *The Happy Prince* on television.

I am hoping that my reading Oscar Wilde's story will touch the students' emotions and that we can afterwards discuss the notion of sacrifice.

As I begin to read the story, the students are quiet and attentive. So I read how the little swallow is about to go to sleep at the feet of the statue of the Happy Prince: "but just as he was putting his head under his wing a large drop of water fell on him." I hardly speak these words or several kids start grinning and glancing at each other as if they have just heard a grotesque joke. Stupidly I do not immediately realize what they are so animated about, and I stop reading: "What is so funny?" Now almost the whole class starts shrieking: "The Prince is peeing on his head. . . . "

"Okay, now, let's not be immature. What really is going on?" I desperately try to repair the situation. I do not want the fragile sphere of the story to be broken. I resume my reading aloud, continuing with a tender tone of voice. "The eyes of the Happy Prince were filled with tears, and tears were running down his golden cheeks." In the past I myself have become quite emotionally stirred while reading the story to my students. But something has happened this time. Some of the children mouth "Gross!" as they hear how the little swallow "plucked out the Prince's eye." And they laugh at the "weeping" of the little bird. I try to read on, admonishing the restless listeners with my eyes. "I am glad that you are going to Egypt at last, little Swallow," said the Prince, "you have stayed too long here; but you must kiss me on the lips, for I love you." At reading these words more than a few students begin to grimace. And before I can even say anything, Jackie calls out: "He is gay! They are both gay!" "Homosexual, you mean," corrects Tim. "Gross," shouts Teresa.

I realize that the emotional power of the story has evaporated.

Inexperienced or naive teachers are sometimes surprised that life in classrooms seems to have a quality of irrationality so totally at odds with the degree that the teacher feels primed to teach the planned lesson. The novice teacher may have thought that, as long as you are very well prepared, you can just walk in and teach the material. And as long as you knew it all, expressed it all, and involved the students, the task would be done. The measure of how well it would have been done would depend on how carefully you had thought through exactly what you would need to say and do and to the extent that the students caught on and responded to what you were trying to do. But experienced teachers know that real teaching is not just a technique. Children may be understandable, but they are ultimately not predictable. This does not mean that teachers should not attempt to influence the students in the course of a lesson; influence, habits, routines, and even manipulation are part of the relational realities of everyday life inside and outside classrooms. But the benign practice of pedagogical routines and manipulation should always be rooted in thoughtfulness—tentative and attentive to the uniqueness of the moment and the singularity of experiential reality of the students.

Not unlike comedians on their first-night performance, teachers realize that their preparations may fall flat, lessons become ineffectual, and the teaching-learning situations lack the sparkle and inspiration they had hoped for. Stand-up comedians have a word for the test of an act: "stand and deliver"—the interpretive ability to deliver one's lines in fine attunement with the contingencies of the moment and the mood of the audience. Good teachers know there is a practical ethical dimension to teaching that is not incidental to the life of the classroom but rather belongs to it essentially.

The nature of teaching is even more demanding than that of stage acting because teaching is not a rehearsed performance but rather a dynamic personal and interpersonal, active and interactive process; unlike stage actors, teachers can never be sure of their next lines. The practice of teaching requires the improvisational tact of instantly knowing how to act in ever-changing situations, a sense of timing, immediately knowing what to do, what to say, how to say it, how to present something, how to hold back, how to create the right tone, how to turn to a text, what to do and when with a piece of technology or media. Even a good lecture demands that the lecturer knows how to sense the audience, how to initiate contact, how to gesture, what posture, what tone of voice, when and where to pause, when to exchange a meaningful look, how to draw attention to an image, and so forth.

It is tempting to call these demands of teaching "the aesthetic" dimension. And, indeed, much has been written about the "art" or "craft" of teaching. A good teacher must be like an actor sometimes—know how to tell a compelling story, dramatize the process of teaching, improvise the performance, and conduct the learning orchestra. But there is something that is easily glossed by the notion of art and craft, and that is not the aesthetic but the ethical aspect of teaching. Seeing a teacher with children is to discern a broadly ethical scene. We may ask: Is that how the teacher should gesture? Is that the proper tone of voice? Is that how the teacher should start a discussion? Should the teacher smile? Or look serious? and so forth. Pedagogy poses the ethical demand of instantly distinguishing what is good from what is not good or less appropriate in dealing with children or young people. In this sense every instant of every moment and act of teaching is ethical. The pedagogical question is always: Is that how this teacher should act, here in this moment, with this child or these students?

Undoubtedly teachers must have available bodies of content knowledge, understandings of curriculum materials, policies, and programs; possess professional expertise and didactical competencies for effectively assessing, planning, and evaluating learning processes and outcomes; and have instructional and classroom management techniques. Indeed, the entire corpus of theories, knowledge, guides, skills, and competencies constitute the rational dimension of teaching and of education. However, within the contemporary context this rationalization of all aspects of education translates into practices that have become increasingly instrumental and technological.

Ontotheology is a term used by Kant and especially Heidegger (1977, 2002) to describe the metaphysical undercurrents of Western culture that condition the technological nature of all human forms of inquiry. The ontotheological roots feeding the technologizing of professional knowledge have not diminished. On the contrary, the influence of communication and information technologies and market economies in the administration of schools and educational systems may have pushed the technological ontotheology even more deeply into the metaphysical sensibilities of Western cultures (Gumbrecht, 2014; Thomson, 2005).

Contemporary educational commentators such as Iain Thomson point out how our technological understanding of being produces a calculative mentality that tends to quantify all qualitative relations, reducing entities to bivalent, programmable information. There is a certain irony in the fact that even the increasing popularity of qualitative inquiry in the professional fields has not prevented professional practice becoming cemented ever more firmly into preoccupations with calculative policies and technological solutions regarding the productivity of outcomes, the accountability of standards of practice, the measurement of effectiveness in terms of institutional ranking, the codification of ethics governing programs of research, and so forth.

The ethical predicament is that there is never adequate knowledge at hand to know what to say or do in this very instant. If such knowledge were available, then the pedagogy of the moment would indeed cease to be ethical. Teachers who rely on rules, prescriptions, or methods in their moment-to-moment acting have thereby forfeited the essentially ethical demand of pedagogy. The pedagogy of teaching requires of teachers that they engage in nontechnical, noninstrumental ways of approaching and interacting with their students.

> Student: "I was not able to complete my assignment before the deadline. May I have one more day to finish?"
> Teacher: "Well, you know the rule: assignments that are late will not be accepted. And so I will have to enter a grade of zero for this assignment."

If the teacher is indeed "blindly" applying the rule to this situation, this teacher's response to the student's request lacks ethical discretion. The point is not necessarily that the student may deserve a second chance or there may exist circumstances that warrant giving an extension for the deadline. Or the teacher could provide a more pedagogically sensitive response rather than routinely falling back on a rule. However, it is also possible that the teacher is fully reflective of the appropriateness of referring to the rule in this particular situation. Thus, the criterion of the ethics of the moment depends on the teacher's active thoughtfulness.

The things we say and do, the acts we perform, the atmosphere we create, the tone of voice, posture, gestures, and glances—these cannot be mechanized or instrumentalized without losing their claim to ethical authenticity. If I say something because it is the rule to say so, then I have succumbed to technocratic behavior; I am not ethically thoughtful. The reality is that there is not a rule book or a checklist that can determine or prescribe what is appropriate for children in contingent situations. And yet without being able to rely on rules or routines in pedagogically sensitive situations and relations, one cannot really "know" what to do. So the predicament of teaching is paradoxical: the teacher must know what to do without knowing what to do.

The challenge of pedagogy is that from moment to moment one never has adequate knowledge to decide what to say or do. This does not mean that we must feel impotent in our actions; it is hoped that we usually act with a certain tact, confidence, and thoughtfulness. But the point is that if we had to give rational justifications for our acting in this situation in a particular way, we would realize that we cannot do so. We cannot act pedagogically by resorting to a technology of teaching: rules, principles, strategies, steps, methods, theories, and so forth. A teacher who operates exclusively within a technology of teaching has become a mere "instructor."

The predicament of pedagogy is two-fold. On the one hand, pedagogical situations and relations are ethical and cannot be approached or handled in a technical manner. On the other hand, the ability to reflect deliberatively about what one should say or do in the immediacy of an interactive event is limited in a temporal and relational sense. Recall that the god of time, Kairos, demands of us the right thing at the right time. Only the right action at the right time will do.

There are many ways of illustrating the essential ethical contingency of teaching-learning situations. From one moment to the next, preparations may go amiss, assignments may create difficulties, group work may lead to unexpected troubles, class discussions may stall, presentations may falter, and there may also be interruptions from outside of the classroom. These examples can also be stated positively. Students' responses to a lesson or a learning situation take a challenging new direction, the teacher senses the need for a new initiative, and so forth. It seems that the life of teaching-learning consists of an ongoing flux of pedagogical moments that constantly require the teacher's tactful actions. However, the immediacy of the interactive pedagogical processes is very difficult to describe because any description tends to suffer from the simplification of some reconstructed logic as one places the experience at a reflective distance for one's contemplation.

What teachers apparently must realize is that the ethical contingencies of the moment, the mood of the class, the dynamics of personal relations, and the readiness of students make demands for a certain improvisational competence, a ready fitness, on the part of the teacher. I have suggested that this fitness may be best captured with the notion of tact. Pedagogical tact is the active alertness, ethical sensitivity, and practical flexibility that educators demonstrate when they are dealing with young people in everyday educational situations. Teachers who have a high degree of pedagogical tact distinguish themselves for being able to say and do just the right things with students in situations that are always particular, sensitive, always unique, never quite the same. If you hesitate then the Kairic moment has passed, all you will be left with is regret. Tactful teachers know what to do when they don't know what to do.

So it should be clear that the practical significance of pedagogical tact should not be sought in instrumental action, efficiency, or technical efficacy; rather, the significance of a pedagogical tact lies in its formative power, issuing from the sensitizing effects and affects of phenomenological reflections on our lived experiences. Phenomenological understanding inheres in the sense and sensuality of our embodied being and practical actions, in encounters with others, and in the ways that our bodies are responsive to the things of our world, and to the situations and relations in which we find ourselves (van Manen, 1997, 2014). Phenomenology of practice is an ethical corrective of the technological and calculative modalities of contemporary life. It finds its source and impetus in phenomenological reflection that opens up possibilities for creating formative relations between being and acting, self and other, interiorities and exteriorities, between who we are and how we act.

Presence and Hope in an Uncertain World

It is not surprising that people increasingly think that we live in a world that is doomed to destroy itself. Climate change, polluting practices, dying oceans, and melting arctic ice are said to be unstoppable events. Religious wars, brutal terrorism, greedy capitalism, extreme inequalities of wealth, and global poverty are the realities that define our contemporary world. It is difficult not to smile cynically at any positive program in the shadow of disaster. It seems easier to shrug fatalistically, to despair, to sigh that the worst is yet to come. Yet those of us who live with children cannot afford to be so nihilistic; we cannot abandon the pedagogical place we occupy in the lives of our children. Children are hope.

A hopeless world has no room for children. But for as long as there are children in your life, in your home, in your classroom, have a look, a good look—a pedagogical look. What you see is hope. Having "seen" your children, hope is now present in your life. In living with children, new parents often gain the sudden conviction that the world should—must—continue to exist. Now that I am a father or grandfather to this child, I can no longer turn away from the political insanities that threaten the world. I experience my children as living hope. I must act. Hope has activated me.

Hope is there from the very beginning, from the first stirring of the fetus. However mixed up and confused the feelings of expectant mothers and fathers may sometimes appear, one of the earliest and deepest sensations is the experience of hope, which particularizes itself in thoughts such as, "I hope this baby will be healthy." The woman who is expecting a child is literally inhabited by hope.

Pedagogical hope animates the way a parent or teacher lives with a child: it gives meaning to the way an adult stands in the world, represents the world to the child, takes responsibility for the world, and embodies or stylizes the forms of knowledge through which the world is known, shown, and explained to children. Those who are inhabited by hope are "true" fathers, "true" mothers, and "true" teachers to children. We forsake our responsibility when we fail or refuse to show how a life of hope is to be lived. Our irresponsibility may turn entire generations of young people into cynics, adults without hope, grown-ups who have no sense of commitment, who refuse to model how life is to be lived. The German author Günter Grass knew this well. In *The Tin Drum* (2010) Oskar simply refused to grow up, for he had no reason to do so.

Hope is not just a passive kind of optimism that somehow things will work out in the end; hope implies commitment and work. Even in the most absurd and painful of circumstances we cannot and must not give up on our children. How ironic! So much can go wrong in our lives, especially these days, and yet it is precisely in this time of perceived hopelessness that the vulnerability of our children makes hope once again a possible and necessary human experience.

To be a parent or a teacher is to have expectations and hope for a child. But *hope* is only a word, and words have ways of becoming overworked, clichéd, superficial, empty utterances. So we must examine how living with children is experienced as hope, how what we do is hope. The most important aspect of our living hope is a way of being with children. It is not what we say and do, first of all, but a way of being present to the child. We may say, "I hope that..." with reference to particular expectations and desires: "I hope that my child will do well in school" or "I hope he can do his homework" or "I hope she will get along." These are the hopes that come and go with the passing of time. But children make it possible for adults to transcend themselves and say, "I hope," "I live with hope," "I live life in such a way that I experience children as hope."

This experience of hope distinguishes a pedagogical life from a nonpedagogical one. It also makes clear that we can only hope for children we truly love in a pedagogical sense. What hope gives us is this simple confirmation: "I will not give up on you. I know you can make a life for yourself." Hope refers to all that gives us patience, tolerance, and belief in the possibilities for our children. Hope is our experience of the child's possibilities. It is our experience of confidence that a child will show us how life is to be lived, no matter how many disappointments we may have experienced. Thus hope gives us pedagogy. Or is it pedagogy that gives us hope?

Let us focus for a moment on the languages of "knowledge production," "program delivery," "outcomes-based instruction," or "management by objectives." The industrial model, computer technology, information processing, and marketplace thinking has deeply invaded schooling, and we constantly hear educational theorists and administrators use it to define educational practice. What are we to make of these kinds of discourses to describe teaching?

In them we can spot a profound contradiction. On the one hand, these languages are used so that teachers will be encouraged to make a difference in their pedagogical lives. But they are at best only ambiguously imbued with hope. Yet it is almost exclusively a language of doing for the future, not of being now. It permits no description of our "being" with children as being present with hope. The language of outcomes, delivery, assessment, inputs, and consumer satisfaction is a disembodied language of hope from which hope itself has been systematically purged. It is the language of hopeless hope. It is an impatient language that does not truly awaken. It is a language that so chops up hope into small bits that neither the king's horses nor the king's men will ever put it together again.

"Having measurable objectives" differs from "having hope." Of course, teachers need to have expectations, set goals and objectives, evaluate progress and growth. But they must also have a deeper trust and larger view of the power of teaching and the wonder of learning and growing up. Expectations and anticipations easily degenerate into desires, wants, certainties, predictions. Thus, teachers may close themselves off from possibilities that lie outside the direct or indirect vision of those expectations. To hope is to believe in possibilities. Hope strengthens and builds.

The point is not that the curricular language of program delivery, management objectives, or learning outcomes is wrong. Seen in proper perspective, this language is probably a useful administrative convenience. Teachers have always planned what should take place in a particular course, class, program, or lesson. The problem is that the "administrative" and "technocratic" values and practices have so penetrated the very lifeblood of our existence that parents and teachers are in danger of forgetting a certain other type of understanding: what it means to hope for and bear children and then to take care of and hope for them. Recalling what thus seems to be forgotten belongs to being a parent or a teacher (Saevi, 2015).

Not to do so has dire consequences. Teacher burnout, for instance—it is a contemporary example of nihilism. Higher values are losing heart. There is no answer to the question: What's the use? Actually the nihilistic "What's the use?" is less a question than a sigh, a shrugging off of any suggestion that there might be cause for hope. Teacher burnout is not necessarily a symptom of excessive effort, of being overworked; it is the condition of no longer knowing why we are doing what we are doing. Burnout is the evidence of hopelessness, of no longer being able to find a positive answer to the sigh, "What's the use?"

"I wish I could be young again but know what I know now." Many of us are nostalgic about our childhood, and not because we want to be children again. What we really want to do is be able to experience the world the way a child does. We long to recapture a sense of possibility and openness—a confidence that almost anything is possible.

A young child knows that he or she cannot really perform superhuman feats, yet in play the child experiences that possibility. All kinds of things are possible when one is young, and the reward for both parents and teachers is the presence of hope. That is what a child can teach us. It is what a child must teach us if we are to be true and good parents, grandparents, and teachers.

The way we understand our children is a telltale indication of the way we understand ourselves. We truly open ourselves to a child's way of being when we are able to experience openness ourselves. The child needs that openness to make something of him or herself. As parents and teachers, we need that openness to be what we are and to examine what we have made of ourselves. We must openly examine ourselves in front of children, for we must model asking ourselves how life is to be lived so that children, used to the question, will freely ask it of themselves. To live responsibly as an adult is to always remain open to the question of how life is to be lived. "Am I living my best life?" Thus, my living becomes a constant example for the child. Whether I like it or not, my life will be saying, "This is the way one may live." My responsibility toward a child constantly confronts me with the need to act, constantly makes me express and conduct myself in such a manner that the child is asked to recognize in me and through me an image of mature adulthood.

That is the way we must learn from our children. We must be even better learners than they are, because they in turn must learn from us.

Damages

As educators we must act ongoingly in our living with children. We may take some time out, personal time or simply time away from children. But even so, there really is no time off, short of running away from life itself. Once a parent, always a parent. Once a teacher, always a teacher. We love and respect our children, yet we cannot help but do damage to them.

So what should we do with the guilt of being an imperfect mother, father, teacher, grandparent? We should do what I have urged throughout this book: look closely at our children. Children are natural forgivers. Of course, that makes our responsibility to be "good" parents and teachers, in a sense, even more urgent. As teachers and parents, we are so aware of this unconditional forgiveness that, somehow, it is at the heart of our guilt. We know that as true pedagogues, we must always strive to live up to the worth and trust bestowed upon us by the children. We must not abuse their forgiveness.

Indeed, children are natural forgivers. Children forgive their parents simply by loving them. It would be difficult to overestimate the significance of a child's attachment to a parent. A child may have been hurt physically or emotionally, but the need to reestablish a loving relationship with the parent is always there. As children grow older there is often a time when they are more distant for a while, more inclined to judge parents for their failings and limitations. But usually these feelings get resolved, and then forgiveness is rooted in "understanding."

The same holds for teachers. The teacher, *in loco parentis*, uses the primordial parent-child relationship in which the child wants to please the parent as a resource for developing a pedagogical relationship. In some important respects a teacher is like a parent. Young people need a teacher who recognizes them and believes in them. The power of teacher recognition and belief in a child's identity, learning, and development is truly inestimable.

Yes, teaching is a pedagogical task; therefore, the teacher cannot help, at times, but act mistakenly and make misjudgments in his or her relations with students. But the important question is: How do the students experience the teacher's care? A teacher who takes responsibility and actively cares for the young people he or she teaches stands in a state of grace with them.

Contrary to a common saying, to forgive is not necessarily to forget. But forgiving has its own pedagogical value: restoring the relationship between mother or father and son or daughter, between teacher and student or, generally, between a caring older person and a child or young person through love and understanding.

Appendix A

Ethical-Pedagogical Perspectives

Pedagogy is a practice and theory that requires a sensitive understanding of the nature of childhood. It requires understanding what kinds of lives children are living in various social, cultural, and family environments and what are the interests, play spaces, technologies, and media that preoccupy children and young people and to which they are exposed. So pedagogical theory and practice presupposes a sensible knowledge of child psychology, sociology, ethnography, and philosophy. But at the heart of these sensibilities lies the realization that pedagogy is in essence always already a relational ethics: the ethics of distinguishing what is good from what is not good, appropriate from inappropriate for the children and young people who are entrusted to our care—as parents, teachers, childcare professionals, family members, neighbors, and so forth. Practically, there is the ethical requirement of knowing how to act in the best interest of the child or children before us. In addition, when reflecting on our actions, or when being accountable for our actions, we may need to resort to ethical considerations that are in a sense external to the ethics that already inheres in pedagogy itself.

Sometimes, when we sense that a child has problems or needs some kind of support, we may opt for a certain ethical approach in our dealing with the child. In other words, pedagogy suggests or asks for a certain ethics that feeds our pedagogical thoughtfulness. This ethical and moral thoughtfulness and tact cannot easily be caught in the neat conceptual frames of existing ethical theories and moral philosophies. And yet it may be helpful to explore how the various ethical and moral philosophies could be translated into ethical pedagogical perspectives.

Pedagogical ethics is not unlike bioethics except that the focus is on the ethical relation between adults and children or young people rather than on the ethical relation between health science practitioners and patients or ill people. Especially in the medical domain of pediatrics and neonatology,

Pedagogical Tact: Knowing What to Do When You Don't Know What to Do, by Max van Manen, 195–202.
© 2015 Taylor & Francis. All rights reserved.

the ethics of health-care practice and decision making regarding sick children, premature or newborn babies with medical issues, are situated less likely in abstract theories but rather in the concrete face-to-face encounters between health-care practitioners and the parents of the infants and children. As Michael van Manen describes in his study of (in)decisions in the NICU (neonatal intensive care unit), the "phenomenal meaning of an ethical decision lies neither wholly in the subjective nor in the objective realm" (2014, p. 1).

In the following paragraphs common ethical perspectives such as deontologism (principle ethics), utilitarianism (hedonistic ethics), consequentialism (teleological ethics), contractualism (consensual ethics), virtue ethics (moral character ethics), situational ethics (existential ethics), and relational ethics (alterity-oriented ethics) are briefly examined for their possible pedagogical import. These seven ethical perspectives provide different responses to the question: Is it good or ethically appropriate for an adult to act with children in this or that manner in this or that situation? Deontological, utilitarian, consequentialist, and contractual ethical perspectives lend themselves especially to moral reasoning, theorizing, and moral judgment. Virtue ethics, situational ethics, and relational ethics are perhaps more attuned to understanding the ethical experience, comportment, intuition, thoughtfulness, and tact in an adult's pedagogical practice.

Deontological Pedagogy

Deontological pedagogical action and reflection is primarily guided by moral norms, obligations, rules of conduct, and principles such as the categorical imperative. Immanuel Kant argued that one should "act only according to that maxim that could or should become a universal law." Deontological ethics posits that it is the action itself, not the consequence of an action that should determine whether it is right or wrong, just or unjust. Deontology means the study (*logos*) of duty (*deon*). Deontological ethics is also called principle ethics.

The principle of the golden rule can also be formulated as, "Don't do unto others what you would not want to be done unto yourself." In dealing with others we should always ask ourselves if that is how we would want to be treated ourselves. Or in interacting with children we should ask whether we would treat our own children in the same manner. The philosopher Kant proposed that we can distinguish good actions from bad actions by rationally examining the thought upon which the action is based. He suggested that people are inclined to do the right or good thing if only they know what is right or good.

There are duties-based and rights-based deontological ethics. A duties-based ethics posits that one adheres to the moral norms and principles that are accepted as binding. Kant argued that one should always be honest and tell the truth and never lie. One should never use a person as a means (for someone else's benefit) but always as an end. From a deontological perspective, morally right action has priority over what is good. It is possible that a certain action may produce outcomes that are good and desirable from a consequentialist perspective, but the action may be morally wrong from a deontological ethics. For example, a deontological ethicist may insist that one should never lie, not even to one's enemies, who could take advantage of one's refusal to lie.

The problem is, however, that it is not necessarily clear what, in actual concrete situations, the contents of right and wrong, duties and obligations consist of. For example, when deontological ethics mandates that we should always treat children with respect, then it is not necessarily clear what respect means in particular situations and relations with young children.

Utilitarian Pedagogy

Utilitarianism is sometimes called hedonistic ethics because actions are judged to be good to the degree that they bring about happiness or pleasure. Jeremy Bentham (Bentham and Mill, 1987) argued that good acting should be useful and have utility with respect to certain goals and purposes. Bentham thought that the ultimate purpose in life consists in attaining as much pleasure and happiness as possible. Indeed, in thinking back about their past family and school life, some people feel that they largely enjoyed a happy childhood; others feel that their childhood was marred by neglect or abuse from their parents or insensitivities and cruelties from teachers and other people. Many parents are surely hoping that what they do is good: they want to give their children a happy childhood and lead them to a happy life.

A utilitarian pedagogy tries to do what gives students happiness and avoid what gives pain. If actions lead to more happiness and well-being and to less suffering and frustration, then the actions are morally good. Should teachers share the outcomes of tests publicly with the whole class? Some students likely will take pleasure in hearing how well they have done in front of their peers, but other students may prefer receiving their grades in private. Utilitarian criteria for acting in certain ways sometimes lead to problems. What if the majority of the students like to hear their grades in public, whereas a few students will feel hurt when their academic standing is exposed?

Not everything we do with and for the children in our care is pleasurable for them in the present moment. At school children may have to engage in learning activities and test their abilities, which can be challenging. A child studying music may need to spend many hours practicing certain skills that will eventually lead to good musicianship but are not very pleasant in the moment. Thus, the utilitarian idea that something is good if it brings pleasure to the largest number is not necessarily without ambiguity.

Consequentialist Pedagogy

Consequentialism is the contemporary variation of utilitarian ethics, sometimes termed teleological ethics (*telos* is the Greek word for purpose, end, or goal). As the term suggests, consequentialism stresses the importance of the effects and the outcomes of actions. The question of whether an act is morally right or wrong depends solely on the consequences of that act itself. However, upon closer examination there are many ethical issues associated with identifying the moral goodness of acts with their moral consequences. Therefore, philosophy has produced several varieties of consequentialist perspectives, depending, for example, upon the moral value of the consequences, the actual as opposed to the intended consequences of one's actions, or the consequences that maximize the goodness of actions in the world. Martha Nussbaum (2000) uses the phrase "sensible consequentialism" to indicate that one needs to take a balanced view of the moral status and value of consequences. For example, pedagogical actions are good when they maximize the happiness as well as the capabilities of children.

So, from a pedagogical point of view courses of actions should be chosen on the basis of the relevant effects of those actions and the states of affairs that are their consequences, and relevant to what is in the child or children's interest. Parents and teachers should always do what maximizes the good of the consequences for the children in their care. And the good has to be relevant to the present and the future lives of children.

In general we want our children's lives and futures to be happy. So consequentialist pedagogy wants to understand the significance and the meaning of the happiness and joy that follows from certain actions. For example, it is good when children experience the pleasure of success and positive recognition. But is it good to give pleasure to some if it is enjoyed at the cost of others? Giving praise may increase a student's self-esteem, but too much praise can lead to unrealistic confidence in one's abilities or talents. Obviously not everything that is pleasurable is good for us. Should parents allow unlimited access to screen time on television, computer, or mobile devices? Should children be permitted unlimited junk food because these give them pleasure? Surely not. And yet some children are permitted to live unhealthy lifestyles.

Contractualist Pedagogy

Contractualism is consensual ethics: an action is right to the extent that it is justifiable, based on agreement and guided by rational and emotional consent. In research and medical contexts the participants or patients are commonly required to sign informed-consent documents, attesting that they agree to certain medical interventions that could involve risky predicaments or outcomes. In pedagogical contexts consent may be required to be given by the parent when the child is too young to understand the issues. But as children get older they too should be involved in consent decisions.

The difficulty is that young people of the same age do not necessarily possess the maturity or wisdom that they should be asked to give consent to actions or participation in situations that could be dangerous or morally questionable. So parents often must take substitutive responsibility for their children. For example, schools ask parents to sign consent forms to seek their agreement to participate in activities that could raise social or health concerns or pose risks of conflicting values (e.g., sex education lessons, participating in research conducted in classrooms, field trips, etc.).

Teachers too are often considered to act *in loco parentis* when it comes to certain pedagogical responsibilities. Contractualist pedagogy hinges on the question of whether certain activities in which children are engaged can be justified in terms of agreements and consensus from the children themselves or from their responsible parents or teachers, who act *in loco parentis*, when the children can only carry diminished responsibilities for giving their consent.

Virtue Pedagogy

Virtue ethics refers to the pedagogical qualities, moral character, moral wisdom, pedagogical motives, and intents of the adult. The notion of virtue is a common translation of the Greek word for excellence, *arete*. The *aretai*, the excellences or virtues, were simply the qualities that made a particular life exemplary, good, admirable, or excellent. Abstract, deontological moral concepts such as the Good, Equality, and Justice do little to guide the thousand and one interactions of our daily lives. Educators, therefore, need to point to richer and more concrete forms of acting that are thoughtful, tactful, and sensitive to the child's experience.

Virtue ethics promotes pedagogical qualities such as understanding a learner's difficulties, knowing how to listen, seeing each child as unique and different, understanding fears and vulnerabilities, encouraging success, remaining patient and supportive, and being reliable, trusted, and available to children. The interesting point about virtues is that they are not reducible to rules or moral principles; virtues are the qualities that support the ethical integrity of a pedagogical practice. In *After Virtue* Alistair MacIntyre (1981) points out that virtues are necessary to attain the internal good of a practice such as pedagogy. In addition, virtues sustain habits, routines, and traditions that enable appropriate pedagogical practices within contingent social and historical contexts.

Ever since the ancient Greeks, specific virtues have usually been explained narratively—through story, poem, anecdote, parable, myth, or theater—by referring to virtuous individuals or virtuous actions as examples. In contemporary life too we tend to use stories and anecdotes when we wish to explain that good parents should have patience or that good teachers should "know" their children. Often what happens is that we tell concrete anecdotes about things that a pedagogically tactful person would do who possesses this or that quality. Thus, virtues are indications of the ethical character of a person. They answer the question of whether a person is well prepared for certain life tasks and responsibilities. This is true for adults and for children. Virtues are commonly acquired through the formation of good habits or customs that parents instill in children. And virtues are also the pedagogical qualities that should be developed and encouraged in teachers and other childcare specialists—and, of course, in parents.

So from the perspective of virtue pedagogy, more important than rules and regulations are the pedagogical character traits of the "being" of the teacher. Pedagogical virtues (qualities) of teaching have been discussed throughout the educational literature. They include qualities such as love for knowledge and wanting to act as a mediator between student and knowledge; being dependable in word and deed; being available and reachable to children and students; being able to have confidence and believe in children, even if the confidence and belief seem unreasonable; being trustworthy and trusting of children; being patient with children; having active hope; acting with dedication and diligence; having balanced expectations of children; being able to act with interpretive intelligence and pedagogically sensitive humor that makes it possible to recognize and relativize the limits of one's own task and possibilities as teacher or parent or childcare professional—we are not almighty, we cannot do everything or for everyone.

Situational Pedagogy

Situational pedagogy focuses on the intrinsic rightness and goodness of what is required in the concrete situation itself—it is not concerned with some abstract principle or the eventual consequences of action. Somehow the pedagogical ethics of good acting—what is good or in the best interest of children—are to be found in the situation in which we find ourselves with these children. And every situation has its own cultural, social, and personal contexts. Situation ethics has roots in existentialist ethics that grew out of the post–World War II experience and the disillusionment with the fact that traditional deontological values and morals somehow permitted the atrocities of the Holocaust and permit the present-day horrors of terrorism and tribal and nationalistic conflicts.

Situation ethics also has roots in the unselfish ethic of *agape*—what is expected of us in every ethical situation is that we act with love. We cannot blame the commands of superiors for our wrongdoings; we cannot lay the blame at the door of so-called higher values of serving our nation. Similarly we cannot exonerate our actions by saying that we are simply following the orders or policies of the larger system within which we work. Situation ethics stresses that in every concrete situation we are personally responsible for our actions. We must do what is best for the child or student, even if it means ignoring the curriculum or violating school policy. As a teacher, I am responsible for what I do or fail to do in this particular situation with this or that child or group of children.

Situationism posits that whatever we do should be out of pedagogical "love" for the children in our care. But love is not a norm or a rule. It does not concretely tell us what to do. Situational pedagogy throws us back onto our own responsibility and our freedom to act responsibly. Responsibility and freedom are intrinsically tied. Without freedom there is no responsibility—we can only act responsibly in freedom. We cannot defer our responsibilities by claiming that we are constrained to do what we should do. Jean-Paul Sartre's famous phrase is that we are condemned to freedom, meaning that we cannot fall back on external rules, principles, or excuses for acting the way we do. We are personally responsible for our responsibilities. The possibilities and criteria for exercising our responsibilities lie in each existential situation in which we find ourselves with the children or students in our care.

Relational Pedagogy

Relational ethics is based on an ethically responsible responsiveness to the need, vulnerability, and weakness of the other whom we encounter and for whom we experience moral responsibility. Relational ethics presumes that one must be able to overcome an orientation to the world that seems to come naturally with human beings, the attitude of seeing oneself at the center of all things. According to Emmanuel Levinas (1998, 2003), I do not really experience the subjectivity of the other until I am able to overcome the centeredness of the self in my world. The fascinating thing is that my possibility of the experience of the otherness of Other originates in my experience of the vulnerability of the other. It is when I see that the other is a person who can experience hurt, distress, pain, suffering, anguish, weakness, grief, or despair that I may be opened to the singularity, the alterity of the other.

Strangely, when I encounter the other in a true I-Other relation, the ethical relation has turned into a relational nonrelation. In this nonrelation the other now has relational primacy over the self. Within the terms of relational ethics the vulnerability of the other has become the weak spot in the armor of the self-centered world. For example, I see a child who is hurt or who is in agony, and, temporarily at least, I forget my present preoccupations. No longer am I driven by my personal agenda. For the moment I am just there for this child, for this other person. And with this recognition of the other comes the possibility of acting ethically for the sake of the other.

And so when I stand in an ethical relation to a child and I actually "see" this child in his or her singularity and vulnerability, then I am in a pedagogical position to do something good for this child. In fact, most likely the relational situation is such that I find myself responding, acting, and orienting to the child before I even think about it. Wilfried Lippitz points out how the primal internal meaning of pedagogy already constitutes its ethical relational significance:

> [M]y responsibility springs from an obligation brought about by the Other, who acts as my master (maître). He or she enables me to do what I am not able to do myself: to discover myself as an I in my responsibility for the Other, to step out of the maelstrom of my own self-referential, economic existence. Thus the establishment of a pedagogical responsibility ensues from the internal pedagogical dimension of the ethical relation. In other words, the Other, the stranger, the child is the condition for the possibility of my pedagogical activity. (Lippitz, 1990, p. 59)

Of course, in a real sense every human being is vulnerable; every human being is mortal and subject to fears and dangers. And so every human being is my other. The other is actually or potentially weak and vulnerable (just as I know myself to be actually or potentially weak and vulnerable). However, the existence of other does not merely manifest itself as my feelings of pity or compassion for the hurt or suffering of this other person. From the perspective of relational ethics, I experience the face of the other as a moral demand, the voice of the other as an appeal to me. And this is what we mean when we speak of our living with children as a vocation, as a calling.

Appendix B

Historical Notes

It may be worth remembering that the etymology of the word "pedagogy" consists of two parts: *paides,* which means child or young person, and *agogy,* which means to give guidance, to accompany, to help, or to lead. So the origin of the term "pedagogy" signifies the supporting of young people. In the wider literature the term pedagogy may appear in such disciplinary phrases as social and cultural pedagogy (examining and discussing how children are seen and to be treated in various societal and cultural contexts), school pedagogy (focusing on the pedagogical relations between educators such as teachers or administrators and their students), historical pedagogy (considering how childhood and children have been seen, understood, and treated through the ages), political pedagogy (primarily preoccupied with government and institutional policies affecting young people, such as in citizenship education, and young-offenders legislation), pedagogy as an agogical science (studying childcare practices in various professions such as child psychology, counseling, social work, and health care), ortho-pedagogy (which deals with special education of handicapped children), pedagogy of technology (that examines how technology affects the way children grow up and are affected by new media and technologies), and andragogy (the ethical practices of dealing with adults and with adult education concerns).

In this book pedagogy (in particular the topic of pedagogical thoughtfulness and tact) focuses primarily on that sphere and relational reality where adults play a role in the education and bringing up of children and young people. To act pedagogically always means to support and to strengthen the (young) person, never to break down or diminish the person for whom we carry pedagogical responsibility. So, the term pedagogy refers to what parents, teachers, and other adults do when interacting with children or young people, but the term may also be appropriate in relational activities between adults who have become students again, such as in advanced levels of education, apprenticeship, mentorship, or university studies.

Informal equivalent terms of the formal term pedagogy are childrearing, raising children, parenting, upbringing of children, or helping young people grow up toward independence, and mature adulthood. However, none of these English terms are quite equivalent to what in other languages is commonly referred to as *opvoeding* (Dutch), *Bildung* (German), *utbildning* (Swedish), *utdanning* (Norwegian), *élever* (French), *allevare* (Italian), and so forth. In Dutch or German there is a distinction between instruction: *onderwijs* (Dutch), *Unterrichtung* or *Unterweisung* (German) and upbringing: *opvoeding* (Dutch), *Erziehung* or *Bildung* (German). But in English, both terms *onderwijs* and *opvoeding* translate as *education*. The confusion is that the term "education" more commonly applies to "schooling" and less commonly to "pedagogy" or "the upbringing of and caring for children." Thus we need to see that the term pedagogy is "richer" and means more than education: pedagogy means education but also *opvoeding*, *Bildung*, *utbildning*, *utdanning*, *élever*, *allevare*.

In schooling contexts the currency of the term *pedagogy* dates at least to the French *pédagogie* in 1495. It was used to refer to the place of teaching such as a school, college, or university. For example, in the fifteenth century the University of Glasgow was also called the Pedagogy of Glasgow. The British usage of the term "pedagogy" (pedagogue, pedagogical, etc.) was actually rather limited—it has been mainly used to refer to the art, practice, and occupation of teaching and to the theories, principles, and methods on which these practices have been based. In recent history the use of the term pedagogy has acquired pedantic overtones in the English language.

Human Science Pedagogy

Pedagogy has a long history in early Greek and Continental philosophies. A list of prominent thinkers of pedagogy usually includes Plato, Seneca, Augustine, Erasmus, Montaigne, Comenius, Locke, Rousseau, Pestalozzi, and Herbart. But with Dilthey, Nohl, Litt, and Flitner the study of pedagogy entered the philosophical period of the human sciences (*Geisteswissenschaften*). The *Geisteswissenschaften* was a cultural reaction to the enlightenment rationalism of previous periods in Continental thought.

Some of the main recent proponents of the pedagogical movements were psychologists, whereas others were philosophers, as the chair of philosophy was often responsible for pedagogy at Western European universities. And yet *Geisteswissenschaftliche Pädagogik* should not be confused with "philosophy of education," at least not as we know it in North America and Britain. The Continental movements were very different from the later British and North American fields of analytic philosophy of education. In the German, Dutch, and Scandinavian traditions the study of pedagogy was seen as a theoretical and practical discipline in its own right rather than as the application of philosophical concerns or concepts *to* education.

From approximately 1910 to the late 1950s in Germany and from the end of World War II to the mid-1960s in the Netherlands, several generations of educational scholars participated in an emerging form of inquiry and thinking that became known as *Geisteswissenschaftliche Pädagogik* in Germany and as *fenomenologische pedagogiek* in the Netherlands. As these terms suggest, the German tradition was more hermeneutic in orientation, whereas the Dutch tradition was more oriented to the phenomenology of the pedagogical lifeworld. In Germany the first major proponents of the *Geisteswissenschaftliche* tradition in education were Herman Nohl (1879–1960) and his contemporaries Theodor Litt (1880–1962), Eduard Spranger (1882–1963), Max Frischeisen-Köhler (1878–1923), and somewhat independently Peter Petersen (1884–1952).

As a student of Wilhelm Dilthey (1833–1911), Herman Nohl (1879–1960) was largely responsible for working out a pedagogical theory on the basis of Diltheyan starting points and formulations. To the second generation belong Nohl's students such as Erich Weniger (1894–1961), Wilhelm Flitner (1889–1990), and Otto Friedrich Bollnow (1903–1999) as well as Josef Derbolav (1912–1987), Theodor Ballauf (1911–1985), and Klaus Schaller (1925). The thinking and the theoretical corpus of this group became known as the Dilthey-Nohl School. This movement was primarily oriented to explicating the meaning of pedagogy in human life. Pedagogy was first of all a notion that the *Geisteswissenschaftliche Pädagogik* approached on the basis of two modes of manifestation: pedagogy as a primordial human phenomenon and pedagogy as a cultural phenomenon (Hintjes, 1981).

Thus, pedagogy became an emergent field of studies and theorizing. First pedagogy became a theme in the hermeneutic human sciences of Dilthey, Nohl, and Litt. Subsequently the emphasis shifted to the phenomenological pedagogy of Langeveld, Bollnow, Vermeer, and Beets. Both were eventually displaced by the critical pedagogy of Wolfgang Klafki (1927–) and Klaus Mollenhauer (1928–1998) in Germany and somewhat differently by Paulo Freire (1921–1997) in Brazil.

In the eighteenth and nineteenth centuries the norms and values of the church (Catholicism, Protestantism, and other denominational belief systems) strongly influenced the education and upbringing of children. With the emergence of the human sciences (*Geisteswissenschaften*) the taken-for-granted beliefs and practices of the old normative pedagogies were increasingly questioned and philosophically interrogated. It is in this context that phenomenology and hermeneutics became strong philosophical platforms for the attempts at developing pedagogical approaches that could be freed from the normativities and habituated presumptions and prejudices of the milieus in which they operated.

Wolfgang Klafki

While in North America the field of education tends to be discussed in terms of the coupling "curriculum and instruction," in Continental educational discourses the common coupling is "pedagogy and didactics." In recent years curriculum scholars like Ian Westbury, Stefan Hopmann, and Kurt Riquarts (2010) have aimed to bridge and develop conversations between the discourses of Curriculum and the discourses of *Didaktik*. However, the meaning of the concept of pedagogy remained largely unexplored in these comparative conversations between the North American theories of Curriculum and the German or Continental theories of *Didaktik*.

The problem is that the concept of pedagogy is partially entwined with the concept of *Didaktik*. Initially, Klafki (1964) places his *Didaktik* in the context of the pedagogical traditions of Pestalozzi, Herbart, Fröbel, and Schleiermacher. Pedagogy is discussed as *Bildung*: the formative growth, educational development, and ethical growth of the person. *Bildung* and *Didaktik* presuppose each other. Every decision of *Didaktik* presumes something about *Bildung*. Therefore, Klafki formulates seven guiding principles of the pedagogy of educational forming (*Bildung*): (1) Forming involves a dialectic tension between individuality and sociality; (2) Forming is a unifying process that does not distinguish between the inner (of the subject) and the outer (of the world)—person and world mutually influence each other; (3) Forming must make it possible to live with and tolerate tension and imperfections; (4) Forming is not static but requires an attitude of openness, flexibility, and change; (5) Forming shapes social conscience which opposes social inequality and injustice; (6) Forming is not ego-centric or ethno-centric but global in intent; (7) Forming involves responsibility and the conscious acceptance of moral principles such as loyalty, trust, honesty, dependability, courage, openness, etc. It is clear that for Klafki the coupling of *Pedagogik* and *Didaktik* has consequences for the educational growth and also for the character development of the students.

Klafki distinguishes dimensions that are of importance in the deliberation of aims and content in the *Didaktik*. For example, one must ask, what are the formative possibilities of each subject matter at the particular age/level of the students? Klafki discusses at length what is elemental (or basic) in determining what is to be taught. Since not everything can be included in the courses of study, one needs to focus on general insights, lawful relationships and structures. *Didaktik* must relate specificity to generality, particularity to universality. This relationship of the general to the particular can take various elemental forms (1964, pp. 441-451):

- *Exemplary content:* for example in physics the law of gravity is demonstrated with the particular case of a falling stone;

totalitarianism in history is taught with the example of Franco in Spain.
- *Typical content:* the typical is a pregnant case of other similar cases. For example in geography we study the Sahara desert as a typical case of other deserts, with consequences for ecology, plants, animals, etc.
- *Classic content:* for example, a certain moral quality is taught at the hand of a single individual.
- *Representative content:* for example those aspects of history are taught that have contemporary relevance.

The teacher must determine the formative (*Bildung*) value of *Didaktik* decisions (Klafki, 1985). For example, the teacher must ask, how is this exemplary, typical, classic, and representative content related to a larger instructional theme or goal? What possible place or significance does the knowledge or competencies associated with this content have for the life experience of a child at this age/level? Wherein lies the significance of this *didaktical* theme for the future of the children? And so forth.

John Dewey

In Continental historical contexts there is a considerable literature of past authors such as Rousseau, Pestalozzi, Fröbel, and Montessori who preoccupied themselves with pedagogical questions regarding the practice of schooling and bringing up children and ethical questions of how children are or should be cared for in families, schools, and communities. In Continental cultural contexts these past traditions have contemporary proponents. In the United Kingdom and North America there is, strangely perhaps, very little comparable pedagogical literature and scholarship. Only critical pedagogy became a hotly debated field of concern in curriculum studies.

The main educational thinker in North America was no doubt the highly productive author and educational philosopher John Dewey. In his well-known *Credo* Dewey (1929) explicates what education is, what the school is, what the subject matter of education is, what the nature of method is, and what the school and social progress is. In other places Dewey speaks of the intellectual and the personal qualities of the teacher. But nowhere does Dewey address the relational qualities that carry the pedagogical experiences of the child. Dewey gets closest to the idea of a pedagogical relation when he talks of the political context of teaching and the notion of democratic classrooms. And, of course, by reading between the lines one can attribute to Dewey certain interests. For example, when he explains how

> the child lives in a somewhat narrow world of personal contacts. Things hardly come within his experience unless they touch, intimately and obviously, his own

well-being, or that of his family and friends. His world is a world of persons with their personal interests, rather than a realm of facts and laws. Not truth, in the sense of conformity to external fact, but affection and sympathy, is its keynote. (Dewey, 1902, p. 5)

And yet it is the pedagogical attentiveness to the child's experience and how we need to deal with the child in pedagogical moments that seem less evident in Dewey's writings. Of course, this is not meant as a critique of Dewey, but rather as an observation that Dewey's massive influence on all aspects of educational thought and practice did not really extend to the pedagogical relation between adult and child, which is the main focus of this book.

Johann Friedrich Herbart on Pedagogical Tact

Herbart's 1802 lecture is little known even amongst Herbart scholars—except in the German educational literature (Metz, 1995). Jakob Muth (1962) was the first scholar who articulated and developed important distinctions with regard to Herbart's notion of tact in German.

In his "Lecture on Pedagogy" Herbart argues that in everyday teaching-learning situations theories of teaching and learning are not effective and appropriate guides for pedagogical actions. And yet from moment to moment a teacher must act and know what to say or do (or refrain from doing). Herbart suggests that this instant acting is best described with tact. But strangely, perhaps, after this initial lecture Herbart never again mentioned the notion of pedagogical tactfulness in any of his many subsequent publications.

So, it may be helpful to examine some excerpts from Johann Friedrich Herbart's first Lecture on Pedagogy (Herbart 1851, pp. 63-74). I have translated these excerpts (with some collegial assistance). The text dates to the very beginning of Herbart's career as a university teacher, when he presented these two talks to pedagogy students at the University of Göttingen in 1802. But the manuscript of Herbart's Lecture on Pedagogy was not published until after his death in 1841. The second part of the lecture is only partially retained as a fragment. From today's perspective the Lecture on Pedagogy may seem discontinuous with Herbart's subsequent writings, or at least incompatible with the "systematic Herbart" as we know him.

Herbart was a philosopher, psychologist, and scholar of pedagogy. He had studied with the Swiss educator Pestalozzi and initially lectured at Göttingen. In 1809 he was appointed to the chair of philosophy at Königsberg, formerly occupied by the famous philosopher Immanuel Kant. Herbart argues in his *Allgemeine Pädagogik* (2005) that the science of pedagogy consists of a fusing of ethics with psychology. A major theme of Herbart's work concerns the meaning of character and character education in young people.

So it could be argued that Herbart's interest in the development of character in both the educator and the student is in some way a follow-through of his initial interest in the development pedagogical tact in educators. Herbart's psychological and philosophical works profoundly influenced Continental and North American theories of education, and his Herbartian educational systems of teaching are still evident in contemporary educational practices. But discussions of Herbart's notion of pedagogical tact are rather limited to the German educational literature (Metz, 1995).

In his "Lecture on Pedagogy" Herbart coins and elaborates on the concept of pedagogical tact. He begins his discussion by posing the issue of practice in epistemological terms. He argues that scientific knowledge is not an appropriate source for the active practice of teaching, because any particular scientific theory is always too narrow, only focusing on a small segment and limited aspect of reality. But theory is also too broad in that it aims to describe universal and general lawful dimensions of the physical and social worlds. In the words of Herbart:

> In the school of science, therefore, one learns always simultaneously too much and too little for practice.

A scientist who is deeply engaged in theory may still not be a good practitioner. Think of the scholar who possesses much theoretical knowledge about child psychology but who does not know how to interact with children. And yet, in everyday situations one must continuously act.

> No matter how good the theorist is when he applies his theory, then an *intermediate* part, in the form of a certain tact, will insert itself quite involuntarily between theory and practice, although not in those cases where the person applies the theory with the same pedantic slowness as a pupil who does a mathematical calculation.

At this epistemological level Herbart simply points out that the structure of instant acting can be described as tact. It would be virtually impossible to support every action in which we engage with deliberative theoretical knowledge. Our actions would become too slow, too cumbersome, too awkward, and too technical. Therefore, Herbart says, tact is

> a mode of action that is less the result of one's thinking, but instead gives vent to one's inner movement, expressing how one has been affected from without, and exhibiting one's emotional state.

This could be called the ontological aspect of tact: it expresses who we *are* and who we have *become* as a result of past life *experience*. In this embodied sense our practical interactions take the shape of instant acting—which is tact. However, Herbart still perceives a "space" between theory and practice which shows that he is still wedded to a theory-practice epistemology:

> *Inevitably* tact occupies the place that theory leaves vacant, and thus tact becomes the immediate ruler (regent) of our practice. This would all be fortunate, without doubt, if this regent is at the same time a truthfully obedient servant of the theory—of which the correctness here is presupposed. The big question, which determines whether one would be a good or a bad educator is solely this: *how* is this tact formed in a person? And is this tact faithful or unfaithful to the laws which science pronounces in its generality?

It seems that at first Herbart implicitly makes the case that there is actually nothing special about tact. Since in the instant of the moment of acting we do not really have theoretical knowledge that can guide our actions, tact becomes the spontaneous substitute for theory in spontaneous acting. Thus, Herbart does not want to declare scientific theory irrelevant. He points out that although theory is not fitted for instant practical acting, it should still ultimately lie at the base of our actions. Theory informs our actions indirectly by preparing and shaping our "being," as we say in contemporary language. For Herbart theory is still the ultimate arbiter for "good" practical acting. But, at Herbart's time an ontological sense of epistemology-of-practice (knowledge as personal "being") was not yet current.

Second, Herbart makes the critical claim that we should judge whether someone is a good teacher or good other educator by the kind or quality of tactfulness that has formed the pedagogical character of the educator. So whereas tact is inevitably the structure of instant acting, only tact that is internalized in the person while also rooted in good scientific theory will be indicative of the good educator. So the preparation for tactful acting is the study of the "science" of education (a term that Herbart would have used more broadly and philosophically than we currently use the term "science"). But the practice of tact is especially formed by practice itself and by our subsequent reflections, ethical-emotional responses, and thoughtful examinations of our practices.

> Let us meditate a bit further, on which effective causes and what influences determine the manner in which educational tact becomes implanted in us. It is formed during practice, it is formed by the influence of practice on our feelings that we exercise in this practice. This effect would be different and would become different, as far as we are different and as far as we are differently attuned. We must and can influence our attunement by reflection. It depends upon the correctedness and weight of this reflection, upon the interest and moral willingness with which we give ourselves up to it.

In this insistence on the role of reflection on practice for the preparation of the possibility of tactful acting lies also the possibility to see tact as the action dimension of a thoughtfulness that has been shaped by reflection on experience. Thus, Herbart in a sense prepares for the possibility of conceptualizing an inner thoughtfulness that constitutes the phenomenological coupling with tact. Thoughtfulness expresses itself in practical action as pedagogical tact.

Herbart also makes the important observation that tactful (instant) actions cannot be planned because tact is improvisational. But by extending Herbart's thinking, we can say that, while tact is unplannable, it can be reflectively conditioned as a style of thoughtfulness.

> The educator must prepare not how he is going to act in specific cases in the future but rather he must prepare himself—this means his mood, his head, his heart, in order to correctly perceive, apperceive, feel and judge the phenomena that await him and the situation in which he may be placed. This must be done through thinking, reflecting, inquiring, through science. If he has anticipatingly indulged in extensive plans, the practical circumstances will mock him. But if he has equipped himself with fundamental principles, then his experiences will be clear to him and teach him every time what is to be done in every case. If he does not know how to distinguish what is significant from what is insignificant, he will waste his effort on what is useless and fail to do what is necessary and wear himself out on what is useless.

And, as we see in the above quote, for Herbart, ultimately science is the arbiter of good tactful action .

> There is then—this is my conclusion—a preparation for the art by science, a preparation of both the head and the heart before we start the enterprise, by virtue of which the experience, which we can obtain only in performing the enterprise itself, will become instructive to us. Only in acting do we learn the art and acquire tact, aptness, quickness, skill; but even in acting only he learns the art who in previous thinking has learned the science, has made it his own, has attuned himself by it—and has predetermined the impressions that are made upon him by experience.

Tact is unplannable and also unruly. It cannot be regulated by certain techniques, rules, or instruments.

> From preparation one should not at all expect that out of its hands one will emerge as an infallible master of the [educator's] art. One should not even ask from it the special instructions about how to act. One should have faith that one will have enough inventiveness to hit upon the particular thing that needs to be done in any instant. One should expect to learn from the mistakes themselves that one is going to make; and one may do this in pedagogy rather than in a thousand other occupations, because here, usually, every single action of the educator as such is trivial—infinitely more important is the totality of action. One must not appear again, to feel constantly the myriad of little things that will be observed with him in his memory. But on the other hand one has to fill all of those considerations that affect the dignity, the importance of the main tools of education.

Even in the above paraphrases from Herbart's speech there is evident a somewhat mechanistic conceptualization of the mediating role of tact between theory and practice. For Herbart science is ultimately the source and arbiter for the practice of tact. The point is that tact does not lie between the continents of theory and practice. Theory—as empirical science and speculative theory—aims for truth and the discovery of scientific facts. Practice—*Praxis, Kunde,* and *Kunst*—as the other side of theory, deals with skills, routines, habits, and practical arts. But tact is of an entirely different order. Therefore, tact needs a different language to express and sponsor itself in our day-to-day living and acting.

For this reason, we may distinguish several modalities of thoughtful "knowing" that are noncognitive in a pathic sense. Rather than speak of possessing a "body of knowledge" we could speak of "body knowledge". More experientially, we feel that our knowing resides in our actions, situations, relations, and, especially, in our bodies. And phenomenologically that is indeed the case. In our daily living we experience our knowing how and what to do through our actions, through the situations in which we find ourselves, through our relations with others and the world around us, and through our embodied being or corporeal existence. To say this differently:

a. Actional knowing: in moments of tactful practice, we may feel that our knowledge, as knowing what to do, resides in our actions: knowledge is action. In a sense we discover what we know, in how we act, in what we can do. This actional knowledge is experienced as confidence in acting, as personal style, as practical tact, and also as habituations, routines, kinesthetic memories, and so on.

b. Situational and thingly knowing: in moments of tactful practice, we may feel that our knowledge resides situationally in the things of our world. Indeed, we discover what we know and "who we are" through the things around us and in the things that belong to us and to which we belong. This situational knowledge is experienced as the way we know ourselves through place, space, the objects, the thingly contingencies of our daily existences. We experience situations by way of recognition, memory, feeling at home, familiar mood, and so on.

c. Relational knowing: in moments of tactful practice, we may feel that our knowledge resides in relations. We discover what we know in our relations with others, for example, as relations of shared experience, trust, recognition, intimacy; as relations of dependence, dominance, equality, expertise, and so forth. In some relations, we feel comfortable, sure of ourselves, and in discussions with others we may surprise ourselves with how much we know, what we can say, and so on. It may also happen that in some relational circumstances, we feel uncomfortable, unsure of ourselves, and awkward. Most of us may have experienced teachers with whom we felt bright and knowledgeable, while with other teachers we felt insecure and stupid.

d. Corporeal knowing: in moments of tactful practice, we may feel that our knowledge resides in our corporeal being. We discover what we know in our immediate corporeal sense of things and others, and in our gestures, demeanor, and so on. Even more broadly than in tactful acting, we trust the body in our daily living and our activities. Thanks to our body knowledge and body memories, we can confidently pick up a hot teapot and pour the drink without spilling. Our body knows how to move around in familiar spaces and places, and how to drive the car in routine traffic. Corporeal knowing also expresses itself in the smell of the city in which we live, the particular smell and feel of the autumn leaves under our feet, the familiar smell of supper in our kitchen at home.

All these modalities of noncognitive or pathic knowing intermingle in our everyday tactful actions and perhaps also in our more reflective actions. The phenomenology of body, relation, situation, and temporality is complex and also politically, ethnically, and existentially charged (Friedman and Stoddard Holmes, 2003; Grumet, 2003). Ordinary cognitive discourses are not well suited to address noncognitive dimensions of professional experience. A pathic language is needed in order to evoke and reflect on pathic meanings. Pathic understanding requires a language that is sensitive to the experiential, moral, emotional, and personal dimensions of professional life (van Manen, 2014, pp. 270, 271).

So, rather than see tact as an epistemological device for mediating theory and practice we may see tact as an onto-epistemological notion that can help us to overcome the problematic epistemological parallel between theory and practice. And rather than understand tact as a process of making instant "decisions" and practical "judgments" (phronesis), we may reconceive pedagogical tact as a mindfully perceptive mode of being that permits us to act in the instant of the moment contingently and yet thoughtfully in our living with children and young people.

By interpreting and extending Herbart's notion of tact phenomenologically, it might be termed an onto-epistemology where our instant "knowledge" is experienced as ethically thoughtful actions, relations, situations, and embodied temporalities. In other words, tact as instant practice of thoughtfulness is already experienced as embedded, embodied knowledge.

Languages of Pedagogy

One may wonder why it is that some cultures seem to have a language or words for things that another lacks. Of course, it is commonplace to point out environmental determinants: how the Inuit living in the Northern Arctic have a highly differentiated vocabulary for snow and ice, whereas in most societies one only has a few general terms. The physical environment of human beings provides for experiences that people in different geographical locations may not encounter. And therefore, the language forms associated with these experiences may not be translatable into languages where the ecological conditions are very different. But how does this sit with terms that describe human relationships? More particularly, does the absence of an equivalent for the word pedagogy in some languages reflect a different preoccupation with children? A different approach to children? Or even culturally different ways of perceiving and thinking about children?

The example of Britain is suggestive of such a question. In an earlier paper entitled "Why No Pedagogy in England?" Brian Simon (1981) states that the concept of pedagogy has actually been shunned in England. Why, when in the nearest continental countries such as the Netherlands, Belgium, Germany, and in Scandinavian countries, the concept of pedagogy has a very extensive and widely discussed tradition? According to Simon, this occurred partly because the members of the most prestigious educational institutions, such as the ancient universities of Oxford and Cambridge, have contemptuously rejected the idea that a professional knowledge base is required for the job of teaching. Simon argues that the class system in England led to an emphasis on socialization. Even though the teacher had certain pastoral care responsibilities in terms of upbringing, in the situation of upper-middle-class culture there was an emphasis on traditional rules and values in the operation of the public school systems. In such private boarding schools kids were being brought up by their peers, older kids. The suffering of excessive pestering, bullying, cruel practices, sexual abuse, and rigid routines took their toll among the children, but problems such as these did not allow for systematic pedagogical questioning of how to be attentive to children's experiences and how to deal with them appropriately.

Another reason pedagogy did not fare well among the scholarly elite in England seems to be the cultural assumptions about inborn talent. The concept of pedagogy is rooted in the recognition of the human potential for personal learning, emotional development, moral growth and in the general human condition of sensitivity to children. A more class-oriented view sees education as a selective instrument. Simon feels that certain assumptions of innate intelligence with the educational elite did not seriously allow for the idea that whatever a teacher could do would make a real difference in a child's future social status.

As a footnote to Simon's reflections on the question "Why no pedagogy in England?" it should be pointed out as well that he interprets the concept of pedagogy primarily in a technical manner. He seems especially interested in the reason for the absence of inquiry into the methods and effective techniques of teaching. He understands his own question as asking, "Why no science of pedagogy in England?" But hereby he already gives a very different twist to the notion of pedagogy—different from the way it has been part of the educational tradition just across the Channel separating England from the rest of the continent. There the notion of pedagogy has a long and complex history. As a practice, pedagogy describes the relational values, the personal engagement, the pedagogical climate, the total lifeworlds, and, especially, the emotional and ethical dimensions of life with children at school, at home, and in the community. And as an academic discipline, pedagogy problematizes the conditions of appropriateness of educational practices and aims to provide an ethical and child sensitive knowledge base for professionals who must deal with childhood difficulties, traumas, and problems of childrearing. Central to the idea of pedagogy is the ethical normativity of distinguishing between what is appropriate and what is less appropriate for children and what are appropriate ways of teaching and giving assistance to children and young people.

Pedagogy Without *Paides*

The situation in North America, Canada, and Australia seems somewhat different. The term pedagogy is no longer avoided in English-speaking communities. On the contrary, shortly after the 1980s the term "pedagogy" has turned into a genuine fashion word. It now appears frequently across a great variety of educational and other theoretical discourses. And yet if we look somewhat closer at these usages, then it appears that this language of pedagogy very often covers things that have little, if anything, to do with understanding the lifeworlds of children.

There are three main developments with reference to the notion of pedagogy in the English-speaking world (outside of the UK). One trend is toward an increased substitution of the term pedagogy for the vocabulary of teaching, curriculum, and so forth. A second trend is the appropriation of the term pedagogy by new theorists. A third trend seems to be searching for a new language to express and address pedagogical preoccupations. In looking at the larger picture, the strange situation is that the popularization of the term pedagogy may actually be aiding the process toward an erosion of the sensibility of pedagogy (as the normative practice of dealing with children), while at the same time there is a movement toward a normative pedagogical sensibility in education but under a different nomenclature: the language of moral education and moral discourse about teaching and life in classrooms.

With respect to the first trend, there is obviously an increasingly widespread usage of the term pedagogy. If we do word searches of publications and articles with pedagogy in the title, then we see a curious phenomenon. Up to the early 1970s the term pedagogy was scarcely used. Between 1975 and 1985 books and articles with pedagogy in the title became increasingly noticeable, especially, of course, in the literature of critical pedagogy, which is still popular and important (Apple, 2014; Freire, 1970; Giroux, 2011, 2015). And after the mid-1980s there seems to have been an explosive usage of the term pedagogy.

But as suggested above, in the general domain of education the new coinage of the term pedagogy may be responsible for a certain erosion of pedagogical sensitivities. It appears that the term pedagogy has often simply been used as a buzzword that has replaced the terms teaching, instruction, or curriculum. So instead of speaking of the "teaching of mathematics" or "whole-language curriculum," one now tends to speak of the "pedagogy of mathematics" and "whole-language pedagogy." And yet, like most fashion words, there is a certain extra something that is expressed in the usage of the term.

I have asked teachers what they feel is the sense of meaning of the term pedagogy—for example: What do you feel is the difference between the expression "language pedagogy" and "language teaching"? Teachers say things such as, "The word 'pedagogy' seems to add a philosophic element, it seems to hint at what is at work behind the phenomena." And invariably they immediately ask, "Well, what does pedagogy *really* mean?" This response is not surprising. Often fashion words are fuzzier and less clearly delineated than the terminology that has more established currency. The word may not yet be completely functional in the relevant language games that belong to people's lifeworlds.

In education fashion words often get formally sanctioned by certain major figures in the educational power hierarchy after the term has already functioned in the progressive, creative, but still marginal labors of less influential, less well-connected scholars. This is the reality of the "sociology of research" that is rarely acknowledged in critical studies. Just as in the designer fashion industry, ideas from street culture sometimes get picked up and formally introduced to the fashion world, so the term pedagogy has become appropriated by the research leadership—but, ironically, sometimes for non-pedagogical ends.

The second trend describes how pedagogy has become a key term in new theory discourses and in what is sometimes called "new order theory." In the broad domain of new theories there also occurs a kind of erosion of pedagogy, especially in the "new" discourse of pedagogy. This erosion is a function of needing a language for radicalizing consciousness but having no use for the reference to *paides* or child. Some commentators speak of a new order, where the old notion of pedagogy as dealing with children is deconstructed and a new pedagogical project is produced that involves approaches such as psychoanalytic readings of contemporary culture, media studies, cultural studies, literary criticism, gender politics, management studies, and so on. Thus, McWilliam (McWilliam and Taylor, 1996) can say in her introduction to the edited volume *Pedagogy, Technology, and the Body*, "Despite its etymology, much of the current writing about pedagogy does not refer specifically to the science of educating children" (p. 1). Instead, a whole array of new topics is unfolded.

Some of this literature does, however, examine the relations that teachers and other professionals maintain with children. These titles cover an exotic range of topics: *Beyond the Missionary Position: Teacher Desire and Radical Pedagogy* by Erica McWilliam; *Eros, Eroticism and the Pedagogical Process* by bell hooks; *Visualizing Safe Sex: When Pedagogy and Pornography Collide* by Cindy Patton; and *Queer Theory, Homosexual Teaching Bodies, and Infecting Pedagogy* by Peter G. Taylor. These works include "the interrogation" of the meaning of professional relations between professional pedagogues and the children or adults they serve. The literature of the new theorists reads like some kind of porn-pedagogy: "Medics, ministers, priests and pedagogues—all stand unfrocked in the new order. And this sensitivity is due in no small measure to the work of feminists who have challenged the cult of personality in the classroom," according to McWilliam and Jones (1996, p. 127).

Why use the word *defrocked*? Ostensibly the intent is to deconstruct the supposed higher values of the practice of pedagogy by hinting at its shady sides. For example, Jane Gallop (1988) explodes the meaning of pedagogy in a manner of suspicion that is provocatively accusative. She winkingly points to the Greek link between pedagogy and pederasty (child molesting). In the words of Gallop: "Pederasty is undoubtedly a useful paradigm for classic European pedagogy. A greater man penetrates a lesser man with his knowledge. The student is empty, a receptacle for the phallus; the teacher is the phallic fullness of knowledge" (1988, p. 43). New-order theorists describe teaching as the erotic seduction of the innocent student (coded as female) by the desirous teacher (coded as male). The teacher intro(se)duces the student into a lifelong scholastic love affair with a "body of knowledge," but in this process the teacher's own body may become the literal body that the student comes to crave and desire and vice versa.

In educational contexts it seems that the public constantly hears of cases where teachers, priests, police, psychologists, sports coaches, and other professions responsible in various ways for the welfare of children have betrayed their sacred trust. Sexual abuse and harassment seem rampant. But this literature goes much further than merely scrutinizing predatory practices; it sees the forces of erotic needs, wants, demands, and desires embedded deeply in our cultural psyche and hidden in our discursive practices in such a way that only psychoanalytic or critical inquiries are able to retrieve things like the sexual politics of the pedagogical relationship.

So the new theorists help us to become aware of how complex, ambiguous, implicative, and fragile human relationships are and how nothing is sacred in our new post-postmodern and posthuman world. Even those who are critical of the sometimes excessive nature of the new-order theories may be willing to admit that our knowledge forms and practices are often built on naive assumptions concerning the intentionality of human motivations, inclinations, predicaments, and propensities. And yet the so-called new pedagogies are subject to their own vulnerabilities. New theorists themselves run the risk of becoming enchanted with the accusatory or titillating products of their own obsessions, polemics, and fascinations. The provocative pedagogies of the teacher as rapist of children may have distasteful shock value, but it can also function as the expression of a hidden craving of the theorizer, whose provocative metaphors and discourses about the pedagogy of desire mask voyeuristic and ambiguous desires, equally insidious to the welfare of children. In other words, just as biographic and critical investigations into Sigmund Freud's theorizing have unmasked some shady sides of the great psychiatrist, so the post-Lacanian new theorists could benefit from critical "self-interrogations" to unmask their own hidden obsessions, perversions, narcissisms, and manias.

But quite apart from the above issues, the main argument here is that the term pedagogy is being depredated from our children under the well-intentioned guise of their liberation from systemic cultural oppression and abuse. This appropriation away from a child-oriented discourse of the term pedagogy by new theorists, cultural theorists, and psychoanalytically oriented educationists is unsettling insofar as it contributes to an erosion of the fragile spirit of pedagogy: the caring commitment to remain interested in the question of how to live responsibly and appropriately with children, not for our benefit but for theirs.

A Continually Unfolding of a Language and Practice of Pedagogy

Against these drifts in the erosion of pedagogy in continental contexts a more hopeful trend emerged in the 1990s. Partly as a reaction, it seems, against the influence of increasingly rationalistic, technocratic, and corporatist movements in education, there is a renewed interest in the question of the ethos of pedagogical practices. First, there were educators who sought to recover something that had been long absent, especially from North American educational thought: an ethics-sensitive language of teaching and an epistemology of practice that is guided by an interest in the child's experience and in the personal relational sphere between teachers and their students.

And yet the most recent push in education in our twenty-first century is toward even more pronounced rationalized practices. We see this in developments such as schools that are set up on the marketplace model, outcomes-based evaluations of teachers, privatization of government responsibilities (e.g., monitoring and testing of achievement levels by for-profit companies), and corporate funding of educational institutions in exchange for advertising visibility. What we are witnessing is a new form of postcapitalist entrepreneurship in education, based on the thought that teaching is simply an instructional skill with commodity value in the market place.

But in spite of these developments, it is significant that there is simultaneously a strong counter-current noticeable in this conversion to free-market ideology and technocratic, solution-based approaches. Educators who worry about this trend argue that we need to ask what it would mean if teachers were treated as moral agents with a practical professional language. Gert Biesta (2006) has compellingly shown how languages of education have been reduced to "a new language of learning" that effectively leads teachers to think of their vocation in terms of measurable learning outcomes. He argues that "there is a need to reclaim a language *of* education *for* education. To do so, however, cannot simply mean a return to the language or languages that were used in the past (2006, p. 14). It is in the spirit of a pedagogy-sensitive language that this book on pedagogical tact has been written. A new and sensitive language of pedagogy allows teachers to think of their daily practices as essentially pedagogical interactions. And the expansion of a pedagogical language (being attentive to student experience, recognition, teacher-student contact, teacher tact, personal pedagogies, etc.) enables teachers to talk about their everyday activities in a manner that many of them experience as freeing, thoughtful, relevant and uncannily inspiring.

In various countries we currently see an emergence of contemporary articulations of pedagogies that take their starting points in the phenomenological or experiential lifeworlds of children, young people, their families, and school classrooms. They focus on the pedagogical role and value of teachers and parents in children's and young people's lives and in the complexities of the pedagogical relation between teachers and students, parents and children, and between childcare workers and young people.

In the Netherlands, a national project (www.NIVOZ.nl) initiated in 2012 by Luc Stevens and focusing on pedagogical tact was originally inspired by *The Tact of Teaching* (van Manen, 1991). The Dutch book *Pedagogische Tact*, edited by Stevens and Bors, 2013, offers narrative contributions from teachers and school leaders at several levels of education.

Pedagogy and the Philosophy of Caring

While in the above chapters the terms "care" and "caring" have been frequently employed to refer to the ethical nature of the theory and practice of pedagogy, in North America theories and elaborations of the concept of care have been the cause of a separate productive literature. This literature should be briefly commented upon even though none of the care scholars, such as Nel Noddings, Debra Shogan, Peta Bowden, and Sara Ruddick, have related their literature to the extensive continental tradition of pedagogy. This should be somewhat surprising since there ought to be a relevant potential fusing of concerns and insights, as shown in chapter 5. But perhaps, because of language issues, the dominant educational scholarship in the USA has remained somewhat insular. It has even been observed that the North American management- and consumer-oriented instrumental paradigms of educational thought and policies have been displacing and eroding the pedagogical traditions and practices in schools and academic institutions.

The exploration into the meanings of care is a kind of phenomenological puzzle. It concerns the question of the relation between the commonly-accepted meanings of the term "caring" and the lived experience of caring, especially as in the primordial context of caring for someone who is vulnerable due to age, health, or circumstance. And I am thinking here especially in terms of the relation between parents and children. In Dutch language the equivalent term for care is *zorgen*. In German the word is almost identical, *Sorge*, and in Scandinavian languages too there are similar terms.

Now, when I think of *zorgen* in the Dutch language I have a very different felt-understanding than the term care or caring evokes in English. Yet, it is not so easy to articulate the difference. In the English, caring seems primarily (but not exclusively) to be a nice and pleasant word and indeed many want to claim to be in the caring business, especially those who *are* in business: we can see advertisements for car care, lawn care, skin care, carpet care, and many other profitable caring practices. It seems that the concept of care has been watered down to "providing attention" and even in expressions like "childcare" we do not really expect that the care goes much beyond institutional supervision. In contrast, the Dutch term for care, *zorgen*, seems to be a more ambiguous term having strong connotations not only of caring but also of being burdened by worries. These are not associations of meaning that business people find attractive for their advertisements.

I imagine a caring look that expresses *zorg* in the Dutch or *Sorgen* in German or *omtänksam* in Swedish or *omsorg* in Norwegian language. This is a different and more ambivalent kind of caring look: it is literally a look that is not carefree, not without worry. It may express affection, but it does not escape me that this face has worry-wrinkles. A parent who looks with caring-Sorgen at his or her child seems to be loving, yes, but also always in some sense worried, though not in the negative worry sense that self-help psychologists have problems with.

In her popular *The Challenge to Care in Schools*, Noddings has chapters on caring for self, caring for strangers, caring for animals, caring for plants, caring for ideas, caring for the world, etc. While this is an interesting philosophical elaboration, it unwittingly shows how the English concept of "care" takes in too much and too little. We are encouraged to care for and about almost everything and yet the more fundamental pedagogical aspect of worry seems to have disappeared from the felt-sense of the word "care" in our everyday language. Her earlier book *Caring: A Feminine Approach to Ethics and Moral Education* (1984) has become a classic text. The title *A Feminine Approach* (1984) was later replaced by the title *A Relational Approach* though the contents of the two books are identical (2013). Indeed, it is questionable why the caring relation should be approached with a feminine or feminist methodology that excludes a sensitivity to the father's and other men's experiences of care for children. It should be noted as well that nowhere do authors such as Noddings engage with the extensive continental literature on pedagogical care and related literature that is the main concern of this book. Only the early philosophical text *On Caring* by Milton Mayeroff (1971) takes a more pedagogical approach to the meaning of caring (without referring to pedagogy) by interpreting caring as helping the other grow.

The Dutch term *zorgen* translates as care, but also as worry. Opening a Dutch (van Dale, 2001) dictionary we read that a *zorgenkind* (literally a child who requires care) is a problem child, a child who causes concern, or who causes one to worry in an even more pronounced manner than is already usually implied in the term *zorgen*. It is curious, however, that when one consults the English-Dutch dictionary for the equivalent of the English term "worry" then one reads the Dutch term "*zorg*" and "*zorgenkind*"; and when one looks for the equivalent of the English term "care" one again finds the Dutch term "*zorg*." Thus, where in English these two terms care and worry are kept separate, in Dutch, German and some other languages these meanings are inextricably wound up in the pedagogical mode of life described by the equivalents caring and *zorgen*. Even in the term *verpleegzorg*, meaning nursing-care, there are similar meaning associations: there is a substrate of worry in this meaning. In general, *zorgen* for someone is to care for someone in a worrying kind of manner that is not carefree. And yet, worrying in this sense is a positive sensibility rather than the negative sense of worrying that psychologists would like to help you get rid of.

As a person whose first language is Dutch, I have always been struck by this strangely different emphasis of meaning in comparing the terms "*zorgen*" and "caring." It made me wonder about the significance of the experiential qualities of these terms. Does this mean that Dutch caregivers generally tend to experience caring in a somewhat different and more worrying modality than North Americans? I doubt it. It is interesting, of course, that in the English language, too, the term worry is associated with care, as when we feel that young children should be carefree (and when adults purchase retirement property in Carefree, Arizona, they may want to do so because they want to be again like children, carefree, free of worry). So why has the meaning of care-as-worry survived in some expressions but has been seemingly lost in most other usages? Has the meaning of caring changed over time?

The *Klein Etymological Dictionary* indeed strongly associates the earliest meaning of care with sorrow and anxiety. Interestingly, the etymology of the term sorrow derives from the Danish, Swedish, Dutch, and German equivalents of *Sorge, zorg* meaning anxiety and worry. Incidentally, the expression sorry, meaning "it causes me pain and regret," also finds its origin in this development from *Sorge* and sorrow. When we say "I'm sorry" then we actually say, "I care."

Modern dictionaries too retain the reference to worry. So when we consult the concise Oxford Dictionary the first equivalent to the noun care is listed as worry and anxiety; and the expanded Oxford Dictionary first lists the terms "mental suffering, sorrow, grief, trouble" and secondly "burdened state of mind arising from fear, doubt, or concern about anything." Webster's, too, lists the synonyms "care, concern, solicitude, anxiety, and worry." So it is noteworthy that both the earliest and more recent dictionary explications of care are heavily invested with the sense of worry.

Why is this noteworthy? Because when we examine the indexes of texts on caring by knowledgeable authors such as Jean Watson (1985), Nel Noddings (1986; 2013), Debra Shogan (1988), Susan Ruddick (1989), Peta Bowden (1997), and Marcia Hills and Jean Watson (2011), we look in vain for the term "worry"; and in the body of these texts too the term "worry" is virtually absent. In *Caring: Gender-Sensitive Ethics,* Bowden comments on the works by Noddings, Ruddick, and others. She writes that she is less interested in theoretical explications of caring than in analyzing how caring actually occurs in the practices of everyday life—in mothering, friendship, nursing, and citizenship. Indeed, the caring literature seems to need more phenomenological attention to how caring is actually experienced rather than as it is conceptualized and conceptually analyzed. And yet, in Bowden's text, too, there seems to be no mention (as far as I could tell) of the pervasive sense of worry that is phenomenologically associated with the act of caring. Mostly Bowden engages in argument with the earlier professional and feminist texts and pays less attention to empirical accounts or literary sources that may reveal how caring is really experienced in everyday life.

In the early nineties Janice Morse and colleagues published two studies presenting a "Comparative Analysis of Conceptualizations and Theories of Caring" (1991), using the categories: human trait, moral imperative, affect, interpersonal interaction, and therapeutic intervention. They also included 23 definitions culled from the studies they examined. Again the term "worry" does not occur in these definitions although some definitions contain related notions such as solicitude and concern. Why this absence of the term "worry" in the caring literature? Does the sense of care-as-worry not fit well into frames of professionalized relations? Is worry too problematic or psychologically negative concept for care theorists in education and the health sciences? Of course, I do not know the answer.

There is one health science context where the notion of care-as-worry is broadly discussed in both a practical and a theoretical way. I am referring, of course, to baby-care literature. It is interesting that in the weeks following the death of Dr. Benjamin Spock early in 1998, all across North America debates raged on radio and television about the legacy of Spock's advice to young parents. Was his influence positive or negative? Apparently his book *Baby and Child Care* helped millions of parents with their inevitable anxieties and worries associated with caring for young children. Ironically, Spock's main message has always been for parents to trust their own feelings and inclinations; and that there is no way to be a perfect mother or a perfect father. The first two sections of the opening chapter are entitled: "Trust Yourself" and "Parental Doubts Are Normal" (Spock and Rothenberg, 1992). However, critics have argued that, instead of alleviating worries, Spock actually instilled worries and anxieties—especially in mothers— since his books implicitly suggest that some ways of dealing with children are more appropriate than others ways. Thus, feminist critics argue that young mothers may worry that they cannot live up to the idealized versions of the perfect mother that, because of Spock's book, they may have constructed for themselves or that society may have constructed for them. However, it is important to note here that for these critics of Spock, the issue of worrying has shifted from care for one's child to care for one's self.

Of course, I am not arguing that self-care is unimportant. Caring for others is difficult if not impossible if in an obvious as well as a deeper sense one's own house is not in order, so to speak. And yet I would like to place some question marks over the assumption that self-care must therefore have priority over care for others. I will use Michel Foucault as an example to problematize the priority of caring for one's self (Foucault, 1986).

In his *Technologies of the Self*, Foucault establishes ancient relations between caring and self-knowledge (Foucault, 1988). He argues that the concern for "taking care of oneself" was one of the principles of practice in early Greek society. Even the oracular "Know Thyself" implied the requirement of knowing how to ask the right questions for the practice of self-scrutiny: the *techne* or practical wisdom regarding how to take care of one's body and soul. These technologies that Foucault has inventoried include self-disclosure, letter writing, confession, self-training, the examination of self and conscience, and so forth.

Foucault finds a foothold for prioritizing the question of self-care in Plato's *Alcibiades*. In this dialogue Socrates becomes the spiritual teacher of

Alcibiades in the latter's quest for self-knowledge. And Foucault asks: "In that relationship, why should Alcibiades be concerned with himself, and why is Socrates concerned with that concern of Alcibiades?" (Foucault, 1988, p. 24). In Plato's text we learn that Alcibiades wants to gain personal and political power over others but that Socrates is able to show him that power over others resides actually in power over self, which requires self-care for its edification. But what Foucault does not consider is that Plato's Alcibiades can also be interpreted as a narrative wherein the meaning of care consists in a pedagogical concern for the other's care as self-care.

In Plato's *Alcibiades* the figure of Socrates is involved in care, namely care for his pupil. This is the story: Socrates is worried about Alcibiades since the latter does not know how to take care of his self or soul. Thus Plato shows, in the example of Socrates, that care as cultivation of self finds its roots in care as concern for others. We can easily translate this idea in everyday pedagogical terms—as parent I care for my child's care as self-care. My pedagogical concern is with the child's taking proper care of his or her body and soul. If I do this not just out of mere parental duty but from a genuine sense of care-as-worrying, then I cannot help but be preoccupied with this other person's welfare.

In this childhood experience of having your parents worry for you and worry about you, the child (as future parent) in turn is encouraged to recognize that the source of understanding this self-care lies in the care for other. Thus teaching self-care also teaches care for the other. It is pedagogically desirable that the child not only demonstrates self-care but also, gradually, begins to demonstrate care-as-worrying for others. While Foucault advocated an archaeology of knowledge, it appears that he was not interested in digging for any originary roots of self-care in the pedagogical example of Socrates' caring for others. For this kind of search we need to consult another French thinker, Emmanuel Levinas (1993; 1998).

Language analysis and etymological sources can help us orient to the semantic variations and meanings of possible human experiences associated with the term caring. But which of these meanings are helpful to our particular practice? And how can we approach the phenomenon of caring without already having become captive inside the limiting frames of the particular conceptualizations that we personally favor or that we find in the literature? This may seem a strange question. Is not every understanding of caring already a conceptualization and thus one that betrays a particular perspective or form of life? For example, Wittgenstein (1958, p. 77) has shown that the meaning of any term is always conditioned by the usage of that term within the social practices of the language games in which we are involved. Therefore, we should not confuse the meanings associated with parental caring with the way caring may be a term used in the discourses of, for example, nursing, medicine, professional childcare, advertising, business enterprises, and so forth. One may argue that it makes little sense to try to determine if there is any core or shared meaning to the idea of caring since the term obviously means different things in different contexts. Perhaps the language-analytical literature of caring is so confused that it is better to simply impose a certain definition or behavioral equivalents on the concept?

But there are dangers in either relativizing the meaning of caring to shifting language games, or, in actually stipulating functional definitions of caring and taking it to mean whatever one wants it to mean. Either way, one stands in danger of forgetting the deeper human meaning of caring as the ethical demand, as the Danish philosopher, Løgstrup, called it (1997), and how the caring encounter may help us understand in a richer way the nature of our profession as a vocation and as a domain of ethical responsibility. The French philosopher Emmanuel Levinas has insistently proposed that caring responsibility can only be understood in its most basic modality if we can somehow transcend the intentional relation toward the world that accompanies all modes of being and thinking.

Thematic Elements of Pedagogical Thoughtfulness and Tact

In the Preface I outlined elements that are thematically woven throughout the chapters of this book. It may be helpful, at the completion of this text, to relist these elements, as they constitute the epistemological dimensions for pedagogical reflecting and acting and for the ontological dimensions in the personal development of pedagogical thoughtfulness and tact:

Child-sense: There is our psychological sensitivity to actively sense what goes on in the life of a particular child or young person in any particular or concrete situation. Teachers tend to develop people-sense and child-sense for knowing what children of a certain age and background are like. We cannot be pedagogically responsive to a child or young person if we do not know what goes on in the inner life of that person.

Personal pedagogy: Our personal background, life experiences, values, knowledge base, and emotional makeup all contribute to a *personal pedagogy* that inclines us to see and interpret pedagogical situations in a personally responsible and responsive manner.

Interpretive reflectivity: We need to develop an intuitive or phenomenological reflectivity that helps us understand the lived meanings of a certain phenomenon (experience) in a child's or young person's life. This reflectivity can be honed by becoming aware of phenomenological methods for determining and describing experiential meaning (van Manen 1997, 2014; Vagle, 2014).

Ontotheology: In our global context we need to possess an ontotheological awareness of the cultural forces that seem to shape not only the character of young people but also the pedagogical character of the adult in positive and negative ways. Do we value competitiveness or cooperation, self-centeredness or altruism, greed or sacrifice, personal happiness or community, and so forth? Negative and even destructive values and motivational forces can unwittingly control our lives and invisibly shape our perceptions of what is worthwhile and desirable.

Pedagogical ethics: Each of us may privilege certain personal and professional forms of ethics that prompt or enable us to actively distinguish "good" from "poor" or inappropriate ways of supporting and dealing with children and youths in particular situations and predicaments. For example, a utilitarian ethics would give us a different ethical motive than a relational ethics for giving guidance to the young.

I hope that this text will contribute to the renewal of a pedagogical impetus in education and other childcare practices.

References

Adams, C. (2006). PowerPoint, habits of mind, and classroom culture. *Journal of Curriculum Studies*, 38(4), pp. 389–411.
Adams, C. (2012). Technology as teacher: Digital media and the re-schooling of everyday life. *Existential Analysis*, 23(2), pp. 262–273.
Allodi, M. W. (2002). Children's experience of school: Narratives of Swedish children with and without learning difficulties. *Scandinavian Journal of Educational Research*, 46(2), pp. 182–205.
Apple, M. (2014). *Official knowledge: Democratic education in a conservative age*. New York: Routledge and Kegan Paul.
Arnal, S., Benjo, C., Letellier, B., and Scotta, C. (Producers), and Cantet, L. (Director). (2008). *The class (Entre les murs)* [Motion picture]. France: France 2 Cinéma.
Arendt, H. (2006). *Between past and future*. New York: Penguin Classics.
Bakker, P. (1944). *Ciske de rat*. Amsterdam/Brussels: Elsevier.
Bentham, J. and Mill, J. S. (1987). *Utilitarianism*. London: Penguin.
Biesta, G. (2006). *Beyond Learning: Democratic Education for a Human Future*. Boulder, CO: Paradigm Publishers.
Bollnow, O. F. (1989). The pedagogical atmosphere. *Phenomenology + Pedagogy*, 7, pp. 64–76.
Bowden, P. (1997). *Caring: gender-sensitive ethics*. London: Routledge.
Brinkmann, M. (2008). Üben–elementares Lernen. Überlegungen zur Phänomenologie, Theorie und Didaktik der pädagogischen Übung. In: Westphal, K., Breibauer, I.M., Mitgutsch, E.S. (Eds). *Dem Lernen auf der Spur. Die pädagogische Perspektive*. Klett-Cotta Verlag, pp. 278–294.
Brooks, D. (2015). *The road to character*. New York: Random House.
Buytendijk, F. J. J. (1998). The first smile of the child. *Phenomenology and pedagogy*, 6(1) pp. 15–24. Translated from Buytendijk, F. J. J. (1961). De eerste glimlach van het kind, inaugurale rede te Nijmegen, 1947. In *Academische Redevoeringen*. Utrecht: Dekker and van de Vegt, NV, pp. 99–117.
Caputo, J. D. (1988). Beyond aestheticism: Derrida's responsible anarchy. *Research in Phenomenology*, 18, pp. 59–73.
Comenius, J. A. (1611/2011). *Orbis sensualium pictus (The world of things obvious to the senses, drawn in pictures)*. Syracuse, NY: Barden Publisher.
Cummings, E. E. (1953/2014). "Who am I?" *The New Republic*, October 14, 2014. Retrieved from: www.newrepublic.com/article/119831/ee-cummings-lectures-about-his-parents-and-poetry
Dahl, K.L. (1995). Challenges in understanding the learner's perspective. *Theory into Practice*, 34(2), pp. 124–130.
Derrida, J. (1995a). *The gift of death*. Chicago: University of Chicago Press.
Derrida, J. (1995b). *On the name*. Stanford, CA: Stanford University Press.
Dewey, J. (1902). *The child and the curriculum*. Chicago: University of Chicago Press.
Dewey, J. (1916). *Essays in experimental logic*. New York: Dover Publications.
Dewey, J. (1929). My pedagogic creed. *Journal of the National Education Association*, 18(9), pp. 291–295.
Dewey, J. (1933). *How we think*. New York: Heath and Co.
Dewey, J. (1964). *John Dewey: selected writings*. New York: The Modern Library.

REFERENCES

Dewey, J. (1973). *The philosophy of John Dewey* (Vols. 1 and 2) (John McDermott, ed.). New York: G. P. Putnam's Sons.
Dilthey, W. (1888). Über die Möglichkeit einer allgemeingültigen pädagogischen Wissenschaft. In F. Nicolin (Ed.) (1969), *Pädagogik als Wissenschaft* (pp. 36–67). Darmstadt: Wissenschaftliche Buchgesellschaft.
Eiseley, L. (1979). *The star thrower*. New York: Random House.
Encyclopedia on early childhood development. Retrieved from: www.child-encyclopedia.com/en-ca/home.html
Flyvbjerg, B. (1991). Sustaining non-rationalized practices: Body-mind, power and situational ethics: An Interview with Hubert and Stuart Dreyfus. *Praxis International*, 11(1), pp. 93–113.
Foucault, M. (1986). *The care of the self*. New York: Pantheon Books.
Foucault, M. (1988). Technologies of the self. In L. H. Martin, H. Gutman, P. H. Hutton (Eds). *Technologies of the self*. Amherst Mass.: The University of Massachusetts Press, pp. 16–59.
Freedman, D.P. and Stoddard Holmes, M. (2003). *The teacher's body: embodiment, authority, and identity in the academy*. Albany, NY: SUNY Press.
Freire, P. (1970). *Pedagogy of the oppressed*. New York: Seabury Press.
Gadamer, H-G. (1975). *Truth and method*. New York: Seabury.
Gallop, J. (1988). *Thinking through the body*. New York: Columbia University Press.
Giddens, A. (1993). *The transformation of intimacy: Sexuality, love and eroticism in modern societies*. Stanford, CA: Stanford University Press.
Giroux, H. A. (2011). *On critical pedagogy*. New York: Bloomsbury.
Giroux, H. A. (2015). The fire this time: black youth and the spectacle of postracial violence. Truthout. Retrieved from: http://www.truth-out.org/news/item/30907-the-fire-this-time-black-youth-and-the-spectacle-of-postracial-violence
Gitlin, M. P., and Scott, R. (Producer), and Figgis, M. (Director). (1994). *The browning version* [motion picture]. UK: Paramount Pictures.
Grass, G. (2010). *The tin drum*. New York: Houghton-Mifflin Harcourt.
Grondin, J. (1994). *Introduction to philosophical hermeneutics*. New Haven: Yale University Press.
Grumet, M. (2003). My teacher's body. In D. P. Freedman and M. Stoddard Holmes (Eds.). *The teacher's body: embodiment, authority, and identity in the Academy*. Albany, NY: SUNY Press, pp. 249–258.
Gumbrecht, H. U. (2014). *Our broad present: Time and contemporary culture*. New York: Columbia University Press.
Gusdorf, G. (1965). *Speaking (La parole)*. Evanston, IL: Northwestern University Press.
Hegel, G. W. F. (1977). *Phenomenology of spirit*. Oxford: Clarendon Press.
Heidegger, M. (1962). *Being and time*. New York: Harper and Row.
Heidegger, M. (1972). *What is called thinking?* New York: Harper and Row Publishers.
Heidegger, M. (1977). *The question concerning technology, and other essays*. New York: Harper and Row.
Heidegger, M. (2002). *Identity and difference*. Chicago: University of Chicago Press.
Herbart, J. F. (1882). Zwei Vorlesungen über Pädagogik (1802). In J. F. Herbart, *Sämtliche Werke* (Erster Band) (K. Kehrbach, Ed.). Langensalza: Druck und Verlag von Hermann Beyer and Søhne.
Herbart, J. F. (2005). *Allgemeine Pädagogik von 1806*. Munich: GRIN Verlag.
Hintjes, J. (1981). *Geesteswetenschappelijke pedagogiek*. Amsterdam: Boom.
Hills, M. and Watson, J. (Eds.) (2011). *Creating a caring curriculum: an emancipatory pedagogy for nursing*. New York: Springer.
Holy Bible. *King James Version*.

REFERENCES

Hood, B. (2012). *The self illusion: How the social brain creates identity.* Oxford: Oxford University Press.
Ihde, D. (2002). *Bodies in technology.* Minneapolis: University of Minnesota Press.
James, W. (1962). *Talks to teachers on psychology.* New York: Dover Publications.
Jay, M. (2005). *Songs of experience: Modern American and European variations on a universal theme.* Berkeley: University of California Press.
Kierkegaard, S. (1983). *Fear and trembling.* Harmondsworth: Penguin Books.
Klafki, W. (1964). *Das pädagogische Problem des Elementaren und die Theorie der kategorialen Bildung.* Weinheim: Verlag Julius Beltz.
Klafki, W. (1985). *Neue Studien zur Bildungstheorie und Didaktik.* Weinheim und Basel: Beltz Verlag.
Langeveld, M. J. (1943/79). *Beknopte theoretische pedagogiek.* Groningen: Wolters-Noordhoff.
Langeveld, M. J. (1967). *Scholen maken mensen* (original title: *Die Schule als Weg des Kindes*). Purmerend: J. Muusses, NV.
Langeveld, M. J. (1975). *Personal help for children growing up. Curry Lecture.* University of Exeter.
Langeveld, M. J. (1983). The secret place in the life of the child. *Phenomenology and Pedagogy,* 1(1), 11–17, and 1(2), 181–191.
Levering, B. (2014). M. J. Langeveld. In H. W. Essen, V. Bussato, and W. Koops (Eds.), *Grondleggers van de pedagogiek.* Amsterdam: Uitgeverij Bert Bakker.
Levinas, E. (1969). *Totality and infinity: An essay on exteriority.* Pittsburgh, PA: Duquesne University Press.
Levinas, E. (1985). *Ethics and infinity: Conversations with Philippe Nemo.* Pittsburgh, PA: Duquesne University Press.
Levinas, E., In F. Rötzer, (Ed.) (1995). *Conversations with French philosophers.* New Jersey: Humanities Press.
Levinas, E. (1993). *Outside the Subject.* London: The Athlone Press.
Levinas, E. (1998). *Entre nous: On thinking-of-the-other.* New York: Columbia University Press.
Levinas, E. (2003). *Humanism of the other.* Urbana and Chicago: University of Illinois Press.
Lingis, A. (2005). Contact. *Janus Head,* 8(2), pp. 439–454.
Lippitz, W. (1983). The child's understanding of time. *Phenomenology + Pedagogy,* 1 (2), pp. 172–180.
Lippitz, W. (1986). Understanding children, communicating with children: Approaches to the child within us, before us, and with us. *Phenomenology + Pedagogy,* 4(3), pp. 172–180.
Lippitz, W. (1990). Ethics as limits of pedagogical reflection. *Phenomenology + Pedagogy,* 8, pp. 49–60.
Lippitz, W. (1993). *Phänomenologische Studien in der Pädagogik.* Weinheim: Deutscher Studienverlag.
Litt, Th. (1925/67). *Führen oder wachsenlassen.* Stuttgart: Ernst Klett Verlag.
Løgstrup, K.E. (1997). *The ethical demand.* Notre Dame: University of Notre Dame Press.
MacIntyre, A. (1981). *After virtue.* Notre Dame, IN: University of Notre Dame Press.
Marion, J. L. (2002). *In excess: Studies of saturated phenomena.* Bronx: Fordham University Press.
Marramao, G. (2007). *Kairos: Towards an ontology of "due time."* Aurora, CO: Davie Group.
Mayeroff, M. (1971). *On caring.* New York: HarperCollins.
McWilliam, E., and Jones, A. (1996). Eros and pedagogical bodies: The state of (non)affairs. In E. McWilliam and P. G. Taylor (Eds.), *Pedagogy, technology, and the body.* New York: Peter Lang, pp. 127–136.
McWilliam, E., and Taylor, P. G. (Eds.) (1996). *Pedagogy, technology, and the body.* New York: Peter Lang.
Merleau-Ponty, M. (1962). *Phenomenology of perception.* London: Routledge and Kegan Paul.

Merleau-Ponty, M. (1964). *The primacy of perception*. Evanston, IL: Northwestern University Press.
Metz, P. (1995). Interpretations of Herbart's pedagogical tact. In Hopman, St., Riquarts, K. (Eds.) *Didaktik and/or Curriculum*. Kiel: Institut für Pädagogik der Naturwissenschaften IPN, pp. 107–123.
Minty, J. (1982). From the diary of Judith Minty, September 19, 1972. In L. Lifshin (Ed.), *Ariadne's threat: A collection of contemporary women's journals*. New York: Harper and Row, pp. 215–219.
Molander, B. (1992). Tacit knowledge and silenced knowledge: Fundamental problems and controversies. In B. Göranzon, and M. Florin, (Eds.), *Skill and education: Reflection and experience*. New York: Springer-Verlag, pp. 46–72.
Mollenhauer, K. (1986). *Vergeten samenhang: Over cultuur en opvoeding*. Meppel, Amsterdam: Boom.
Morse, J. M., Solberg, S., Neander, W., Bottorff, J., Johnson, J. L. (1990). Concepts of caring and caring as a concept. *Advances in nursing science*. 13 (1), pp. 1–14.
Morse, J. M., Bottorff, J., Neander, W., Solberg, S. (1991). Comparative analysis of conceptualizations and theories of caring. *IMAGE: Journal of Nursing Scholarship*. Summer, 23(2), pp. 119–126.
Murchadha, F. O. (2013). *The time of revolution: Kairos and Chronos in Heidegger*. New York: Bloomsbury Publishing.
Muth, J. (1962). *Pädagogischer Takt*. Essen: Verlagsgesellschaft.
Noddings, N. (1984). *Caring: A feminine approach to ethics and moral education*. Berkeley: University of California Press.
Noddings, N. (1992). *The challenge to care in schools*. New York: Teachers College Press.
Noddings, N. (2013). *Caring: A relational approach to ethics and moral education*. Berkeley: University of California Press.
Nohl, H. (1967). *Ausgewählte pädagogische Abhandlungen*. Paderborn: Ferdinand Schöningh.
Nussbaum, M. (2000). The costs of tragedy: Some moral limits of cost-benefit analysis. *Journal of Legal Studies*, 29, pp. 1005–1036.
Ondaatje, M. (1979). *There's a trick with a knife I'm learning to do*. Toronto: McClelland and Stewart.
Plato (1927). Lamb W. R. M. (Transl.). *Plato XII : Charmides, Alcibiades I and II, Hipparchus, Lovers, Theages, Minos, Epinomis*. Harvard: Harvard University Press.
Proust, M. (1981). *Remembrance of things past*. London: Random House.
Rifkin, J. (2006). *The empathic civilization: The race to global consciousness in a world in crisis*. New York: Penguin.
Rilke, R. M. (1982). *The selected poetry of Rainer Maria Rilke* (S. Mitchell, Ed., Trans.). New York: Random House.
Rilke, R. M. (2015). Dauer der Kindheit Retrieved from: http://www.rilke.de/gedichte/kindheitdauer.htm
Ruddick, S. (1989). *Maternal thinking: Toward a politics of peace*. Boston: Beacon Press.
Sandmel, S. (Ed.). 1976. *The new English bible. Oxford study edition*. New York: Oxford University Press.
Schön, D.A. (1983). *The reflective practitioner: How professionals think in action*. New York: Basic Books.
Shogan, D. (1988). *Care and moral motivation*. Toronto: OISE Press.
Simon, B. (1981). Why no pedagogy in England? In B. Simon and W. Taylor (Eds.), *Education in the eighties*. London: Batsford Academic and Educational Ltd., pp. 124–145.
Schleiermacher, F. E. D. (1983). *Ausgewählte pädagogische Schriften*. Paderborn: Ferdinand Schöningh.

Spiecker, B. (1984). The pedagogical relationship. *Oxford Review of Education.* 10(2), pp. 203–209.
Spock, B. and Rothenberg, M.B. (1992). *Dr. Spock's baby and child care.* New York: Dutton.
Saevi, T. (2012). Why Mollenhauer matters. A response to Klaus Mollenhauer's book Forgotten Connections: On Culture and Upbringing. *Phenomenology and Practice,* 6(2), pp. 180–191.
Saevi, T. (2015). Learning and pedagogic relations. In D. Scott and E. Hargreaves (Eds.). *Sage Handbook of Learning.* Thousand Oaks, CA: Sage Publications, pp. 342–352.
Stevens, L. and Bors, G. (Eds) (2013). *Pedagogische tact.* Antwerpen: Garant.
Stiegler, B. (2010). *Taking care of youth and the generations.* Stanford, CA: Stanford University Press.
Stout, M. (2006). *The sociopath next door: The ruthless versus the rest of us.* New York: Harmony Books.
Thomas, M. E. (2013). *Confessions of a sociopath.* New York: Crown Publishers.
Thompson, C. (2008). Brave new world of digital intimacy. *New York Times Magazine.* Retrieved from: www.nytimes.com/2008/09/07/magazine/07awareness-t.html
Thomson, I. D. (2005). *Heidegger on ontotheology: Technology and the politics of education.* Cambridge: Cambridge University Press.
Tyler, S. A. (1986). Post-modern ethnography: From document of the occult to occult document. In J. Clifford and G. E. Marcus, *Writing culture: The poetics and politics of ethnography.* Berkeley, Cal: University of California Press.
Vagle, M. D. (2014). *Crafting Phenomenological Research.* Walnut Creek, CA: Left Coast Press.
Van Dale Groot woordenboek Nederlands-Engels and Van Dale Groot woordenboek Engels-Nederlands. (2001). Utrecht: Van Dale Lexicografie.
Van Manen, M. (1977). Linking ways of knowing to ways of being practical. *Curriculum Inquiry,* 6(3), pp. 205–228.
Van Manen, M. (1979). The phenomenology of pedagogic observation. *Canadian Journal for Studies in Education* (CSSE), 4 (1), pp. 5–16.
Van Manen, M. (1982). Phenomenological pedagogy. *Curriculum Inquiry,* 12(3), pp. 283–299.
Van Manen, M. (1984). Theory of the unique: Thoughtful learning for pedagogic tactfulness. In G. Milburn, and R. Enns (Eds.), *Curriculum Canada.* University of British Columbia Press, pp. 32–41.
Van Manen, M. (1990). *Childhood contingency and pedagogical fitness.* Halifax: Dalhousie University Publication, Robert Jackson Memorial Lecture.
Van Manen, M. (1991). *The tact of teaching: The meaning of pedagogical thoughtfulness.* Albany: SUNY Press; London, Ontario: Althouse Press.
Van Manen, M. (1992). Reflectivity and the pedagogical moment: The normativity of pedagogical thinking and acting. *Journal of Curriculum Studies,* 23(6), pp. 507–536.
Van Manen, M. (1994). Pedagogy, virtue, and narrative identity in teaching. *Curriculum Inquiry,* 24 (2), p. 135.
Van Manen, M. (1997). *Researching lived experience: Human science for an action sensitive pedagogy.* London, Ontario: Althouse Press.
Van Manen, M. (1999). The language of pedagogy and the primacy of student experience. In J. Loughran (Ed.), *Researching teaching: Methodologies and practices for understanding pedagogy.* London: Falmer Press, pp. 13–27.
Van Manen, M. (2000). Moral language and pedagogical experience. *The Journal of Curriculum Studies,* 32(2), pp. 315–327.
Van Manen, M. (2002). *The tone of teaching: The language of pedagogy.* London, Ontario: Althouse Press.

Van Manen, M. (2014). *Phenomenology of practice: Meaning-giving methods in phenomenological research and writing.* Walnut Creek, CA: Left Coast Press.

Van Manen M., and Adams, C. (2014). Phenomenological pedagogy. In Phillips, D.C. (Ed.), *Encyclopedia of Educational Theory and Philosophy.* London, UK: Sage, pp. 606–610.

Van Manen, M., and Levering, B. (1996). *Childhood's secrets: Intimacy, privacy, and the self reconsidered.* New York: Teachers College Press. Retrieved from: www.archive.org/details/childhoodssecret00vanm

Van Manen, M., McClelland J., and Plihal J. (2007). Naming student experiences and experiencing student naming. In D. Thiessen and A. Cook-Sather (Eds.), *International handbook of student experience in elementary and secondary school* (pp. 85–98). New York: Springer Publishing Company.

Van Manen, M. A. (2012). Technics of touch in the neonatal intensive care. *Medical Humanities,* 38(2), pp. 91–96.

Van Manen, M. A. (2014). On ethical (in)decisions experienced by parents of infants in neonatal intensive care. *Qualitative Health Research.* Sage. Retrieved from: http://qhr.sagepub.com/content/early/2014/01/27/1049732313520081.full.pdf

Watson, J. (1985). *Nursing: The philosophy and science of caring.* Boulder Colorado: Colorado Associated University Press.

Westbury, I., Hopmann, S., Riquarts, K. (Eds.) (2010). *Teaching as a reflective practice: The German Didaktik tradition. Studies in Curriculum Theory Series.* New York, NY: Routledge.

Wittgenstein, L. (1968). *Philosophical investigations* (G. E. M. Anscombe, Trans.). Oxford: Basil Blackwell.

Wittgenstein, L. (1972). *On certainty.* New York: Harper and Row Publishers.

Name Index

Adams, Catherine, 14, 39, 136, 227, 323
Allodi, Mara W., 160, 227,
Apple, Michael, 216, 227,
Augustine, Saint, 204,
Arendt, Hannah, 21, 45, 227

Bakker, Piet, 26, 27, 28, 29, 30, 227
Ballauf, Theodor, 205,
Begaudeau, François, 23,
Bentham, Jeremy, 197, 227
Biesta, Gert, 219, 227
Bollnow, Otto F., 21, 120, 205, 227
Bors, Geert, 14, 219, 231
Bowden, Peta, 220, 222, 227
Brooks, David, 45, 46, 227
Buytendijk, Frederik J. J., 111, 227

Caputo, John D., 69, 227
Caravaggio (Michelangelo Merisi or Amerighi), 69, 70
Comenius, John Amos, 43, 204, 227
Cummings, E.E., 149, 150, 227

Dahl, Karin L., 159, 160, 161, 227
Demont-Breton, Virginie, 13
Derbolav, Josef, 205
Derrida, Jacques, 69, 70, 71, 72, 157, 227
Dewey, John, 49, 50, 51, 57, 207, 208, 227, 228
Dilthey Wilhelm, 119, 124, 204, 205, 228

Eiseley, Loren, 84, 228
Erasmus, Desiderius, 204

Flyvbjerg, Bent, 89, 228,
Foucault, Michel, 223, 224, 228
Freedman, Diane P., 228
Freire, Paulo, 205, 216, 228
Frischeisen-Köhler, Max, 205

Gadamer, Hans-Georg, 167, 168, 228
Gallop, Jane, 217, 228
Giddens, Anthony, 174, 228
Giroux, Henry A., 216, 228
Grass, Günter, 191, 228
Grondin, Jean, 122, 228
Grumet, Madeleine, 213, 228
Gumbrecht, Hans U., 188, 228
Gusdorf, Georges, 158, 228

Hegel, Georg W. F., 141, 228
Heidegger, Martin, 122, 123, 188, 228
Herbart, Johann F., 78, 104, 105, 204, 206, 208–213, 228, 230
Hintjes, Jacques, 125, 205, 228
Hills, Marcia, 22, 228
Hooks, Bell, 217
Hood, Bruce, 148, 149, 229
Hopman, Stefan, 206, 230, 232

Ihde, Don, 174, 229

James, William, 105, 106, 229
Jay, Martin, 168, 229
Jones, Alison, 217, 229

Kierkegaard, Søren, 68, 69, 229
Klafki, Wolfgang, 205–207, 229

Langeveld, Martinus J., 21, 37–41, 44, 150–152, 205, 229
Levering, Bas, 44, 172, 229
Levinas, Emmanuel, 20, 37, 68–75, 116, 117, 121, 201, 224, 225, 229
Lifshin, Lyn, 230
Lingis, Alphonso, 110, 111, 229
Lippitz, Wilfried, 14, 202, 229
Litt, Theodor, 124, 125, 204, 205, 229
Locke, John, 204
Løgstrup, Knud E., 225, 229

233

MacIntyre, Alistair, 199, 229
Marion, Jean-Luc, 177, 229
Marramao, Giacomo, 52, 229
Mayeroff, Milton, 221, 229
McClelland, Jerry, 157, 232
McWilliam, Erica, 216, 217, 229
Merleau-Ponty, Maurice, 103, 137, 167, 229, 230
Metz, Peter, 78, 208, 209, 230
Mill, John S., 197, 227
Minty, Judith, 65, 66, 112, 230
Molander, Bengt, 183, 230
Mollenhauer, Klaus, 21, 129, 130, 205, 230
Montaigne, Michel de, 204
Morse, Janice M., 222, 230
Murchadha, Felix O., 52, 230
Muth, Jakob, 97, 208, 230

Noddings, Nel, 67, 220–222, 230
Nohl, Herman, 119, 120, 125, 204, 205, 230
Nussbaum, Martha, 198, 230

Ondaatje, Michael, 17, 18, 22, 230

Patton, Cindy, 217
Pestalozzi, Heinrich, 204, 206–208
Plato, 204, 223, 224, 230
Plihal, Jane, 157, 232
Proust, Marcel, 16, 17, 230

Riquarts, Kurt, 206, 230, 232
Rembrandt, 69–71
Rifkin, Jeremy, 46, 230
Rilke, Rainer Maria, 128, 148, 149, 230

Riquarts, Kurt, 206, 230, 232
Rötzer, Florian, 71, 229
Rousseau, Jean-Jacques, 204, 207
Ruddick, Susan, 220, 222, 230

Saevi, Tone, 14, 141, 193, 231
Schleiermacher, Friedrich E. D., 124, 206, 230
Schön, Donald A., 50, 51, 230
Seneca, Lucius A., 204
Shogan, Debra, 220, 222, 230
Simon, Brian, 214, 230
Spiecker, Ben, 121, 231
Spock, Benjamin, 223, 231
Spranger, Eduard, 205
Stevens, Luc, 219, 231
Stiegler, Bernard, 21, 231
Stoddard Holmes, Martha, 213, 228
Stout, Martha, 46, 231

Taylor, Peter G., 216, 217, 229
Thomas, M. E., 46, 231
Thompson, Clive, 178, 231
Thomson, Iain D., 177, 231
Tyler, Stephen A., 152, 231

Vagle, Mark D., 40, 225, 231
Van Heemskerck, Maarten, 173
Van Manen, Max, 22, 78, 152, 213, 231
Van Manen, Michael A., 14, 107, 212, 196, 227

Watson, Jean, 222, 228, 232
Weniger, Erich, 205
Westbury, Ian, 206, 232
Wittgenstein, Ludwig, 183, 224, 232

Subject Index

Abraham & Isaac, 68–72
acting, action, 18, 33, 46, 88, 92, 113; ethical, 195–202; instant, 38, 39, 58, 208, 212; pedagogical, 37–39, 47, 58, 99, 104, 179–194, 225; everyday practical, 57, 124, 170; reflective, 49–51, 59; tactful, 78–86, 97, 105; thoughtfully, thinkingly, 101, 102, 212, 213
adult–child relation, 11, 20, 21, 85, 120, 121
adulthood, 36, 44, 78, 90, 132, 149, 152, 193, 204; mature, 21, 41, 45, 63, 78, 88, 90, 91, 94, 105, 125, 150, 152, 186, 193, 196, 199, 204
agape, 201
agogy, agogic, 41
alterity, otherness, 79, 114, 121, 201, 173, 196, 201
anecdote, 27, 31, 38, 57, 112, 135, 143, 153, 155, 165–167, 200; writing, 165, 166
antinomies, 124–126
attentive, attentiveness, 17, 18, 22, 35, 36, 40, 62, 63, 66, 79, 83, 88, 101, 121, 127, 134, 153, 171, 186, 187, 208, 214, 219; inattentive, 108, 113, 160
Augenblick, instant of a moment, 18, 35, 52, 58, 60, 77, 78, 81, 82, 91, 101, 104, 105, 108, 140, 164, 168, 170, 182, 187, 208, 210, 211, 213

being, 12, 36, 45, 79, 80, 82, 83, 86, 96, 98, 104, 110, 115, 118, 119, 123, 126, 127, 131, 137, 158, 161, 178, 181, 184, 190–192, 200, 210, 212, 213, 225; a what, a who, 114; seen, 103, 139–155, 167; touched, 103, 104, 109, 168
Bildung, forming, 141, 204, 206, 207
blushing, 143

body language, 24, 98; body skill, 81, 102; mindful body skill, 91

care, 14, 16–19, 33, 38, 40, 41, 63, 88, 112, 115–119, 126, 132, 144, 152, 155, 174, 179, 193–198, 201, 207, 214, 219–225; care-as-worry, 33, 64–75, 179, 222–224; carefree, 140, 220–222; self-care, 94, 223, 224
caring theory, 219–225
character, 11, 12, 24, 45–47, 50, 77, 79, 80, 155, 181, 184, 196, 199, 200, 206, 208–210, 225
child abuse, 12, 29, 42, 46, 110, 153, 154, 194, 197, 214
child-sense, 11, 77, 78, 217
contact, 19, 25, 40, 74, 82, 104, 107–119, 142, 167, 171–178, 187, 207, 219; constant, 142, 171, 175–178; *contingere*, 107; deferential, 113; elective, 116; eye, 103, 108, 109; face-to-face, 177; familial, 112; to have good contact, 109, 110; modes of contact, 111–117; in touchness, 107, 110, 178; presentative & representative, 129–131; responsive, 114, 115; toxic, 110; valuing, 113; virtual, 136, 137, 171–178
content, 92, 117, 130, 134, 167, 168, 188, 207; classic, 207; exemplary, 206, 207; representative, 207; typical, 207
contingency, contingent, 39, 44, 45, 56, 58, 72, 73, 80, 82, 85, 94, 136, 164, 185, 187, 189, 190, 199, 212, 213
control, 90, 91, 125, 147, 175
corporate, corporatism, 43, 87, 88, 110, 218, 219
curriculum, 22, 24, 43, 44, 53, 62, 87, 89, 90, 94, 106, 110, 117, 129–131, 134, 135, 148, 188, 201, 206, 207, 215, 216

235

SUBJECT INDEX

cyber bullying, 174
cyber-pedagogy, 171–178; space, 174

damages, 19, 23, 41, 42, 194
dependence, independence, 18, 20, 41, 47, 62, 125, 126, 139, 173, 175, 179, 181, 204, 212
desire, 16, 24, 27, 30, 49, 62, 67, 68, 100, 104, 105, 109, 115, 125, 141, 172–174, 184, 192, 217, 218
didactics, 44, 130, 188, 206; *Didaktik*, 117, 206
discipline, 34, 54, 59, 83–86, 94, 96–98, 125, 135; *docere*, 84; self-discipline, 120, 125,
doubt, 19, 33, 36, 49, 87, 113, 137, 184, 222, 223

e-learning, 136; e-life, 171; e-work, 171
economism, 14, 46, 80, 110, 188, 202
empathy, 42, 45, 46, 77, 80, 155, 172
epistemology, 55, 82, 102, 134, 209, 210, 213, 218, 225
Erlebnis, 167
Eros, 119, 126, 172, 217
ethics, ethical, 11, 18, 20–23, 33, 37–39, 41, 42, 44, 45, 68, 69, 70, 72, 73, 78, 82, 88, 98, 101, 117, 124, 134, 139, 141, 144, 154, 179–181, 187–189, 195–202, 206, 207, 208, 210, 215, 218, 219, 225; bioethics, 180; discretion, 189; experience, 37, 68, 70, 196; intelligence, 101; pain, 73; perspectives, 195–202; practice, 33, 74, 203, 213; professional, 181; relational, 20, 195, 196, 201, 202, 226; responsibility, 181, 182, 225; sensitivity, 179, 190; uncertainty, 33
evocative, 14, 116, 152, 174
example, 14, 35, 36, 40, 42, 46, 64, 65, 68, 82–84, 89, 103, 105–107, 123, 124, 132, 139, 148, 159, 160, 163, 180, 189, 193, 200, 207, 214, 223, 224

fashion words, 215, 216
freedom, 125, 201

friendship, 42, 85, 89, 90, 120, 222
führen oder wachsenlassen, 124

Gefühl, 97, 105
gesture, 13, 25, 30, 34, 36, 59, 61, 82, 83, 93, 98, 99, 109, 110, 114, 117, 129, 131, 137, 142, 143, 146, 147, 160, 160, 167, 182, 184, 185, 187, 189, 213
glance, 23, 25, 28, 59, 61, 82, 83, 92, 93, 108, 109, 113, 115, 128, 140, 145, 160, 163, 172, 185, 189
goals, 29, 43, 44, 59, 61, 130, 131, 192, 197
goodness, 20, 75, 89, 198, 200

hostage, 117

identity, 16, 109, 121, 137, 139, 142, 143, 146, 158, 162, 167, 169, 194; self-identity, 99, 109, 143–145, 149, 150, 163, 172–175
improvisational, 78, 81, 89, 91, 92, 100, 136; ability, 78, 104, 190; acting, 82, 106, 164; gift, 79; tact, 187, 211
in loco parentis, 34, 86, 194, 199
inceptuality, 20, 148, 149, 150
influence, 13, 16, 17, 23, 42, 46, 47, 63, 79, 80, 84, 94, 95, 101, 102, 123, 149, 164, 173, 181, 187, 188, 205, 206, 208, 210, 218, 223
inner life, 24, 42, 45, 77, 82, 98, 111, 172, 173, 225; innerliness, 111
insight, 21, 24, 29, 40, 47, 48, 51, 52, 63, 68, 74, 77, 82, 86, 100–104, 141, 152, 154, 159, 161, 169, 206, 220
instrumentalism, 14, 41, 43, 62, 91, 105, 110, 128, 188–190, 220
intentional, 50, 81, 98, 99, 102, 119, 120, 218, 225
intersubjective, 139, 145
intimacy, intimate, 107, 108, 116, 127, 150, 152, 157, 158, 165, 167, 172–178; digital, 174, 175–178; online, 42, 173; textual, 174, 176, 177

Kairos, 52, 53, 57, 81, 82, 104, 183, 189; moment, 52, 53, 55, 81, 82, 164, 185; time, 51–53, 58, 81 knowing, 13, 14, 47, 63, 68, 74, 77, 87, 104, 134, 144, 193, 199, 223, 225; actional, 212; as knowing what to do, 81, 85, 99, 104, 184, 187, 189, 195; corporeal, 182, 213; noncognitive, 40, 212, 213; pathic, 126, 213; relational, 212; silent, 182, 183; situational, 212

latency, 14, 15, 16, 118, 119; latent significance, 16, 22, 78, 113, 119
lifeworld, 21, 30, 40, 50, 53, 64, 119, 120, 123–125, 145, 170, 205, 215, 216, 219
lived experience, 12, 39, 87, 152, 154, 159, 160, 166, 167, 168, 190, 220
love, 16, 20, 29, 37, 40, 42, 46, 56, 64, 67, 68, 69, 72, 73, 85, 90, 96, 112, 113, 116, 117, 119–121, 126, 129, 131, 134, 135, 140, 144, 149, 153, 172, 174, 177, 178, 186, 194, 201, 217

managerialism, 14, 87, 110,
meaningfulness, 12, 20, 29, 39, 44, 88, 91, 92, 93, 110, 115, 117–119, 141, 142, 145, 148, 149, 158, 166, 174, 187
mimesis, 118, 133, 137
mindfulness, 67, 79, 91, 102, 104, 105, 106, 149, 213
Momus, 171–173
MOOCs, 137

naming, 64, 157, 158, 161–170; name forgetting, 157, 165, 169
nearness, 174, 176
now, 47, 51–53, 81
nudging, 47, 62, 100, 101, 180

oculesics, 108, 109
ontology, 118, 124, 184; inner, 82
ontotheology, 11, 45–47, 188, 225
openness, 41, 79, 145, 151, 169, 177, 193, 206
originary, 19, 73, 224

paides, 41, 203, 215–218

pathic, 42, 85, 212, 213; dimension, 85, 97; language, 177, 213; quality, 85, 121; sensibility, 42, 85, 213
patience, 40, 135, 185, 192, 199, 200
pedagogical qualities, 43, 135, 185, 192, 200
people-sense, 77, 225
personal becoming, 23, 120
personal pedagogies, 11, 55, 78, 79–82, 154, 219, 225
phenomenality, 148, 196
phenomenology, 11, 14, 19, 24, 39, 40, 42, 47, 50, 53, 56, 59, 109, 110, 141, 151, 152, 154, 158–170, 176, 181, 183, 190, 205, 210, 212, 213, 219, 220, 225
phronesis, 78, 213; practical wisdom, 223
possible, 35, 36, 86–88, 147, 169, 191–193, 196, 207, 224
PowerPoint, 136, 171
practice (such as pedagogical), 21, 23, 39, 42, 48, 51, 55, 56, 77, 85–90, 102, 103, 105, 112, 117, 123, 124, 134, 139, 142, 144, 179, 181, 182–184, 187, 188, 193, 195, 196, 199, 203, 207, 209, 210, 212, 213, 215, 217–220, 223; *agogical*, 41; effective, 73, 88; epistemology of, 55, 209, 210; ethical, 33, 35, 74, 203; informal, marginal, 89, 91, 96; intuitive, 59; ontologies of, 98, 99, 184; phenomenology of, 152, 190; professional, 47, 48, 72, 74, 86, 188; reflective, 49–60, 95; tactful, 212, 213; thoughtful, 91, 100, 213
praise, 45, 139, 142–144, 198
predator, 174, 217
prereflectivity, 22, 40, 72, 154, 168, 169
presentative, representative, 129–131, 207
productionist, 87

recognizing, recognition, regard, 16, 24, 63, 77, 108, 116, 119, 139–155; the incognito, 116; the unrecognizable, 116

reflection in action, 38, 39, 50, 51, 53, 57, 58
reflective, 11, 14, 19, 20, 22, 23, 25, 33, 38, 39, 40, 42, 72, 78, 81, 86, 94, 100, 102, 111, 124, 125, 150, 151, 154, 168, 169, 177, 179, 182, 183, 189, 190, 211; actions, 49, 213; practice, 49–60, 95; teaching, 58, 122
reflectivity, 11, 92, 122; interpretive, 11, 225
responsibility, 20, 21, 23, 34, 40–42, 44, 47, 50, 68–75, 84, 86, 88, 95, 104, 112, 114, 120, 121, 124, 125, 131, 146, 181, 191, 193, 194, 199–206, 225; for the other, 37, 70, 202; response-ability, 19, 37; self-responsibility, 41, 120

self, 16, 37, 58, 59, 99, 139, 141–151, 163, 169, 173, 174, 177, 190, 201, 220, 223, 224; -awareness, 139, 141, 152; -care, 223, 224; -centered, 45, 121, 202, 226; -confidence, 55, 131, 144, 184; -consciousness, 54, 58, 111, 122, 147; -control, 125; -creating, 152; -critical, 47; -defeating, 142; -deprecating, 57; -determination, 44; -development, 17; -discipline, 120; -disclosure, 223; -discovery, 148, 149, 150; -doubt, 113; -destructive, 91; -education, 37; -esteem, 45, 46, 139, 142, 144, 198; -experience, 148, 150; -forgetful, 59, 121, 182; -formative, 62, 146; -hatred, 113; -identity, 99, 109, 143, 144, 145, 149, 150, 163, 172, 173; -illusion, 148; -help, 220; -image, 150; -indulgent, 65; -interest, 47, 98; -interrogation, 218; -knowledge, 223, 224; -legitimating, 95; -occupied, 177; -presentation, 150; -punishment, 163; -realization, 144; -recognition, 149; -referential, 202; -reflective, 102, 122; -reflexive, 11; -respect, 144; -responsibility, 41, 44, 94, 120; -sacrifice, 46, 155; -scrutiny, 223; -training, 223; -understanding, 17, 150
selfhood, 87, 143, 158
selfishness, 45, 47, 201
singularity, 70, 71, 73, 78, 105, 114, 121, 150, 157, 158, 169, 172, 173, 178, 187, 201, 202
Smart Boards, 136, 171
social networks, 48, 142, 171, 173, 176
sociopath, psychopath, 46
sorgen, zorgen, 67, 220, 221
star thrower, 84

tactics, 98
tactus, 101, 103
Taktgefühl, 97
tangere, 103
technocratic, 14, 45, 87, 89, 95, 105, 146, 189, 193, 218, 219,
technologism, 110
technology, 78, 87, 90, 110, 171, 172, 174, 187, 189, 192, 203, 217
thinking on your feet, 50
thinkingly acting, 49, 51, 82,
toxic, 110; contact, 110; teachers, 110

unforgettable, 134
uniqueness, 35, 40, 62, 72, 78, 90, 91, 97, 105, 114, 121, 137
unplannable, 98, 211
untouchability, 116

vulnerability, 19, 40, 46, 54, 70, 73, 74, 79, 114, 115, 117, 121, 177, 191, 199, 201, 202, 218, 220

who am I?, 147–150
worry, 19, 33, 40, 64–68, 72–75, 88, 117, 180, 219–224; care-as-worry, 72, 73–75, 179, 222–224

About the Author

Max van Manen is emeritus Professor in Research Methods, Pedagogy and Curriculum Studies in the Faculty of Education at the University of Alberta, and Adjunct Professor at the University of Victoria. He is the leading proponent of the practice and meaning of phenomenological inquiry in pedagogy, psychology, health science, and the human sciences. He is author of *Phenomenology of Practice* (2014), *Childhood's Secrets* (with Bas Levering) (1996), *The Tact of Teaching* (1991), *Researching Lived Experience* (1990/1997), *The Tone of Teaching* (1986/2002), and author-editor of *Writing in the Dark* (2002). He has had his books translated into many languages, and he has authored numerous articles and chapters. Max van Manen was granted an Honorary Doctorate, and is the recipient of the Lifetime Achievement Award by the Curriculum Division of the American Educational Research Association among many other awards and distinctions.

Van Manen is also the editor of Left Coast's Phenomenology of Practice series.

For Product Safety Concerns and Information please contact our EU representative GPSR@taylorandfrancis.com
Taylor & Francis Verlag GmbH, Kaufingerstraße 24, 80331 München, Germany

www.ingramcontent.com/pod-product-compliance
Lightning Source LLC
Chambersburg PA
CBHW071353290426
44108CB00014B/1523